John G. Paton, Missionary to the New Hebrides

JOHN G. PATON.

An Autobiography.

John G. Paton.

JOHN G. PATON,

MISSIONARY TO THE

NEW HEBRIDES.

An Autobiography.

EDITED BY HIS BROTHER.

WITH A PORTRAIT AND MAP.

SECOND THOUSAND.

London:
HODDER AND STOUGHTON,
27, PATERNOSTER ROW.
MDCCCLXXXIX.

Butler & Tanner,
The Selwood Printing Works,
Frome, and London.

PREFACE.

THE Manuscript of this Volume, put together in a rough draft amid ceaseless and exacting toils, was placed in my hands and left absolutely to my disposal by my beloved brother, the Missionary.

It has been to me a labour of perfect love to re-write and revise the same, pruning here and expanding there, and preparing the whole for the press. In the incidents of personal experience, constituting the larger part of the book, the reader peruses in an almost unaltered form the graphic and simple narrative as it came from my brother's pen. But, as many sections have been re-cast and largely modified, especially in those Chapters of whose events I was myself an eye-witness, or regarding which I had information at first hand from the parties concerned therein,—and as circum-

stances make it impossible to submit these
in their present shape to my brother before
publication,—I must request the Public to
lay upon me, and not on him, all responsibility
for the final shape in which the Autobiography
appears.

I publish it, because Something tells me
there is a blessing in it.

January, 1889.   JAMES PATON.

NOTE TO SECOND EDITION.

THE Editor desires very gratefully to acknowledge his joy in receiving, not only through
Press Notices, but from Correspondents in
every rank, most ample confirmation of the
assurance expressed by him in the last sentence
of the Original Preface—" There is a blessing
in it."

He has been urging his Brother to complete,
as soon as he possibly can, Part Second of the
Autobiography ; and he hopes that the call for
this Second Edition of Part First at so early a
date will successfully enforce his appeal.

February, 1889.

CONTENTS.

CHAPTER VII.

MISSION LEAVES FROM TANNA.

CHAPTER VIII.

MORE MISSION LEAVES FROM TANNA.

CHAPTER IX.,

DEEPENING SHADOWS.

CHAPTER X.

FAREWELL SCENES.

APPENDIX.

I.

EARLIER DAYS.

CHAPTER I.

EARLIER DAYS.

Introductory Note.—Kirkmahoe.—Torthorwald Village.— Our
Villagers.—Nithsdale Scenes.—Our Cottage Home.—Our
Forebears.—An Idyll of the Heart.—A Consecrated Father.
—Accepted Vows. — Happy Sabbath Days. — Golden
Autumn of Life.

WHAT I write here is for the glory of God.
For more than twenty years have I been
urged to record my story as a missionary of the
Cross; but always till now, in my sixty-fourth year,
my heart has shrunk from the task, as savouring
too much of self. Latterly the conviction has been
borne home to me that if there be much in my experience which the Church of God ought to know,
it would be pride on my part, and not humility, to
let it die with me. I lift my pen, therefore, with that
motive supreme in my heart; and, so far as memory
and entries in my note-books and letters of my own
and of other friends serve or help my sincere desire
to be truthful and fair, the following chapters will
present a faithful picture of the life through which
the Lord has led me. If it bows any of my readers

3

under as deep and certain a confidence as mine, that
in "God's hand our breath is, and His are all our
ways," my task will not be fruitless in the Great Day.

On the 24th May, 1824, I was born in a cottage
on the farm of Braehead, in the parish of Kirkmahoe,
near Dumfries, in the south of Scotland.   My father,
James Paton, was a stocking manufacturer in a small
way ; and he and his young wife, Janet Jardine
Rogerson, lived on terms of warm personal friendship
with the "gentleman farmer," so they gave me his
name, John *Gibson ;* and the curly-haired child of
the cottage was soon able to toddle across to the
mansion, and became a great pet of the lady there.
More than once, in my many journeyings, have I
met with one or another, in some way connected
with that family, and heard little incidents not
needing to be repeated here, showing how beautiful
and tender and altogether human was the relation-
ship in those days betwixt the landlord and the
cottars on his estate.   On my last visit to Scotland, sixty years after, I drove to Braehead in company with my youngest brother James and my
cousin David,—the latter born the same week as I,
and the former nearly twenty years my junior ; and
we found no cottage, nor trace of a cottage, but
amused ourselves by supposing that we could dis-
cover by the rising of the grassy mound, the outline
where the foundations once had been !   Of ten
thousand homes in Scotland, once sweet and beau-

tiful, each a little possible Paradise in its own well-cultivated plot, this is true to-day; and where are the healthy, happy peasant boys and girls that such homes bred and reared? They are sweltering and struggling for existence in our towns and cities. I am told that this must be—that it is all the result of economic laws; but I confess to a deepening conviction that it need not be, and that the loss to the nation as a whole is vital, if not irreparable.

While yet a mere child, five years or so of age, my parents took me to a new home in the ancient village of Torthorwald, about four and a quarter miles north from Dumfries, on the road to Lockerbie. At that time, about 1830, Torthorwald was a busy and thriving village, and comparatively populous, with its cottars and crofters, large farmers and small farmers, weavers and shoemakers, cloggers and coopers, blacksmiths and tailors. Fifty-five years later, when I last visited the scenes of my youth, the village proper was literally extinct, except for five thatched cottages where the lingering patriarchs were permitted to die slowly away,—when they too would be swept into the large farms, and their garden plots ploughed over, like sixty or seventy others that had been obliterated! Of course the Village Smithy still survives, but its sparks are few and fading,—the great cultivators patronizing rather the towns. The Meal Mill still grinds away,—but nothing like what it did when every villager bought or cultivated his few acres of corn, and every crofter and farmer in the parish sent all his grist to the mill. The Grocer's Shop still recalls the well-known name of Robert Henderson; but so few are the mouths now to be fed, that his warm-hearted wife and universal favourite, the very heroine of our village life, "Jean Grier," is retiring from it in disgust, and leaving it to her son-in-law, declaring that "these Tory landlords and their big farms hae driven our folks a' awa', and spoiled the Schule and the Shop, the Kirk and the Mill." And verily the School is robbed of its children, and the Parish Church of its worshippers, when five families only are reared where twenty once flourished!. Political economy may curse me, if it will; but I heard with grim satisfaction that this system of large farming, which extinguishes our village homes, and sends our peasantry to rear their children in lanes and alleys, in attics and cellars of populous towns, was proving ruinous at length to the landlords and factors, who had in many cases cruelly forced it on an unwilling people for mere selfish gain.

The Villagers of my early days—the agricultural servants, or occasional labourers, the tradesmen, the small farmers—were, generally speaking, a very industrious and thoroughly independent race of people. Hard workers they had to be, else they would starve; yet they were keen debaters on all affairs both in Church and State, and sometimes in the "smiddy" or the "kiln," sometimes in a happy knot on the "village green," or on the road to the "kirk" or the "market," the questions that were tearing the mighty world beyond were fought over again by secluded peasants with amazing passion and bright intelligence.

From the Bank Hill, close above our village, and accessible in a walk of fifteen minutes, a view opens to the eye which, despite several easily understood prejudices of mine that may discount any opinion that I offer, still appears to me well worth seeing amongst all the beauties of Scotland. At your feet lay a thriving village, every cottage sitting in its own plot of garden, and sending up its blue cloud of " peat reek," which never somehow seemed to pollute the blessed air ; and after all has been said or sung, a beautifully situated village of healthy and happy homes for God's children is surely the finest feature in every landscape ! There nestled the Manse amongst its ancient trees, sometimes wisely, some-times foolishly tenanted, but still the " man's-house," the man of God's house, when such can be found. for it. There, close by, the Parish School, where rich and poor met together on equal terms, as God's children ; and we learned that brains and character make the only aristocracy worth mentioning. Yonder, amid its graves, that date back on crumbling stone five hundred years, stands the Village Church ; and there, on its little natural hill, at the end of the village, rises the old tower of Torthorwald, frowning over all the far-sweeping valley of the Nith, and telling of days of blood and Border foray. It was one of the many castles of the Kirkpatricks, and its enormous and imperishable walls seem worthy of

him who wrote the legend of his family in the blood
of the Red Comyn, stabbed in the Greyfriars Church
of Dumfries, when he smote an extra blow to that of
Bruce, and cried, "I mak' siccar." Beyond, betwixt
you and the Nith, crawls the slow-creeping Lochar
towards the Solway, through miles and miles of moss
and heather,—the nearest realization that I ever be-
held of a "stagnant stream." Looking from the
Bank Hill on a summer day, Dumfries with its
spires shone so conspicuous that you could have
believed it not. more than two miles away ; the
splendid sweeping vale through which Nith rolls to
Solway, lay all before the naked eye, beautiful with
village spires, mansion houses, and white shining
farms ; the Galloway hills, gloomy and far-tumbling,
bounded the forward view, while to the left rose
Criffel, cloud-capped and majestic ; then the white
sands of Solway, with tides swifter than horsemen ;
and finally the eye rested joyfully upon the hills of
Cumberland, and noticed with glee the blue curling
smoke from its villages on the southern Solway
shores. Four miles behind you lie the ruins of the
Castle of the Bruce, within the domains of his own
Royal Burgh of Lochmaben ; a few miles in front,
the still beautiful and amazing remains of Caerlave-
rock Castle, famous in many a Border story ; all
around you, scattered throughout the dale of Nith,
memories or ruins of other baronial " keeps," rich in
suggestion to the peasant fancy ! Traditions lost
nothing in bulk, or in graphic force, as they were

retold for the thousandth time by village patriarchs around the kindly peat fire, with the younger rustics gaping round. A high spirit of patriotism, and a certain glorious delight in daring enterprises, was part of our common heritage.

There, amid this wholesome and breezy village life, our dear parents found their home for the long period of forty years. There were born to them eight additional children, making in all a family of five sons and six daughters. Theirs was the first of the thatched cottages on the left, past the "miller's house," going up the "village gate," with a small garden in front of it, and a large garden across the road; and it is one of the few still lingering to show to a new generation what the homes of their fathers were. The architect who planned it had no ideas of art, but a fine eye for durability! It consists at present of three, but originally of four, pairs of "oak couples" (Scotticé *kipples*), planted like solid trees in the ground at equal intervals, and gently sloped inwards till they meet or are "coupled" at the ridge, this coupling being managed not by rusty iron, but by great solid pins of oak. A roof of oaken wattles was laid across these, till within eleven or twelve feet of the ground, and from the ground upwards a stone wall was raised, as perpendicular as was found practicable, towards these overhanging wattles, this wall being roughly "pointed" with sand and clay and lime. Now into and upon the roof was woven and intertwisted a covering of thatch, that defied all

winds and weathers, and that made the cottage
marvellously cosey,—being renewed year by year,
and never allowed' to remain in' disrepair at any
season. But the beauty of the construction was and
is its durability, or rather the permanence of its
oaken ribs! There they stand, after probably not
less than four centuries, japanned with "peat reek"
till they .are literally shining, so hard that no
ordinary nail can be driven into them, and perfectly
capable for service for four centuries more on the
same conditions. The walls are quite modern, having
all been rebuilt in my father's time, except only the
few great foundation boulders, piled around the
oaken couples; and parts of the roofing also may
plead guilty to having found its way thither only in
recent days ; but the architect's one idea survives,
baffling time and change—the ribs and rafters of oak.

Our home consisted of a "but" and a "ben"
and a "mid room," or chamber, called the "closet."
The one end was my mother's domain, and served
all the purposes of dining-room and kitchen and
parlour, besides containing two large wooden erec-
tions, called by our Scotch peasantry "box-beds";
not holes in the wall, as in cities, but grand, big,
airy beds, adorned with many-coloured counterpanes,
and hung with natty curtains, showing the skill of
the mistress of the house. The other end was my
father's workshop, filled with five or six "stocking
frames," whirring with the constant action of five or
· six pairs of busy hands and feet, and producing right

genuine hosiery for the merchants at Hawick and Dumfries. The "closet" was a very small apartment betwixt the other two, having room only for a bed, a little table, and a chair, with a diminutive window shedding diminutive light on the scene. This was the Sanctuary of that cottage home. Thither daily, and oftentimes a day, generally after each meal, we saw our father retire, and "shut to the door"; and we children got to understand by a sort of spiritual instinct (for the thing was too sacred to be talked about) that prayers were being poured out there for us, as of old by the High Priest within the veil in the Most Holy Place. We occasionally heard the pathetic echoes of a trembling voice pleading as if for life, and we learned to slip out and in past that door on tiptoe, not to disturb the holy colloquy. The outside world might not know, but we knew, whence came that happy light as of a new-born smile that always was dawning on my father's face: it was a reflection from the Divine Presence, in the consciousness of which he lived. Never, in temple or cathedral, on mountain or in glen, can I hope to feel that the Lord God is more near, more visibly walking and talking with men, than under that humble cottage roof of thatch and oaken wattles. Though everything else in religion were by some unthinkable catastrophe to be swept out of memory, or blotted from my understanding, my soul would wander back to those early scenes, and shut itself up once again in that Sanctuary Closet, and, hearing still the echoes of those cries to

God, would hurl back all doubt with the victorious appeal, "He walked with God, why may not I ?"

A few notes had better here be given as to our "Forebears," the kind of stock from which my father and mother sprang. My father's mother, Janet Murray, claimed to be descended from a Galloway family that fought and suffered for Christ's Crown and Covenant in Scotland's "killing time," and was herself a woman of a pronouncedly religious development. Her husband, our grandfather, William Paton, had passed through a roving and romantic career, before he settled down to a douce deacon of the weavers of Dumfries, like his father before him.

Forced by a press-gang to serve on board a British man-of-war, he was taken prisoner by the French, and thereafter placed under Paul Jones, the pirate of the seas, and bore to his dying day the mark of a slash from the captain's sword across his shoulder for some slight disrespect or offence. Determining with two others to escape, the three were hotly pursued by Paul Jones's men. One, who could swim but little, was shot, and had to be cut adrift by the other two, who in the darkness swam into a cave and managed to evade for two nights and a day the rage of their pursuers. My grandfather, being young and gentle and yellow-haired, persuaded some kind heart to rig him out in female attire, and in this costume escaped the attentions of the press-gang more than once ; till, after many hardships, he bargained with the captain of a coal sloop to stow him away amongst his black diamonds, and thus, in due time, he found his way home to Dumfries, where he tackled bravely and wisely the duties of husband, father, and citizen for the remainder of his days. The smack of the sea about the stories of his youth gave zest to the talks round their quiet fireside, and that, again, was seasoned by the warm evangelical spirit of his Covenanting wife, her lips " dropping grace."

Of their children, two reproduced the disposition of their father, and two that of their mother. William took to the soldier's career, and died in Spain ; May, the only daughter, gave her heart and hand to John Wood, a jolly and gallant Englishman, who fought at Waterloo, and lived to see his hundredth birthday. John and James, the latter being my father, both learned the stocking manufacturing business of their fathers, and both followed their mother's piety and became from their early teens very pronounced and consistent disciples of the Lord.

On the other side, my mother, Janet Rogerson, had for parents a father and mother of the Annandale stock. William Rogerson, her father, was one of many brothers, all men of uncommon strength and great force of character, quite worthy of the Border rievers of an earlier day. Indeed, it was in some such way that he secured his wife, though the dear old lady in after-days was chary about telling the story. She was a girl of good position, the ward of two un-scrupulous uncles who had charge of her small estate, near Langholm ; and while attending some boarding school she fell devotedly in love with the tall, fair-haired, gallant young blacksmith, William Rogerson. Her guardians, doubtless very properly, objected to the "connection"; but our young Lochinvar, with his six or seven stalwart brothers and other trusty "lads," all mounted, and with some ready tool in case of need, went boldly and claimed his bride, and she, willingly mounting at his side, was borne off in the light of open day, joyously married, and took possession of her "but and ben," as the mistress of the blacksmith's abode.

The uncles had it out with him, however, in another way. While he was enjoying his honeymoon, and careless of mere mundane affairs, they managed to dispose of all the property of their ward, and make good their escape with the proceeds to the New World. Having heard a rumour of some such sale, our young blacksmith on horseback just reached the scene in time to see the last article—a Family Bible—put up for auction. This he claimed, or purchased, or seized, in name of the heiress—but that was all that she ever inherited. It was used devoutly by her till her dying day, and was adorned with the record of her own marriage and of the birth of a large and happy family, whom by-and-by God gave to her.

Janet Jardine bowed her neck to the self-chosen yoke, with the light of a supreme affection in her heart, and showed in her gentler ways, her love of books, her fine accomplishments with the needle, and her general air of ladyhood, that her lot had once been cast in easier, but not necessarily happier, ways. Her blacksmith lover proved not unworthy of his lady bride, and in her old days found a quiet and modest home, the fruit of years of toil and hopeful thrift, their own little property, in which they rested and waited a happy end. Amongst those who at last wept by her grave stood, amidst many sons and daughters, her son the Rev. James J. Rogerson, clergyman of the Church of England, who, for many years thereafter, and till quite recently, was spared to occupy a distinguished position at ancient Shrewsbury, and has left behind him there an honoured and beloved name.

One thing else, beautiful in its pathos, I must record of that dear old lady. Her son, Walter, had gone forth from her, in prosecution of his calling, had corresponded with her from various counties in England, and then had suddenly disappeared; and no sign came to her, whether he was dead or alive. The mother-heart in her clung to the hope of his return; every night she prayed for that happy event, and before closing the door, threw it wide open, and peered into the darkness with a cry, "Come hame, my boy Walter, your mither wearies sair;" and every morning, at early break of day, for a period of more than twenty years, she toddled up from her cottage door, at Johnsfield, Lockerbie, to a little round hill, called the "Corbie Dykes," and, gazing with tear-filled eyes towards the south for the form of her returning boy, prayed the Lord God to keep him safe and restore him to her yet again. Always, as I think upon that scene, my heart finds consolation in reflecting that if not here, then for certain *there*, such deathless longing love will be rewarded, and, rushing into long-delayed embrace, will exclaim, " Was lost and is found."

From such a home came our mother, Janet Jardine Rogerson, a bright-hearted, high-spirited, patient-toiling, and altogether heroic little woman; who, for about forty-three years, made and kept such a wholesome, independent, God-fearing, and self-reliant life for her family of five sons and six daughters, as constrains me, when I look back on it now, in the light of all I have since seen and known of others far differently situated, almost to worship her memory. She had gone with her high spirits and breezy disposition to gladden, as their companion, the quiet abode of some grand or great-grand-uncle and aunt, familiarly named in all that Dalswinton neighbourhood, " Old Adam and Eve." Their house was on the outskirts of the moor, and life for the young girl there had not probably too much excitement. But one thing had arrested her attention. She had noticed that a young stocking maker from the " Brig End," James Paton, the son of William and Janet there, was in the habit of stealing alone into the quiet wood, book in hand, day after day, at certain hours, as if for private study and meditation. It was a very excusable curiosity that led the young bright heart of the girl to watch

him devoutly reading and hear him reverently reciting
(though she knew not then, it was Ralph Erskine's
"Gospel Sonnets," which he could say by heart sixty
years afterwards, as he lay on his bed of death); and
finally that curiosity awed itself into a holy respect,
when she saw him lay aside his broad Scotch bonnet,
kneel down under the sheltering wings of some tree,
and pour out all his soul in daily prayers to God.
As yet they had never spoken. What spirit moved
her, let lovers tell—was it all devotion, or was it a
touch of unconscious love kindling in her towards
the yellow-haired and thoughtful youth? Or was
there a stroke of mischief, of that teasing, which so
often opens up the door to the most serious step
in all our lives? Anyhow, one day she slipped in
quietly, stole away his bonnet, and hung it on a
branch near by, while his trance of devotion made
him oblivious of all around; then, from a safe retreat
she watched and enjoyed his perplexity in seeking
for and finding it! A second day this was repeated;
but his manifest disturbance of mind, and his long
pondering with the bonnet in hand, as if almost
alarmed, seemed to touch another chord in her heart
—that chord of pity which is so often the prelude of
love, that finer pity that grieves to wound anything
nobler or tenderer than ourselves. Next day, when
he came to his accustomed place of prayer, a little
card was pinned against the tree just where he knelt,
and on it these words :—

"She who stole away your bonnet is ashamed of

what she did ; she has a great respect for you, and asks you to pray for her, that she may become as good a Christian as you."

Staring long at that writing, he forgot Ralph Erskine for one day; taking down the card, and wondering who the writer could be, he was abusing himself for his stupidity in not suspecting that some one had discovered his retreat, and removed his bonnet, instead of wondering whether angels had been there during his prayer,—when, suddenly raising his eyes, he saw in front of old Adam's cottage, through a lane amongst the trees, the passing of another kind of angel, swinging a milk-pail in her hand and merrily singing some snatch of old Scottish song. He knew, in that moment, by a Divine instinct, as infallible as any voice that ever came to seer of old, that she was the angel visitor that had stolen in upon his retreat—that bright-faced, clever-witted niece of old Adam and Eve, to whom he had never yet spoken, but whose praises he had often heard said and sung—"Wee Jen." I am afraid he did pray "for her," in more senses than one, that afternoon ; at any rate, more than a Scotch bonnet was very effectually stolen ; a good heart and true was there bestowed, and the trust was never regretted on either side, and never betrayed.

Often and often, in the genial and beautiful hours of the autumntide of their long life, have I heard my dear father tease "Jen" about her maidenly intentions in the stealing of that bonnet; and often with quick mother wit have heard her happy retort, that had his motives for coming to that retreat been altogether and exclusively pious, he would probably have found his way to the other side of the wood, but that men who prowled about the Garden of Eden ran the risk of meeting some day with a daughter of Eve!

Somewhere in or about his seventeenth year, my father passed through a crisis of religious experience, and from that day he openly and very decidedly followed the Lord Jesus. His parents had belonged to one of the older branches of what now we call the United Presbyterian Church; but my father, having made an independent study of the Scotch Worthies, the Cloud of Witnesses, the Testimonies, and the Confession of Faith, resolved to cast in his lot with the oldest of all the Scotch Churches, the Reformed Presbyterian, as most nearly representing the Covenanters and the attainments of both the first and second Reformations in Scotland. This choice he deliberately made, and sincerely and intelligently adhered to; and was able at all times to give strong and clear reasons from Bible and from history for the principles he upheld. Still his sympathies and votes always went with the more progressive party in that ancient Church. He held it to be right that Cameronians, like other citizens, should exercise the municipal and political franchise, and he adhered to the "Majority Synod," which has since been incorporated with the Free Church of Scotland.

While glorying in the Psalms, he rejoiced to sing
other hymns and spiritual songs (thanks to Ralph
Erskine's "Sonnets," perhaps, for that!) from his earliest days, at least everywhere except in the ordinary
Public Worship; and long before he died, though
he still held the Psalms to be supreme, he had learned
to hear with glowing delight vast congregations singing the hymns of modern days, had learned joyfully
to join in these songs of Zion, and was heard often
to confess his belief that God had greatly owned and
blessed the ministry of song in the service of the
Gospel.

Besides his independent choice of a Church
for himself, there was one other mark and fruit of
his early religious decision, which looks even fairer
through all these years. Family Worship had heretofore been held only on Sabbath day in his father's
house; but the young Christian, entering into con-
ference with his sympathising mother, managed to
get the household persuaded that there ought to be
daily morning and evening prayer and reading of
the Bible and holy singing. This the more readily,
as he himself agreed to take part regularly in the
same and so relieve the old warrior of what might
have proved for him too arduous spiritual toils. And
so began in his seventeenth year that blessed custom
of Family Prayer, morning and evening, which my
father practised probably without one single omission
till he lay on his deathbed, seventy-seven years of
age; when, even to the last day of his life, a portion

of Scripture was read, and his voice was heard softly joining in the Psalm, and his lips breathed the morning and evening Prayer,—falling in sweet benediction on the heads of all his children, far away many of them over all the earth, but all meeting him there at the Throne of Grace. None of us can remember that any day ever passed unhallowed thus ; no hurry for market, no rush to business, no arrival of friends or guests, no trouble or sorrow, no joy or excitement, ever prevented at least our kneeling around the family altar, while the High Priest led our prayers to God, and offered himself and his children there. And blessed to others, as well as to ourselves, was the light of such example! I have heard that, in long after years, the worst woman in the village of Torthorwald, then leading an immoral life, but since changed by the grace of God, was known to declare, that the only thing that kept her from despair. and from the hell of the suicide, was when in the dark winter nights she crept close up underneath my father's window, and heard him pleading in family worship that God would convert " the sinner from the error of wicked ways and polish him as a jewel for the Redeemer's crown." "I felt," said she, "that I was a burden on that good man's heart, and I knew that God would not disappoint *him.* That thought kept me out of Hell, and at last led me to the only Saviour."

My father had a strong desire to be a minister of the Gospel; but when he finally saw that God's will had marked out for him another lot, he reconciled himself by entering with his own soul into this solemn vow,—that if God gave him sons, he would consecrate them unreservedly to the ministry of Christ, if the Lord saw fit to accept the offering, and open up their way. It may be enough here to say that he lived to see three of us entering upon and not unblessed in the Holy Office;—myself, the eldest born; my brother Walter, several years my junior; and my brother James, the youngest of eleven, the Benjamin of the flock.

Our place of worship was the Reformed Presbyterian Church at Dumfries, under the ministry, during most of these days, of Rev. John McDiarmid— a genuine, solemn, lovable Covenanter, who cherished towards my father a warm respect, that deepened into apostolic affection when the yellow hair turned snow-white and both of them grew patriarchal in their years. The minister, indeed, was translated to a Glasgow charge; but that rather exalted than suspended their mutual love. Dumfries was four miles fully from our Torthorwald home; but the tradition is that during all these forty years my father was only thrice prevented from attending the worship of God—once by snow so deep that he was baffled and had to return; once by ice on the road, so dangerous that he was forced to crawl back up the Roucan Brae on his hands and knees, after having descended it so far with many falls; and once by the terrible outbreak of cholera at Dumfries. All intercourse betwixt the town and the surrounding villages was publicly prohibited; and the farmers and villagers, suspecting that no cholera would make my father stay at home on Sabbath, sent a deputation to my mother on the Saturday evening, and urged her to restrain his devotions for once! That, however, was needless; as, where the life of others was at stake, his very devotion came to their aid. Each of us, from very early days, considered it no penalty, but a great joy, to go with our father to the church; the four miles were a treat to our young spirits, the company by the way was a fresh incitement, and occasionally some of the wonders of city-life rewarded our eager eyes. A few other pious men and women of the best evangelical type, went from the same parish to one or other favourite minister at Dumfries,— the parish church during all those years being rather miserably served; and when these God-fearing peasants "forgathered" in the way to or from the House of God, we youngsters had sometimes rare glimpses of what Christian talk may be and ought to be. They went to the church, full of beautiful expectancy of spirit—their souls were on the outlook for God; they returned from the church, ready and even anxious to exchange ideas as to what they had heard and received of the things of life. I have to bear my testimony that religion was presented to us with a great deal of intellectual freshness, and that it did not repel us but kindled our spiritual interest. The talks which we heard were, however, genuine; not the make-believe of religious conversation, but the sincere outcome of their own personalities. That, perhaps, makes all the difference betwixt talk that attracts and talk that drives away.

We had, too, special Bible Readings on the Lord's Day evening,—mother and children and visitors reading in turns, with fresh and interesting question, answer, and exposition, all tending to impress us with the infinite grace of a God of love and mercy in the great gift of His dear Son Jesus, our ·Saviour. The Shorter Catechism was gone through regularly, each answering the question asked, till the whole had been explained, and its foundation in Scripture shown by the proof-texts adduced. It has been an amazing thing to me, occasionally to meet with men who blamed this "catechizing" for giving them a distaste to religion; every one in all our circle thinks and feels exactly the opposite. It laid the solid rock-foundations of our religious life. After-years have given to these questions and their answers a deeper or a modified meaning, but none of us have ever once even dreamed of wishing that we had been otherwise trained. Of course, if the parents are not devout, sincere, and affectionate,—if the whole affair on both sides is taskwork, or worse, hypocritical and false,—results must be very different indeed! Oh, I can remember those happy Sabbath evenings; no blinds drawn, and shutters up, to keep out the sun from us, as some scandalously affirm; but a holy, happy, entirely human day, for a Christian father, mother, and children to spend. How my father would parade across and across our flag-floor, telling over the substance of the day's sermons to our dear mother, who, because of the great distance and because of her many living "encumbrances," got very seldom indeed to the church, but gladly embraced every chance, when there was prospect or promise of a "lift" either way from some friendly gig! How he would entice us to help him to recall some idea or other, rewarding us when we got the length of "taking notes" and reading them over on our return; how he would turn the talk ever so naturally to some Bible story, or some martyr reminiscence, or some happy allusion to the "Pilgrim's Progress"! And then it was quite a contest, which of us would get reading aloud, while all the rest listened, and father added here and there a happy thought, or illustration, or anecdote. Others must write and say what they will, and as they feel; but so must I. There were eleven of us brought up in a home like that; and never one of the eleven, boy or girl, man or woman, has been heard, or ever will be heard, saying that Sabbath was dull or wearisome for us, or suggesting that we have heard of or seen any way more likely than that for making the Day of the Lord bright and blessed alike for parents and for children. But God help the homes where these things are done by force and not by love! The very discipline through which our father passed us was a kind of religion in itself. If anything really serious required to be punished, he

retired first to his closet for prayer, and we boys got
to understand that he was laying the whole matter
before God ; and that was the severest part of the
punishment for me to bear ! I could have defied
any amount of mere penalty, but this spoke to my
conscience as a message from God. We loved him
all the more, when we saw how much it cost him to
punish us ; and, in truth, he had never very much
of that kind of work to do upon any one of all the
eleven—we were ruled by love far more than by fear.

As I must, however, leave the story of my father's
life—much more worthy, in many ways, of being
written than my own—I may here mention that his
long and upright life made him a great favourite in
all religious circles far and near within the neighbourhood, that at sick-beds and at funerals he was
constantly sent for and much appreciated, and
that this appreciation greatly increased, instead of
diminishing, when years whitened his long, flowing
locks and gave him an apostolic beauty ; till finally,
for the last twelve years or so of his life, he became
by appointment a sort of Rural Missionary for the
four contiguous parishes, and spent his autumn in
literally sowing the good seed of the Kingdom as
a Colporteur of the Tract and Book Society. His
success in this work, for a rural locality, was beyond
all belief. Within a radius of five miles, he was
known in every home, welcomed by the children,
respected by the servants, longed for eagerly by the
sick and aged. He gloried in showing off the beauti-

ful Bibles and other precious books, which he sold in amazing numbers. He sang sweet Psalms beside the sick, and prayed like the voice of God at their dying beds. He went cheerily from farm to farm, from cot to cot; and when he wearied on the moorland roads, he refreshed his soul by reciting aloud one of Ralph Erskine's "Sonnets," or crooning to the birds one of David's Psalms. His happy partner, "Wee Jen," died in 1865, and he himself in 1868, having reached his seventy-seventh year,—an altogether beautiful and noble episode of human existence having been enacted, amid the humblest surroundings of a Scottish peasant's home, through the influence of their united love by the grace of God; and in this world, or in any world, all their children will rise up at mention of their names and call them blessed!

II.

AT SCHOOL AND COLLEGE.

CHAPTER II.

AT SCHOOL AND COLLEGE.

A Typical Scottish School.—A School Prize.—A Wayward
Master.—Learning a Trade.—My Father's Prayers.—Jeho-
vah Jireh.—With Sappers and Miners.—Harvest Field.—
On the Road to Glasgow.—A Memorable Parting.—Before
the Examiners.—Killing Work.—Deep Waters.—Maryhill
School.—Rough School Scenes.—Aut Cæsar, Aut Nullus.
—My Wages.

IN my boyhood Torthorwald had one of the grand
old typical Parish Schools of Scotland, where
the rich and the poor met together in perfect equality,
where Bible and Catechism were taught as zealously
as grammar and geography, and where capable lads
from the humblest of cottages were prepared in Latin
and Mathematics and Greek to go straight from their
village class to the University bench. Besides, at that
time, an accomplished pedagogue of the name of
Smith, a learned man of more than local fame, had
added a Boarding House to the ordinary School, and
had attracted some of the better class gentlemen and
farmers' sons from the surrounding county, so that
Torthorwald, under his *régime*, reached the zenith

of its educational fame. In this School I was initiated into the mystery of letters, and all my brothers and sisters after me, though some of them under other masters than mine;—my youngest brother James, trained there under a master named Lithgow, going direct from the Village School to the University of Glasgow in his fourteenth year!

My teacher punished severely—rather, I should say, savagely—especially for lessons badly prepared. Yet, that he was in some respects kindly and tenderhearted, I had the best of reasons to know. Seeing me not so "braw" as the well-to-do fellows of my year, and taking a warm interest in me as a pupil, he, concluding probably that new suits were not so easily got in my home as in some of the rest, planned a happy and kind-hearted surprise—a sort of unacknowledged school prize. One evening, when my father was "taking the books," and pouring out his heart in family worship, the door of our house gently opened on the latch, and gently closed again. After prayer, on rushing to the door, I found a parcel containing a new suit of warm and excellent clothes,— seeing which my mother said that "God had sent them to me, and I should thankfully receive them as from His hand, whoever might have brought them." Appearing in them at school next morning, the teacher cheerily saluted and complimented me on my "braws." I innocently told him how they came and what my mother said; and he laughingly replied,—

"John, whenever you need anything after this, just

tell your father to 'tak' the Book,' and God will send
it in answer to prayer!"

Years passed by before I came to know, what the
reader has already guessed, that the good-hearted
schoolmaster's hand lifted the latch that evening
during my father's prayer.

All his influence, however, was marred by occasional bursts of fierce and ungovernable temper,
amounting to savagery. His favouritism, too, was
sometimes disheartening,—as when I won a Latin
prize for an exercise by the verdict of the second
master, yet it was withheld from me, and prizes were
bestowed without merit on other and especially
wealthier boys; so at least I imagined, and it cooled
my ambition to excel. Favouritism might be borne,
but not mere brutality when passion mastered him.
Once, after having flogged me unjustly, on my return
only at my mother's entreaty, he ran at me again,
kicked me, and I fled in pain and terror from his
presence, rushing home. When his passion subsided,
he came to my parents, apologized, and pled with
me to return; but all in vain,—nothing would induce
me to resume my studies there. Undoubtedly at
that time I had a great thirst for education, and a
retentive memory, which made all lessons comparatively easy; and, as no other school was within my
reach, it was a great loss that my heart shrank from
this teacher.

Though under twelve years of age, I started to
learn my father's trade, in which I made surprising

P.   3

progress. We wrought from six in the morning till
ten at night, with an hour at dinner-time and half an
hour at breakfast and again at supper. These spare
moments every day I devoutly spent on my books,
chiefly in the rudiments of Latin and Greek; for I
had given my soul to God, and was resolved to aim
at being a missionary of the Cross, or a minister of
the Gospel. Yet I gladly testify that what I learned
of the stocking frame was not thrown away; the
facility of using tools, and of watching and keeping
the machinery in order, came to be of great value to
me in the Foreign Mission field.

How much my father's prayers at this time impressed me I can never explain, nor could any
stranger understand. When, on his knees and all
of us kneeling around him in Family Worship, he
poured out his whole soul with tears for the conversion of the heathen world to the service of Jesus, and
for every personal and domestic need, we all felt as
if in the presence of the living Saviour, and learned
to know and love Him as our Divine Friend. As
we rose from our knees, I used to look at the light
on my father's face, and wish I were like him in
spirit,—hoping that, in answer to his prayers, I might
be privileged and prepared to carry the blessed Gospel to some portion of the heathen world.

One incident of this time I must record here,
because of the lasting impression made upon my
religious life. Our family, like all others of peasant
rank in the land, were plunged into deep distress,

and felt the pinch severely, through the failure of the potato, the badness of other crops, and the ransom-price of food. Our father had gone off with work to Hawick, and would return next evening with money and supplies; but meantime the meal barrel ran empty, and our dear mother, too proud and too sensitive to let any one know, or to ask aid from any quarter, coaxed us all to rest, assuring us that she had told God everything, and that He would send us plenty in the morning. Next day, with the carrier from Lockerbie came a present from her father, who, knowing nothing of her circumstances or of this special trial, had been moved of God to send at that particular nick of time a love-offering to his daughter, such as they still send to each other in those kindly Scottish shires—a bag of new potatoes, a stone of the first ground meal or flour, or the earliest home-made cheese of the season—which largely supplied all our need. My mother, seeing our surprise at such an answer to her prayers, took us around her knees, thanked God for His goodness, and said to us,—

"O my children, love your heavenly Father, tell Him in faith and prayer all your needs, and He will supply your wants so far as it shall be for your good and His glory."

Perhaps, amidst all their struggles in rearing a family of eleven, this was the hardest time they ever had, and the only time they ever felt the actual pinch of hunger; for the little that they had was mar-

vellously blessed of God, and was not less marvellously utilized by that noble mother of ours, whose
high spirit, side by side with her humble and gracious
piety, made us, under God, what we are to-day.

I saved as much at my trade as enabled me to go
six weeks to Dumfries Academy; this awoke in me
again the hunger for learning, and I resolved to give
up that trade and turn to something that might be
made helpful to the prosecution of my education.
An engagement was secured with the sappers and
·miners, who were mapping and measuring the county
of Dumfries in connection with the Ordnance Survey
of Scotland. The office hours were from 9 a.m. till
4 p.m.; and though my walk from home was above
four miles every morning, and the same by return in
the evening, I found much spare time for private
study, both on the way to and from my work and
also after hours. Instead of spending the mid-day
hour with the rest, at football and other games, I
stole away to a quiet spot on the banks of the Nith,
and there pored over my book, all alone. Our lieutenant, unknown to me, had observed this from his
house on the other side of the stream, and after a
time called me into his office and inquired what I
was studying. I told him the whole truth as to my
position and my desires. After conferring with some
of the other officials there, he summoned me again,
and in their presence promised me promotion in the
service, and special training in Woolwich at the
Government's expense, on condition that I would sign

an engagement for seven years. Thanking him most gratefully for his kind offer, I agreed to bind myself for three years or four, but not for seven.

Excitedly he said, "Why? Will you refuse an offer that many gentlemen's sons would be proud of?"

I said, "My life is given to another Master, so I cannot engage for seven years."

He asked sharply, "To whom?"

I replied, "To the Lord Jesus, and I want to prepare as soon as possible for His service in the proclaiming of the Gospel."

In great anger he sprang across the room, called the paymaster, and exclaimed, "Accept my offer, or you are dismissed on the spot!"

I answered, "I am extremely sorry if you do so, but to bind myself for seven years would probably frustrate the purpose of my life; and though I am greatly obliged to you, I cannot make such an engagement."

His anger made him unwilling or unable to comprehend my difficulty; the drawing instruments were delivered up, I received my pay, and departed without further parley. The men, both over me and beside me, were mostly Roman Catholics, and their talk was the most profane I had ever heard. Few of them spoke at any time without larding their language with oaths, and I was thankful to get away from hearing their shocking speech. But to me personally both officers and men had been extremely kind, for which, on leaving, I thanked them all very cordially, and they looked not a little surprised,—as if unused to such recognitions!

Hearing how I had been treated, and why, Mr. Maxwell, the Rector of Dumfries Academy, offered to let me attend all classes there, free of charge, so long as I cared to remain ; but that, in lack of means of support, was for the time impossible, as I would not and could not be a burden on my dear father, but was determined rather to help him in educating the rest. I went therefore to what was known as the Lamb Fair at Lockerbie, and for the first time in my life took a "fee" for the harvest. On arriving at the field when shearing and mowing began, the farmer asked me to bind a sheaf; when I had done so, he lifted it by the band, and it fell to pieces! Instead of disheartening me, however, he gave me a careful lesson how to bind, and the second that I bound did not collapse when shaken, and the third he pitched across the field, and on finding that it still remained firm, he cried to me cheerily,—

"Right now, my lad ; go ahead!"

It was hard work for me at first, and my hands got very sore; but, being willing and determined, I soon got into the way of it, and kept up with the best of them. The harvesters, seeing I was not one of their own workers, had an eager dispute as to what I was, some holding that I was a painter, and some a tailor ; but the more 'cute observers denied me the rank of tailor from the lack of "jaggings" on my

thumb and finger, so I suppose they credited me with
the brush. The male harvesters were told off to
sleep in a large hay-loft, the beds being arranged all
along the side, like barracks. Many of the fellows
were rough and boisterous, and I suppose my look
showed that I hesitated in mingling with them, for
the quick eye and kind heart of the farmer's wife
prompted her to suggest that I, being so much
younger than the rest, might sleep with her son
George in the house,—an offer, oh, how gratefully accepted! A beautiful new steading had recently been
built for them; and during certain days, or portions of
days, while waiting for the grain to ripen or to dry,
I planned and laid out an ornamental garden in front
of it, which gave great satisfaction—a taste inherited
from my mother, with her joy in flowers and garden
plots. They gave me, on leaving, a handsome present, as well as my fee, for I had got on very plea-
santly with them all. This experience, too, came to
be valuable to me, when, in long-after days, and far
other lands, Mission buildings had to be erected, and
garden and field cropped and cultivated without the
aid of a single European hand.

Before going to my first harvesting, I had applied
for a situation in Glasgow, apparently exactly suited
for my case; but I had little or no hope of ever hearing of it further. An offer of £50 per annum was
made by the West Campbell Street Reformed Presbyterian Congregation, then under the good and
noble Dr. Bates, for a young man to act as district

visitor and tract distributor, especially amongst the
absentees from the Sabbath school; with the privilege
of receiving one year's training at the Free Church
Normal Seminary, that he might qualify himself for
teaching, and thereby push forward to the Holy
Ministry. The candidates, along with their application and certificates, were to send an essay on some
subject, of their own composition, and in their own
handwriting. I sent in two long poems on the
Covenanters, which must have exceedingly amused
them, as I had not learned to write decent prose!
But, much to my surprise, immediately on the close
of the harvesting experience, a letter arrived, inti-
mating that I, along with another young man, had
been put upon the short leet, and that both were
requested to appear in Glasgow on a given day and
compete for the appointment. Two days thereafter
I started out from my quiet country home on the
road to Glasgow. Literally on the road, for from
Torthorwald to Kilmarnock—about forty miles—had
to be done on foot, and thence to Glasgow by rail.
Railways in those days were as yet few, and coach
travelling was far beyond my purse. A small bundle,
tied up in my pocket handkerchief, contained my
Bible and all my personal belongings. Thus was I
launched upon the ocean of life. " I know thy poverty,
but thou art rich."

My dear father walked with me the first six miles
of the way. His counsels and tears and heavenly
conversation on that parting journey are fresh in my

heart as if it had been yesterday; and tears are on my cheeks as freely now as then, whenever memory steals me away to the scene. For the last half-mile or so we walked on together in almost unbroken silence,—my father, as was often his custom, carrying hat in hand, while his long, flowing yellow hair (then yellow, but in later years white as snow) streamed like a girl's down his shoulders. His lips kept moving in silent prayers for me; and his tears fell fast when our eyes met each other in looks for which all speech was vain. We halted on reaching the appointed parting place; he grasped my hand firmly for a minute in silence, and then solemnly and affection- ately said,—

"God bless you, my son! Your father's God prosper you, and keep you from all evil!"

Unable to say more, his lips kept moving in silent prayer; in tears we embraced, and parted. I ran off as fast as I could, and, when about to turn a corner in the road where he would lose sight of me, I looked back and saw him still standing with head uncovered where I had left him. Waving my hat in adieu, I was round the corner and out of sight in an instant. But my heart was too full and sore to carry me further, so I darted into the side of the road and wept for a time. Then, rising up cautiously, I climbed the dyke to see if he yet stood where I had left him, and just at that moment I caught a glimpse of him climbing the dyke and looking out for me! He did not see me, and after he had gazed eagerly in

my direction for a while, he got down, turned his face
towards home, and began to return—his head still
uncovered, and his heart, I felt sure, still rising in
prayers for me. I watched through blinding tears,
till his form faded from my gaze; and then, hasten-
ing on my way, vowed deeply and oft, by the help of
God, to live and act so as never to grieve or dishonour
such a father and mother as He.had given me. The
appearance of my father, when we parted,—his
advice, prayers and tears,—the road, the dyke, the
climbing up on it and then walking away, head
uncovered, have often, often, all through life, risen
vividly before my mind,—and do so now while I am
writing, as if it had been but an hour ago. In my
earlier years particularly, when exposed to many
temptations, his parting form rose before me as that
of a guardian Angel. It is no Pharisaism, but deep
gratitude, which makes me here testify that the
memory of that scene not only helped, by God's
grace, to keep me pure from the prevailing sins, but
also stimulated me in all my studies, that I might not
fall short of his hopes, and in all my Christian duties,
that I might faithfully follow his shining example.

I reached Glasgow on the third day, having slept
one night at Thornhill, and another at New Cum-
nock; and having needed, owing to the kindness of
acquaintances upon whom I called by the way, to
spend only three half-pence of my modest funds.
Safely arrived, but weary, I secured a humble room
for my lodging, for which I had to pay one shilling

and sixpence per week. Buoyant and full of hope and looking up to God for guidance, I appeared at the appointed hour before the examiners, as did also the other candidate; and they, having carefully gone through their work, asked us to retire. When re-called, they informed us that they had great difficulty in choosing, and suggested that the one of us might withdraw in favour of the other, or that both might submit to a more testing examination. Neither seemed inclined to give it up, both were willing for a second examination, but the patrons made another suggestion. They had only £50 per annum to give; but if we would agree to divide it betwixt us, and go into one lodging, we might both be able to struggle through; they would pay our entrance fees at the Free Normal Seminary, and provide us with the books required; and perhaps they might be able to add a little to the sum promised to each of us. By dividing the mission work appointed, and each taking only the half, more time also might be secured for our studies. Though the two candidates had never seen each other before, we at once accepted this proposal, and got on famously together, never having had a dispute on anything of common interest throughout our whole career.

As our fellow-students at the Normal were all far advanced beyond us in their education, we found it killing work, and had to grind away incessantly, late and early. Both of us, before the year closed, broke down in health, partly by hard study, but principally,

perhaps, for lack of nourishing diet. A severe cough
seized upon me; I began spitting blood, and a doctor
ordered me at once home to the country and forbad
all attempts at study. My heart sank; it was a
dreadful disappointment, and to me a bitter trial.
Soon after, my companion, though apparently much
stronger than I, was similarly seized. He, however,
never entirely recovered, though for some years he
taught in a humble school; and long ago he fell
asleep in Jesus, a devoted and honoured Christian man.

I, on the other hand, after a short rest, nourished
by the hill air of Torthorwald and by the new milk of
our family cow, was ere long at work again, and got
an appointment to teach a small school at Girvan.
There I received the greatest kindness from Rev.
Matthew G. Easton of the Reformed Presbyterian
Church, now Dr. Easton of the Free Church, Darvel,
and gradually but completely recovered my health.

Having saved £10 by my teaching, I returned to
Glasgow, and was enrolled as a student at the
College; but before the session was finished my
money was exhausted—I had lent some to a poor
student who failed to repay me—and only nine
shillings remained in my purse. There was no one
from whom to borrow, had I been willing; I had
been disappointed in securing private tuition; and
no course seemed open for me, except to pay what
little I owed, give up my College career, and seek
for teaching or other work in the country. I wrote
a letter to my father and mother, informing them of

my circumstances; that I was leaving Glasgow in quest of work, and that they would not hear from me again till I had found a suitable situation. I told them that if otherwise unsuccessful, I should fall back on my own trade, though I shrank from that as not tending to advance my education; but that they might rest assured I would do nothing to dishonour them or my Christian profession. Having read that letter over again through many tears, I said,—I cannot send that, for it will grieve my darling parents; and therefore, leaving it on the table, I locked my room door and ran out to find a place where I might sell my few precious books, and hold on a few weeks longer. But, as I stood on the opposite side and wondered whether these folks in a shop with the three golden balls would care to have a poor student's books, and as I hesitated, knowing how much I needed them for my studies, conscience smote me for doing a guilty thing; I imagined that the people were watching me as if I were about to commit a theft, and I made off from the scene at full speed, with a feeling of intense shame at having dreamed of such a thing! Passing through one short street into another, I marched on mechanically; but the Lord God of my father was guiding my steps, all unknown to me.

A certain notice in a window, into which I had probably never in my life looked before, here caught my eye, to this effect—"Teacher wanted, Maryhill Free Church School; apply at the Manse." A coach

or 'bus was just passing, when I turned round; I
leapt into it, saw the minister, arranged to undertake
the school, returned to Glasgow, paid my landlady's
lodging score, tore up the letter to my parents and
wrote another full of cheer and hope, and early next
morning entered the school and began a tough and
trying job. The minister warned me that the school
was a wreck, and had been broken up chiefly by
coarse and bad characters from mills and coal-pits,
who attended the evening classes. They had abused
several masters in succession; and, laying a thick
and heavy cane on the desk, he said,—

"Use that freely, or you will never keep order
here!"

I put it aside into the drawer of my desk, saying,—
"That will be my last resource."

There were very few scholars for the first week—
about eighteen in the day school and twenty in the
night school. The clerk of the mill, a good young
fellow, came to the evening classes, avowedly to learn
book-keeping, but privately he said he had come to
save me from personal injury.

The following week, a young man and a young
woman began to attend the night school, who showed
from the first moment that they were bent on mischief. By talking aloud, joking, telling stories, and
laughing, they stopped the work of the school. On
my repeated appeals for quiet and order, they became the more boisterous, and gave great merriment
to a few of the scholars present. I finally urged the

young man, a tall, powerful fellow, to be quiet or at
once to leave, declaring that at all hazards I must
and would have perfect order; but he only mocked
at me, and assumed a fighting attitude. Quietly
locking the door and putting the key in my pocket,
I turned to my desk, armed myself with the cane,
and dared any one at his peril to interfere betwixt
us. It was a rough struggle, he smashing at me
clumsily with his fists, I with quick movements
evading and dealing him blow after blow with the
heavy cane for several rounds, till at length he
crouched down at his desk, exhausted and beaten,
and I ordered him to turn to his book, which he did
in sulky silence. Going to my desk, I addressed
them and asked them to inform all who wished to
come to the school, "that if they came for education,
everything would be heartily done that it was in my
power to do; but that any who wished for mischief
had better stay away, as I was determined to
conquer, not to be conquered, and to secure order
and silence, whatever it might cost. Further, I assured them that that cane would not again be lifted
by me, if kindness and forbearance on my part could
possibly gain the day, as I wished to rule by love
and not by terror. But this young man knew he was
in the wrong, and it was that which had made him
weak against me, though every way stronger far than
I. Yet I would be his friend and helper, if he was
willing to be friendly with me, the same as if this
night had never been.'

A dead silence fell on the school ; every one buried face diligently in book ; and the evening closed in uncommon quiet and order.

Next morning, two of the bigger boys at the day school, instead of taking their seats like the rest, got in under the gallery where coals and lumber were kept, and made a great noise as if dog and cat were worrying each other. Pleading with them only increased the uproar; so I locked the doors, laid past the keys, and proceeded with the morning's work. Half an hour before the mid-day rest, I began singing a hymn, and marched the children round as if to leave ; then the two young rascals came out, and, walking in front, sang boisterously. Seizing the first by the collar, I made him stagger into the middle of the floor, and dragging the other beside him, I raised my heavy cane and dared them to move. Ordering the children to resume their seats, I appointed them a jury to hear the case and to pass sentence. The two were found guilty, and awarded a severe lashing. I proposed, as this was their first offence, and as I only used the cane for a last resource, to forego all punishment, if they apologized and promised to be attentive and obedient in the future. They both heartily did so, and became my favourite scholars. Next evening I had little difficulty, as the worst characters did not at once return, guessing that they had got a bit of lion in the new dominie, that was more likely to subdue than to be subdued.

On the following day, the parents of some children,

getting alarmed by the rumours of these exploits, waited on me with the minister, and said their children were terrified to come. I said that no *child* had been beaten by me, but that I insisted upon order and obedience; I reminded the minister that of my immediate predecessors three had suffered from these rowdies in the evening class—one actually going wrong in the mind over the worry, another losing his health and dying, and the third leaving in disgust; and finally I declared that I must either be master, at whatever cost, or leave the school. From that time perfect order was established, and the school flourished apace. During next week, many of the worst characters returned to their class work in the evening; but thenceforward the behaviour of all towards me was admirable. The attendance grew, till the school became crowded, both during the day and at night. During the mid-day hour even, I had a large class of young women who came to improve themselves in writing and arithmetic. By-and-by the cane became a forgotten implement; the sorrow and pain which I showed as to badly done lessons, or anything blameworthy, proved the far more effectual penalty.

The School Committee had promised me at least ten shillings per week, and guaranteed to make up any deficit if the fees fell short of that sum; but if the income from fees exceeded that sum, all was to be mine. Affairs went on prosperously for a season; indeed, too much so for my selfish interest. The committee, regarding the arrangement with me as

P. 4

only temporary, took advantage of the larger attendance and better repute of the school, to secure the services of a master of the highest grade. The parents of many of the children, resenting this, offered to take and seat a hall if I would remain and carry on an opposition school; but, besides regarding this as scarcely fair to the committee, however unhandsomely they had treated me, I knew too well that I had neither education nor experience to compete with an accomplished teacher, and so declined the proposal, though grateful for their kind appreciation. Their children, however, got up a testimonial and subscription, in token of their gratitude and esteem, which was presented to me on the day before I left; and this I valued chiefly because the presentation was made by the young fellows who at first behaved so badly, but were now my warm friends.

Once more I committed my future to the Lord God of my father, assured that in my very heart I was willing and anxious to serve Him and to follow the blessed Saviour, yet feeling keenly that intense darkness had once again enclosed my path.

III.

IN GLASGOW CITY MISSION.

CHAPTER III.

IN GLASGOW CITY MISSION.

"He leadeth me."—A Degraded District.—The Gospel in a
Hay-Loft.—New Mission Premises.—At Work for Jesus.—
At War with Hell.—Sowing Gospel Seeds.—Publicans on
the War Path—Marched to the Police Office.—Papists
and Infidels.—An Infidel Saved.—An Infidel in Despair.—
A Brand from the Burning.—A Saintly Child.—Papists in
Arms.—Elder and Student.

BEFORE undertaking the Maryhill school, I had
applied to be taken on as an agent in the
Glasgow City Mission ; and the night before I had
to leave Maryhill, I received a letter from Rev.
Thomas Caie, the superintendent of the said Mission,
saying that the directors had kept their eyes on me
ever since my application, and requesting, as they
understood I was leaving the school, that I would
appear before them the next morning, and have my
qualifications for becoming a Missionary examined
into. Praising God, I went off at once, passed the
examination successfully, and was appointed to spend
two hours that afternoon and the following Monday
in visitation with two of the directors, calling at every
house in a low district of the town, and conversing

with all the characters encountered there on their eternal welfare. I had also to preach a "trial" discourse in a Mission meeting, where a deputation of directors would be present, the following evening being Sunday; and on Wednesday evening, they met again to hear their reports and to accept or reject me. All this had come upon me so unexpectedly, that I almost anticipated failure; but looking up for help I went through with it, and on the fifth day after leaving the school they called me before a meeting of directors, and informed me that I had passed my trials most successfully, and that the reports were so favourable that they had unanimously resolved to receive me at once as one of their City Missionaries. It was further explained that one of their number, Matthew Fairley, Esq., an elder in Dr. Symington's congregation, had guaranteed the half of my salary for two years, the other half to be met by the resources of the Mission voluntarily contributed,—the whole salary at that time amounting to £40 per annum. The district allocated to me was one especially needful and trying, that had never been occupied, in and around the Green Street of Calton, and I was enjoined to enter upon my duties at once. After receiving many good and kind counsels from these good and kind men, one of them in prayer very solemnly dedicated me and my work to the Lord; and several of them were appointed to introduce me to my district, taking a day each by turns, and to assist me in making arrangements for the on-carrying of the work.

Deeply solemnized with the responsibilities of my'
new office, I left that meeting praising God for all
His undeserved mercies, and seeing most clearly His
gracious hand in all the way by which He had led
me, and the trials by which He had prepared me for
the sphere of service. Man proposes—God disposes.

Most of these directors were men of God, adapted
and qualified for this special work, and very helpful
in counsel as they went with me from day to day, in-
troducing me to my district, and seeing the character
and position of the people dwelling there. Looking
back upon these Mission experiences, I have ever felt
that they were, to me and many others, a good and
profitable training of students for the office of the
Ministry; preparing us to deal with men of every
shade of thought and of character, and try to lead
them to the knowledge and service of the Lord Jesus.
I found the district a very degraded one. Many
families said they had never been visited by any
minister; and many were lapsed professors of religion
who had attended no church for ten, sixteen, or
twenty years, and said they had never been called
upon by any minister, nor by any Christian visitor.
In it were congregated many avowed infidels,
Romanists, and drunkards,—living together, and
associated for evil, but apparently without any effective counteracting influence. In many of its closes
and courts sin and vice walked about openly—naked
and *not* ashamed.

We were expected to spend four hours daily in

visiting from house to house, holding small prayer
meetings amongst those visited, calling them together
also in evening meetings, and trying by all means to
do whatever good was possible amongst them. The
only place in the whole district available for a Sabbath evening Evangelistic Service was a hay-loft,
under which a cow-feeder kept a large number of
cows, and which was reached by an outside rickety
wooden stair. After nearly a year's hard work, I had
only six or seven non-church-goers, who had been
led to attend regularly there, besides about the same
number who met on a week evening in the ground-
floor of a house kindly granted for the purpose by
a poor and industrious but ill-used Irishwoman.
She supported her family by keeping a little shop,
and selling coals. Her husband was a powerful man
—a good worker, but a hard drinker, and, like too
many others addicted to intemperance, he abused and
beat her, and pawned and drank everything he could
get hold of. She, amid many prayers and tears, bore
everything patiently, and strove to bring up her only
daughter in the fear of God. We exerted, by God's
blessing, a good influence upon him through our
meetings. He became a total abstainer, gave up his
evil ways, and attended church regularly with his
wife. As his interest increased, he tried to bring
others also to the meeting, and urged them to become abstainers. His wife became a centre of help
and of good influence in all the district, as she
kindly invited all and welcomed them to the meeting

in her house, and my work grew every day more hopeful.

Seeing, however, that one year's hard work showed such small results, the directors proposed to remove me to another district, as in their estimation the non-church-goers in Green Street were unassailable by ordinary means. I pleaded for six months' longer trial, as I had gained the confidence of many of the poor people there, and had an invincible faith that the good seed sown would soon bear blessed fruit. To this the directors kindly agreed. At our next meeting I informed those present that, if we could not draw out more of the non-church-goers to attend the services, I should be removed to another part of the city. Each one there and then agreed to bring another to our next meeting. Both our meetings at once doubled their attendance. My interest in them and their interest in me now grew apace, and, for fear I might be taken away from them, they made another effort, and again doubled our attendance. Henceforth meeting and class were both too large for any house that was available for us in the whole of our district. We instituted a Bible Class, a Singing Class, a Communicants' Class, and a Total Abstinence Society; and, in addition to the usual meetings, we opened two prayer meetings specially for the Calton division of the Glasgow Police—one at a suitable hour for the men on day duty, and another for those on night duty. The men got up a Mutual Improvement Society and Singing Class also amongst themselves, weekly, on another evening. My work now occupied every evening in the week ; and I had two meetings every Sabbath. By God's blessing they all prospered, and gave evidence of such fruits as showed that the Lord was working there for good by our humble instrumentality.

The kind cow-feeder had to inform us—and he did it with much genuine sorrow—that at a given date he would require the hay-loft, which was our place of meeting ; and as no other suitable house or hall could be got, the poor people and I feared the extinction of our work. On hearing this the ostlers and other servants of Menzies, the coach-hirer, who had extensive premises near our place of meeting, of their own accord asked and obtained liberty to clear out a hay-loft of theirs that was seldom in use, and resolved, at their own expense, to erect an outside wooden stair for the convenience of the people. This becoming known, and being much talked of, caused great joy in the district, arrested general attention, and increased the interest of our work. But I saw that, however generous, it could be at the best only another temporary arrangement, and that the premises might again at any moment be required. After prayer I therefore laid the whole case before my good and great-hearted friend, Thomas Binnie, Esq., Monteith Row, and he, after inquiring into all the circumstances, secured a good site for a Mission Hall in a piece of unoccupied ground near our old hay-loft, on which he proposed to build suitable premises at his own expense. At

that very time, however, a commodious block of
buildings, that had been Church, Schools, Manse, etc.,
came into the market. Mr. Binnie persuaded Dr.
Symington's congregation, Great Hamilton Street, in
connection with which my Mission was carried on,
to purchase the whole property for Mission purposes.
Its situation at the foot of Green Street gave it a
control of the whole district where my work lay;
and so the Church was given to me in which to
conduct all my meetings, while the other halls were
adapted as Schools for poor girls and boys, where
they were educated by a proper master, and were
largely supplied with books, clothing, and even food,
by the ladies of the congregation. The purchasing
and using of these buildings for an evangelistic and
educational Mission became a blessing—a very conspicuous blessing—to that district in the Calton of
Glasgow; and the blessing still perpetuates itself,
not only in the old premises, now used for an Indus-
trial School, but still more in the beautiful and
spacious Mission Halls, erected immediately in front
of the old, and consecrated to the work of the Lord
in that poor and crowded and clamant portion of the
city.

Availing myself of the increased facilities, my work
was all re-organized. On Sabbath morning, at seven
o'clock, I had one of the most deeply interesting and
fruitful of all my Classes for the study of the Bible.
It was attended by from seventy to a hundred of the
very poorest young women and grown-up lads of the

whole district. They had nothing to put on except their ordinary work-day clothes,—all without bonnets, some without shoes. Beautiful was it to mark how the poorest began to improve in personal appearance immediately after they came to our class; how they gradually got shoes and one bit of clothing after another, to enable them to attend our other meetings. and then to go to church; and, above all, how eagerly they sought to bring others with them, taking a deep personal interest in all the work of the Mission. Long after they themselves could appear in excellent dress, many of them still continued to attend in their working clothes, and to bring other and poorer' girls with them to that morning class, and thereby helped to improve and elevate their companions.

My delight in that Bible Class was among the purest joys in all my life, and the results were amongst the most certain and precious of all my ministry. Yet it was not made successful without unceasing pains and prayers. What would my younger brethren in the Ministry, or in the Mission, think of starting out at six o'clock every Sunday morning, running from street to street for an hour, knocking at the doors and rousing the careless, and thus getting together, and keeping together, their Bible Class? This was what I did at first; but, in course of time, a band of voluntary visitors belonging to the class took charge of all the irregulars, the indifferents, and the new-comers, and thereby not only relieved and assisted me, but vastly increased their own personal interest, and became warmly attached to each other.

I had also a very large Bible Class—a sort of Bible-reading—on Monday night, attended by all, of both sexes and of any age, who cared to come or had any interest in the work. Wednesday evening, again, was devoted to a Prayer Meeting for all, and the attendance often more than half-filled the Church. There I usually took up some book of Holy Scripture, and read and lectured right through, practically expounding and applying it. On Thursday I held a Communicants' Class, intended for the more careful instruction of all who wished to become full members of the Church. Our constant text-book was "Patterson on the Shorter Catechism," than which I have never seen a better compendium of the doctrines of Holy Scripture. Each being thus trained for a season, received from me, if found worthy, a letter to the minister of any Protestant Church which he or she inclined to join. In this way great numbers became active and useful communicants in the surrounding congregations, and eight young lads of humble circumstances educated themselves for the ministry of the Church,—most of them getting their first lessons in Latin and Greek from my very poor stock of the same! Friday evening was occupied with a Singing Class, teaching Church music, and practising for our Sabbath meetings. On Saturday evening we held our Total Abstinence meeting, at which the members themselves took a principal part, in readings, addresses, recitations, singing hymns, etc.

Great good resulted from this Total Abstinence work. Many adults took and kept the pledge, thereby greatly increasing the comfort and happiness of their homes. Many were led to attend the church on the Lord's Day, who had formerly spent it in rioting and drinking. But, above all, it trained the young to fear the very name of intoxicating drink, and to hate and keep far away from everything that led to intemperance. From observation, at an early age I became convinced that mere Temperance Societies were a failure, and that Total Abstinence, by the grace of God, was the only sure preventive as well as remedy. What was temperance in one man was drunkenness in another; and all the drunkards came not from those who practised total abstinence, but from those who practised or tried to practise temperance. I had seen *temperance* men drinking wine in the presence of others who drank to excess, and never could see how they felt clear of blame; and I had known ministers and others, once strong temperance advocates, fall through their "moderation" and become drunkards. Therefore it has all my life appeared to me beyond dispute, in reference to intoxicants of every kind, that the only rational temperance is total abstinence from them as beverages, and the use of them only as drugs, and then only with extreme caution, as they are deceptive and deleterious poisons of the most debasing and demoralizing kind. I found also, that when I tried to reclaim a drunkard, or caution any one as to intemperate habits, one of the first questions was,—

"Are you a pledged Abstainer yourself?"

By being enabled to reply decidedly, "Yes, I am," the mouth of the objector was closed; and that gave me a hundred-fold more influence with him than if I had had to confess that I was only "temperate." For the good of others, and for the increase of their personal influence as the servants of Christ, I would plead with every Minister and Missionary, every office-bearer and Sabbath school teacher, every one who wishes to work for the Lord Jesus in the family, the Church, and the world, to be a Total Abstainer from all intoxicating drinks.

I would add my testimony also against the use of tobacco, which injures and leads many astray, especially the very young, and which never can be required by any person in ordinary health. But I would not be understood to regard the evils that flow from it as deserving to be mentioned in comparison with the unutterable woes and miseries of intemperance. To be protected, however, from suspicion and from evil, all the followers of Jesus should, in self-denial (how small!) and consecration to His service, be pledged Abstainers from both of these selfish indulgences, which are certainly injurious to many, which are no ornament to any character, and which can be no help in well-doing. Praise God for the many who are now so pledged! Happy day for poor Humanity, when

all the Lord's people adopt this self-denying ordi-
nance for the good of the race !

Not boastfully, but gratefully, let me record that
my Classes and Meetings were now attended by such
numbers that they were amongst the largest and
most successful that the City Mission had ever
known ; and by God's blessing I was enabled to
develop them into a regular, warmly attached, and
intelligent Congregation. My work, however exacting, was full of joy to me. From five to six hundred
people were in usual weekly attendance ; consisting
exclusively of poor working persons, and largely of
the humbler class of mill-workers. So soon as their
circumstances improved, they were constantly removing to more respectable and healthy localities,
and got to be scattered over all the city. But wherever they went, I visited them regularly to prevent
their falling away, and held by them till I got them
interested in some Church near where they had
gone to live. On my return, many years after, from
the Foreign Mission field, there was scarcely a congregation in any part of the city where some one
did not warmly salute me with the cry, " Don't you
remember me ? " And then, after greetings, came
the well-remembered name of one or other member
of my old Bible Class.

Such toils left me but small time for private studies.
The City Missionary was required to spend four hours
daily in his work ; but often had I to spend double
that time, day after day, in order to overtake what was

laid upon me. About eight or ten of my most devoted young men, and double that number of young women, whom I had trained to become visitors and tract distributors, greatly strengthened my hands. Each of the young men by himself, and the young women two by two, had charge of a portion of a street, which was visited by them regularly twice every month. At a monthly meeting of all our Workers, reports were given in, changes were noted, and all matters brought under notice were attended to. Besides, if any note or message were left at my lodging, or any case of sickness or want reported, it was looked after by me without delay. Several Christian gentlemen, mill-owners and other employers in the Calton, Mile-end, and Bridgeton of Glasgow, were so interested in my work that they kindly offered to give employment to every deserving person recommended by me, and that relieved much distress and greatly increased my influence for good.

Almost the only enemies I had were the keepers of Public-Houses, whose trade had been injured by my Total Abstinence Society. Besides the Saturday night meetings all the year round, we held, in summer evenings and on Saturday afternoons, Evangelistic and Total Abstinence services in the open air. We met in Thomson's Lane, a short, broad street, not open for the traffic of conveyances, and admirably situated for our purposes. Our pulpit was formed by the top of an outside stair, leading to the second flat of a house in the middle of the lane. Prominent

P.   5

Christian workers took part with us in delivering
addresses; an intimation through my classes usually
secured good audiences; and the hearty singing of
hymns by my Mission Choir gave zest and joy to the
whole proceedings. Of other so-called "attractions"
we had none, and needed none, save the sincere pro-
clamation of the Good Tidings from God to men!

On one occasion, it becoming known that we
had arranged for a special Saturday afternoon de-
monstration, a deputation of Publicans complained
beforehand to the Captain of the Police that our
meetings were interfering with their legitimate trade.
He heard their complaints and promised to send
officers to watch the meeting, prevent any disturbance, and take in charge all offenders, but declined to
prohibit the meetings till he received their reports.
The Captain, a pious Wesleyan, who was in full sympathy with us and our work, informed me of the
complaints made and intimated that his men would
be present, but I was just to conduct the meeting as
usual, and he would guarantee that strict justice
would be done. The Publicans, having announced
amongst their sympathisers that the Police were to
break up and prevent our meeting and take the con-
ductors in charge, a very large crowd assembled, both
friendly and unfriendly, for the Publicans and their
hangers-on were there "to see the fun," and to help
in baiting the Missionary. Punctually, I ascended
the stone stair, accompanied by another Missionary
who was also to deliver an address, and announced

our opening hymn. As we sang, a company of
Police appeared, and were quietly located here and
there among the crowd, the serjeant himself taking
his post close by the platform, whence the whole
assembly could be scanned. Our enemies were
jubilant, and signals were passed betwixt them and
their friends, as if the time had come to provoke a
row. Before the hymn was finished, Captain Baker
himself, to the infinite surprise of friend and foe alike,
joined us on the platform, devoutly listened to all
that was said, and waited till the close. The Publicans could not for very shame leave, while he was
there at their suggestion and request, though they
had wit enough to perceive that his presence had
frustrated all their sinister plans. They had to hear
our addresses and prayers and hymns ; they had to
listen to the intimation of our future meetings.
When all had quietly dispersed, the Captain warmly
congratulated us on our large and well-conducted
congregation, and hoped that great good would result
from our efforts. This opposition, also, the Lord overruled to increase our influence, and to give point and
publicity to our assaults upon the kingdom of Satan.

Though disappointed thus, some of the Publicans
resolved to have revenge. On the following Saturday
evening, when a large meeting was being addressed
in our Green Street Church, which had to be entered
by a great iron gateway, a spirit merchant ran his
van in front of the gate, so that the people could not
leave the Church without its removal. Hearing this,

I sent two of my young men to draw it aside and clear the way. The Publican, watching near by in league with two policemen, pounced upon the young men whenever they seized the shafts, and gave them in charge for removing his property. On hearing that the young men were being marched to the Police Office, I ran after them and asked what was their offence? They replied that they were prisoners for injuring the spirit merchant's property; and the officers tartly informed me that if I further interfered I would be taken too. I replied, that as the young men only did what was necessary, and at my request, I would go with them to the Office. The cry now went through the street, that the Publicans were sending the Missionary and his young men to the Police Office, and a huge mob rushed together to rescue us; but I earnestly entreated them not to raise disturbance, but allow us quietly to pass on. At the Office, it appeared as if the lieutenant on duty and the men under him were all in sympathy with the Publicans. He took down in writing all their allegations, but would not listen to us. At this stage a handsomely dressed and dignified gentleman came forward and said,—

"What bail is required?"

A few sharp words passed; another, and apparently higher, officer entered, and took part in the colloquy. I could only hear the gentleman protest, in authoritative tones, the policemen having been quietly asked some questions,—

"I know this whole case, I will expose it to the bottom; expect me here to stand by the Missionary and these young men on Monday morning."

Before I could collect my wits to thank him, and before I quite understood what was going on, he had disappeared; and the superior officer turned to us and intimated in a very respectful manner that the charge had been withdrawn, and that I and my friends were at liberty. I never found out exactly who the gentleman was that befriended us; but from the manner in which he asserted himself and was listened to, I saw that he was well known in official quarters. From that day our work progressed without further open opposition, and many who had been slaves of intemperance were not only reformed, but became fervent workers in the Total Abstinence cause.

Though intemperance was the main cause of poverty, suffering, misery, and vice in that district of Glasgow, I had also considerable opposition from Romanists and Infidels, many of whom met in clubs, where they drank together and gloried in their wickedness and in leading other young men astray. Against these I prepared and delivered lectures, at the close of which discussion was allowed; but I fear they did little good. These men embraced the opportunity of airing their absurdities, or sowing the seeds of corruption in those whom otherwise they could never have reached, while their own hearts and minds were fast shut against all conviction or light.

One infidel Lecturer in the district became very ill.

His wife called me in to visit him. I found him possessed of a circulating library of infidel books, by which he sought to pervert unwary minds. Though he had talked and lectured much against the Gospel, he did not at all really understand its message. He had read the Bible, but only to find food there for ridicule. Now supposed to be dying, he confessed that his mind was full of terror as to the Future. After several visits and frequent conversations and prayers, he became genuinely and deeply interested, drank in God's message of salvation, and cried aloud with many tears for pardon and peace. He bitterly lamented the evil he had done, and called in all the infidel literature that he had in circulation, with the purpose of destroying it. He began to speak solemnly to any of his old companions that came to see him, telling them what he had found in the Lord Jesus. At his request I bought and brought to him a Bible, which he received with great joy, saying, " This is the book for me now ; " and adding, " Since you were here last, I gathered together all my infidel books ; my wife locked the door, till she and my daughter tore them to pieces, and I struck the light that reduced the pile to ashes."

As long as he lived, this man was unwearied and unflinching in testifying, to all that crossed his path, how much Jesus Christ had been to his heart and soul; and he died in the possession of a full and blessed hope.

Another Infidel, whose wife was a Roman Catholic,

also became unwell, and gradually sank under great
suffering and agony. His blasphemies against God
were known and shuddered at by all the neighbours.
His wife pled with me to visit him. She refused, at
my suggestion, to call her own priest, so I accompanied her at last. The man refused to hear one
word about spiritual things, and foamed with rage.
He even spat at me, when I mentioned the name of
Jesus. "The natural man receiveth not the things of
the Spirit of God; for they are foolishness unto him!"
There is a wisdom which is at best earthly, and at
worst "sensual and devilish." His wife asked me to
take care of the little money they had, as she would
not entrust it to her own priest. I visited the poor
man daily, but his enmity to God and his sufferings
together seemed to drive him mad. His yells
gathered crowds on the streets. He tore to pieces
his very bed-clothes, till they had to bind him on
the iron bed where he lay, foaming and blaspheming.
Towards the end I pled with him even then to look to
the Lord Jesus, and asked if I might pray with him?
With all his remaining strength, he shouted at me,—

"Pray for me to the devil!"

Reminding him how he had always denied that
there was any devil, I suggested that he must surely
believe in one now, else he would scarcely make such
a request, even in mockery. In great rage he cried,—

"Yes, I believe there is a devil, and a God, and a
just God, too; but I have hated Him in life, and I
hate Him in death!"

With these awful words, he wriggled into Eternity; but his shocking death produced a very serious impression for good, especially amongst young men, in the district where his character was known.

How different was the case of that Doctor who also had been an unbeliever as well as a drunkard! Highly educated, skilful, and gifted above most in his profession, he was taken into consultation for specially dangerous cases, whenever they could find him tolerably sober. After one of his excessive "bouts," he had a dreadful attack of *delirium tremens.* At one time, wife and watchers had a fierce struggle to dash from his lips a draught of prussic acid; at another, they detected the silver-hafted lancet concealed in the band of his shirt, as he lay down, to bleed himself to death. His aunt came and pled with me to visit him. My heart bled for his poor young wife and two beautiful little children. Visiting him twice daily, and sometimes even more frequently, I found the way somehow into his heart, and he would do almost anything for me and longed for my visits. When again the fit of self-destruction seized him, they sent for me; he held out his hand eagerly, and grasping mine, said,—

" Put all these people out of the room, remain you with me; I will be quiet, I will do everything you ask!".

I got them all to leave, but whispered to one in passing to "keep near the door."

Alone I sat beside him, my hand in his, and kept up a quiet conversation for several hours. After we

had talked of everything that I could think of, and it
was now far into the morning, I said,—

"If you had a Bible here, we might read a chapter,
verse about."

He said dreamily, "There was once a Bible above
yon press; if you can get up to it, you might find it
there yet."

Getting it, dusting it, and laying it on a small
table which I drew near to the sofa on which we sat,
we read there and then a chapter together. After
this, I said, "Now, shall we pray?"

He replied heartily, "Yes."

I having removed the little table, we kneeled down
together at the sofa; and after a solemn pause, I
whispered, "You pray first."

He replied, "I curse, I cannot pray; would you
have me curse God to His face?"

I answered, "You promised to do all that I asked;
you must pray, or try to pray, and let me hear that
you cannot."

He said, "I cannot curse God on my knees; let me
stand, and I will curse Him; I cannot pray."

I gently held him on his knees, saying, "Just try
to pray, and let me hear you cannot."

Instantly he cried out, "O Lord, Thou knowest
I cannot pray," and was going to say something
dreadful as he strove to rise up. But I just took the
words he had uttered as if they had been my own,
and continued the prayer, pleading for him and his
dear ones as we knelt there together, till he showed

that he was completely subdued and lying low at the
feet of God.   On rising from our knees he was manifestly greatly impressed, and I said,—

"Now, as I must be at College by daybreak and
must return to my lodging for my books and an
hour's rest, will you do one thing more for me before
I go?"

"Yes," was his reply.

"Then," said I, "it is long since you had a refreshing sleep; now, will you lie down, and I will sit
by you till you fall asleep?"

He lay down, and was soon fast asleep. After com-
mending him to the care and blessing of the Lord,
I quietly slipped out, and his wife returned to watch
by his side. When I came back later in the day, after
my classes were over, he, on hearing my foot and
voice, came running to meet me, and clasping me in
his arms, cried,—

"Thank God, I can pray now! I rose this
morning refreshed from sleep, and prayed with my
wife and children for the first time in my life; and
now I shall do so every day, and serve God while I
live, who hath dealt in so great mercy with me!"

After delightful conversation, he promised to go
with me to Dr. Symington's church on Sabbath Day;
there he took sittings beside me; at next half-yearly
communion he and his wife were received into mem-
bership, and their children were baptized; and from
that day till his death he led a devoted and most
useful Christian life. Henceforth, as a medical man,

he delighted to attend all poor and destitute cases
which we brought under his care; he ministered to
them for Jesus' sake, and spoke to them of their
blessed Saviour. When he came across cases that
were hopeless, he sent for me to visit them too, being
as anxious for their souls as for their bodies. He
died, years after this, of consumption, partly at least
the fruit of early excesses; but he was serenely prepared for death, and happy in the assured hope of
eternal blessedness with Christ. He sleeps in Jesus;
and I do believe that I shall meet him in Glory as a
trophy of redeeming grace and love!

In my Mission district, I was the witness of many
joyful departures to be with Jesus,—I do not like to
name them "deaths" at all. Even now, at the distance of nearly forty years, many instances, especially
amongst the young men and women who attended
my classes, rise up before my mind. They left us,
rejoicing in the bright assurance that nothing present
or to come "could ever separate them or us from the
love of God which is in Christ Jesus our Lord."
Several of them, by their conversation even on their
death-bed, were known to have done much good.
Many examples might be given; but I can find room
for only one. John Sim, a dear little boy, was carried
away by consumption. His childish heart seemed
to be filled with joy about seeing Jesus. His simple
prattle, mingled with deep questionings, arrested not
only his young companions, but pierced the hearts
of some careless sinners who heard him, and greatly

refreshed the faith of God's dear people. It was the very pathos of song incarnated to hear the weak quaver of his dying voice sing out,—

> " I lay my sins on Jesus,
>   The spotless Lamb of God."

Shortly before his decease he said to his parents, "I am going soon to be with Jesus; but I sometimes fear that I may not see you there."

"Why so, my child?" said his weeping mother.

"Because," he answered, "if you were set upon going to heaven and seeing Jesus there, you would pray about it, and sing about it; you would talk about Jesus to others, and tell them of that happy meeting with Him in Glory. All this my dear Sabbath school teacher taught me, and she will meet me there. Now why did not you, my father and mother, tell me all these things about Jesus, if you are going to meet Him too?"

Their tears fell fast over their dying child; and he little knew, in his unthinking eighth year, what a message from God had pierced their souls through his innocent words. One day an aunt from the country visited his mother, and their talk had run in channels for which the child no longer felt any interest. On my sitting down beside him, he said,—

"Sit you down and talk with me about Jesus; I am tired hearing so much talk about everything else but Jesus; I am going soon to be with Him. Oh, do tell me everything you know or have ever heard about Jesus, the spotless Lamb of God!"

At last the child literally longed to be away, not for rest, or freedom from pain—for of that he had very little—but, as he himself always put it, "to see Jesus." And, after all, that was the wisdom of the heart, however he learned it. Eternal life, here or hereafter, is just the vision of Jesus.

Amongst many of the Roman Catholics in my Mission district, also, I was very kindly received, and allowed even to read the Scriptures and to pray. At length, however, a young woman who professed to be converted by my classes and meetings brought things to a crisis betwixt them and me. She had renounced her former faith, was living in a Protestant family, and looked to me as her pastor and teacher. One night, a closed carriage, with two men and women, was sent from a Nunnery in Clyde Street, to take her and her little sister with them. She refused, and declined all authority on their part, declaring that she was now a Protestant by her own free choice. During this altercation, a message had been sent for me. On arriving, I found the house filled with a noisy crowd. Before them all, she appealed to me for protection from these her enemies. The Romanists, becoming enraged, jostled me into a corner of the room, and there enclosed me. The two women pulled her out of bed by force, for the girl had been sick, and began to dress her, but she fainted among their hands.

I called out,—

Do not murder the poor girl! Get her water,

quick, quick!" and leaving my hat on the table, I
rushed through amongst them, as if in search of
water, and they let me pass. Knowing that the
house had only one door, I quickly slipped the key
from within, shut and locked the door outside, and
with the key in my hand ran 'to the Police Office.
Having secured two constables to protect the girl
and take the would-be captors into custody, I returned, opened the door, and found, alas! that these
constables were themselves Roman Catholics, and at
once set about frustrating me and assisting their own
friends. The poor sick girl was supported by the
arms into the carriage; the policemen cleared the
way through the crowd; and before I could force
my way through the obstructives in the house, the
conveyance was already starting. I appealed and
shouted to the crowds to protect the girl, and seize
and take the whole party to the Police Office. A
gentleman in the crowd took my part, and said to
a big Highland policeman in the street,—

"Mac, I commit that conveyance and party to
you on a criminal charge, before witnesses; you will
suffer, if they escape."

The driver lashing at his horse to get away, Mac
drew his baton and struck, when the driver leapt
down to the street on the opposite side, and threw
the reins in the policeman's face. Thereupon our
stalwart friend at once mounted the box, and drove
straight for the Police Office. On arriving there, we
discovered that only the women were inside with the

sick girl—the men having escaped in the scuffle and the crush. What proved more disappointing was that the lieutenant on duty happened to be a Papist, who, after hearing our statement and conferring with the parties in the conveyance, returned, and said,—

"Her friends are taking her to a comfortable home; you have no right to interfere, and I have let them go." He further refused to hear the grounds of our complaint, and ordered the police to clear the Office.

Next morning, a false and foolish account of the whole affair appeared in the Newspapers, condemnatory of the Mission and of myself; a meeting of the directors was summoned, and the Superintendent came to my lodging to take me before them. Having heard all, and questioned and cross-questioned me, they resolved to prosecute the abductors of the girl. The Nunnery authorities confessed that the little sister was with them, but denied that *she* had been taken in there, or that they knew anything of her case. Though the girl was sought for carefully by the Police, and by all the members of my class, for nearly a fortnight, no trace of her or of the coachman or of any of the parties could be discovered; till one day from a cellar, through a grated window, she called to one of my class girls passing by, and begged her to run and let me know that she was confined there. At once, the directors of the City Mission were informed by me, and Police were sent to rescue her; but on examining that house they found that she had been again removed. The occupiers denied all knowledge of where she had gone, or who had taken her away from their lodging. All other efforts failed to find her, till she was left at the Poor House door, far gone in dropsy, and soon after died in that last refuge of the destitute and forsaken.

Anonymous letters were now sent, threatening my life ; and I was publicly cursed from the altar by the priests in Abercromby Street Chapel. The directors of the Mission, fearing violence, advised me to leave Glasgow for a short holiday, and even offered to arrange for my being taken for work in Edinburgh for a year, that the fanatical passions of the Irish Papists might have time to subside. But I refused to leave my work. I went on conducting it all as in the past. The worst thing that happened was, that on rushing one day past a row of houses occupied exclusively by Papists, a stone thrown from one of them cut me severely above the eye, and I fell stunned and bleeding. When I recovered and scrambled to my feet, no person of course that could be suspected was to be seen ! The doctor having dressed the wound, it rapidly healed, and after a short confinement I resumed my work and my studies without any further serious annoyance. Attempts were made more than once, in these Papist closes, and I believe by the Papists themselves, to pour pails of boiling water on my head, over windows and down dark stairs, but in every case I marvellously escaped ; and as I would not turn coward, their malice tired itself out, and they ultimately left me entirely at peace. Is not this a feature of the lower Irish, and especially Popish population? Let them see that bullying makes you afraid, and they will brutally and cruelly misuse you; but defy them fearlessly, or take them by the nose, and they will crouch like whelps beneath your feet. Is there anything in their Religion that accounts for this? Is it not a system of alternating tyranny on the one part, and terror, abject terror, on the other?

About this same time there was an election of elders for Dr. Symington's congregation, and I was by an almost unanimous vote chosen for that office. For years now I had been attached to them as City Missionary for their district, and many friends urged me to accept the eldership, as likely to increase my usefulness, and give me varied experience for my future work. My dear father, also, himself an elder in the congregation at Dumfries, advised me similarly; and though very young, comparatively, for such a post, I did accept the office, and continued to act as an elder and member of Dr. Symington's kirk session, till by-and-by I was ordained as a Missionary to the New Hebrides, where the great lot of my life had been cast by the Lord, as yet unknown to me.

All through my City Mission period, I was painfully carrying on my studies, first at the University of Glasgow, and thereafter at the Reformed Presbyterian Divinity Hall; and also medical classes at the Andersonian College. With the exception of one session, when failure of health broke me down, I struggled patiently on through ten years. The

P.

6

work was hard and most exacting; and if I never
attained the scholarship for which I thirsted—being
but poorly grounded in my younger days—I yet had
much of the blessed Master's presence in all my
efforts, which many better scholars sorely lacked;
and I was sustained by the lofty aim which burned
all these years bright within my soul, namely,—to
be qualified as a preacher of the Gospel of Christ,
to be owned and used by Him for the salvation of
perishing men.

IV.

FOREIGN MISSION CLAIMS.

CHAPTER IV.

FOREIGN MISSION CLAIMS.

The Wail of the Heathen.—A Missionary Wanted.—Two Souls
  on the Altar.—Lions in the Path.—The Old Folks at
  Home.—Successors in Green Street Mission.—Old Green
  Street Hands.—A Father in God.

HAPPY in my work as I felt, and successful by
  the blessing of God, yet I continually heard,
and chiefly during my last years in the Divinity Hall,
the wail of the perishing Heathen in the South Seas;
and I saw that few were caring for them, while I well
knew that many would be ready to take up my work
in Calton, and carry it forward perhaps with more
efficiency than myself. Without revealing the state
of my mind to any person, this was the supreme
subject of my daily meditation and prayer; and this
also led me to enter upon those medical studies, in
which I purposed taking the full course; but at the
close of my third year, an incident occurred, which
led me at once to offer myself for the Foreign Mission field.

The Reformed Presbyterian Church of Scotland, in
which I had been brought up, had been advertising

for another Missionary to join the Rev. John Inglis
in his grand work in the New Hebrides.   Dr. Bates,
the excellent convener of the Heathen Missions Committee, was deeply grieved, because for two years
their appeal had failed.   At length, the Synod, after
much prayer and consultation, felt the claims of the
Heathen so urgently pressed upon them by the Lord's
repeated calls, that they resolved to cast lots, to dis-
cover whether God would thus select any Minister to
be relieved from his home-charge, and designated as
a Missionary to the South Seas.   Each member of
Synod, as I was informed, agreed to hand in, after
solemn appeal to God, the names of the three best
qualified in his esteem for such a work, and he who
had the clear majority was to be loosed from his
congregation, and to proceed to the Mission field—
or the first and second highest, if two could be secured.   Hearing this debate, and feeling an intense
interest in these most unusual proceedings, I remember yet the hushed solemnity of the prayer before
the names were handed in.   I remember the strained
silence that held the Assembly while the scrutinizers
retired to examine the papers; and I remember how
tears blinded my eyes when they returned to an-
nounce that the result was so indecisive, that it was
clear that the Lord had not in that way provided a
Missionary.   The cause was once again solemnly laid
before God in prayer, and a cloud of sadness appeared to fall over all the Synod.

The Lord kept saying within me, "Since none better

qualified can be got, rise and offer yourself!" Almost
overpowering was the impulse to answer aloud, "Here
am I, send me." But I was dreadfully afraid of mis-
taking my own emotions for the will of God. So I
resolved to make it a subject of close deliberation
and prayer for a few days longer, and to look at the
proposal from every possible aspect. Besides, I was
keenly solicitous about the effect upon the hundreds
of young people and others, now attached to all my
classes and meetings ; and yet I felt a growing assurance that this was the call of God to His servant,
and that He who was willing to employ me in the
work abroad, was both able and willing to provide
for the on-carrying of my work at home. The wail
and the claims of the Heathen were constantly sound-
ing in my ears. I saw them perishing for lack of the
knowledge of the true God and His Son Jesus, while
my Green Street people had the open Bible, and all
the means of grace within easy reach, which, if they
rejected, they did so wilfully, and at their own peril.
None seemed prepared for the Heathen field ; many
were capable and ready for the Calton service. My
medical studies, as well as my literary and divinity
training, had specially qualified me in some ways for
the Foreign field, and from every aspect at which I
could look the whole facts in the face, the voice within me sounded like a voice from God.

It was under good Dr. Bates of West Campbell
Street that I had begun my career in Glasgow—receiving £25 per annum for district visitation in connection

with his congregation, along with instruction under
Mr. Hislop and his staff in the Free Church Normal
Seminary—and oh, how Dr. Bates did rejoice, and
even weep for joy, when I called on him, and offered
myself for the New Hebrides Mission! I returned to
my lodging with a lighter heart than I had for some
time enjoyed, feeling that nothing so clears the vision,
and lifts up the life, as a decision to move forward in
what you know to be entirely the will of the Lord.
I said to my fellow-student, who had chummed with
me all through our course at college,—

"I have been away signing my banishment" (a
rather trifling way of talk for such an occasion).
"I have offered myself as a Missionary for the New
Hebrides."

After a long and silent meditation, in which he
seemed lost in far-wandering thoughts, his answer
was,—

"If they will accept of me, I also am resolved to
go!"

I said, "Will you write the convener to that effect,
or let me do so?"

He replied, "You may."

A few minutes later his letter of offer was in the
post office. Next morning, Dr. Bates called upon
us early, and after a long conversation, commended
us and our future work to the Lord God in fervent
prayer.

My fellow-student, Mr. Joseph Copeland, had also
for some time been a very successful City Missionary

in the Camlachie district, while attending along with me at the Divinity Hall. This leading of God, whereby we both resolved at the same time to give ourselves to the Foreign Mission field, was wholly unexpected by us, as we had never once spoken to each other about going abroad. At a meeting of the Heathen Missions Committee, held immediately thereafter, both were, after due deliberation, formally accepted, on condition that we passed successfully the usual examinations required of candidates for the Ministry. And for the next twelve months we were placed under the special committee for advice as to medical experience, acquaintance with the rudiments of trades, and anything else which might be thought useful to us in the Foreign field.

When it became known that I was preparing to go abroad as Missionary, nearly all were dead against the proposal, except Dr. Bates and my fellow-student. My dear father and mother, however, when I consulted them, characteristically replied, "that they had long since given me away to the Lord, and in this matter also would leave me to God's disposal." From other quarters we were besieged with the strongest opposition on all sides. Even Dr. Symington, one of my professors in divinity, and the beloved Minister in connection with whose congregation I had wrought so long as a City Missionary, and in whose kirk session I had for years sat as an elder, repeatedly urged me to remain at home. He argued, "that Green Street Church was doubtless the sphere for

which God had given me peculiar qualifications, and
in which He had so largely blessed my labours ; that
if I left those now attending my classes and meetings, they might be scattered,. and many of them
would probably fall away ; that I was leaving certainty for uncertainty—work in which God had made
me greatly useful, for work in which I might fail to
be useful, and only throw away my life amongst
Cannibals."

' I replied, "that my mind was finally resolved ;
that, though I loved my work and my people, yet I
felt that I could leave them to the care of Jesus, who
would soon provide them a better pastor than I ; and
that, with regard to my life amongst the Cannibals, as
I had only once to die, I was content to leave the
time and place and means in the hand of God, who
had already marvellously preserved me when visiting
cholera patients and the fever-stricken poor ; on that
score I had positively no further concern, having left
it all absolutely to the Lord, whom I sought to serve
and honour, whether in life or by death."

The house connected with my Green Street Church,
was now offered to me for a Manse, and any reasonable salary that I cared to ask (as against the promised £120 per annum for the far-off and dangerous
New Hebrides), on condition that I would remain at
home.　I cannot honestly say that such offers or
opposing influences proved a heavy trial to me ; they
rather tended to confirm my determination that the
path of duty was to go abroad.　Amongst many who

sought to deter me, was one dear old Christian gentleman, whose crowning argument always was,—

"The Cannibals! you will be eaten by Cannibals!"

At last I replied, "Mr. Dickson, you are advanced in years now, and your own prospect is soon to be laid in the grave, there to be eaten by worms; I confess to you, that if I can but live and die serving and honouring the Lord Jesus, it will make no difference to me whether I am eaten by Cannibals or by worms; and in the Great Day my resurrection body will arise as fair as yours in the likeness of our risen Redeemer."

The old gentleman, raising his hands in a deprecating attitude, left the room exclaiming,—

"After that I have nothing more to say!"

My dear Green Street people grieved excessively at the thought of my leaving them, and daily pled with me to remain. Indeed, the opposition was so strong from nearly all, and many of them warm Christian friends, that I was sorely tempted to question whether I was carrying out the Divine will, or only some headstrong wish of my own. This also caused me much anxiety, and drove me close to God in prayer. But again every doubt would vanish, when I clearly saw that all at home had free access to the Bible and the means of grace, with Gospel light shining all around them, while the poor Heathen were perishing, without even the chance of knowing all God's love and mercy to men. Conscience said louder and clearer every day, "Leave all these results with Jesus your

Lord, who said, 'Go ye into all the world, preach the gospel to every creature, and lo! I am with you alway.'" These words kept ringing in my ears; these were our marching orders.

Some retorted upon me, "There are Heathen at home; let us seek and save, first of all, the lost ones perishing at our doors." This I felt to be most true, and an appalling fact; but I unfailingly observed that those who made this retort neglected these home Heathen themselves; and so the objection, as from them, lost all its power. They would ungrudgingly spend more on a fashionable party at dinner or tea, on concert or ball or theatre, or on some ostentatious display, or worldly and selfish indulgence, ten times more, perhaps in a single day, than they would give in a year, or in half a lifetime, for the conversion of the whole Heathen World, either at home or abroad. Objections from all such people must, of course, always count for nothing among men to whom spiritual things are realities. For these people themselves,—I do, and always did, only pity them, as God's stewards, making such a miserable use of time and money entrusted to their care.

On meeting with so many obstructing influences, I again laid the whole matter before my dear parents, and their reply was to this effect:—"Heretofore we feared to bias you, but now we must tell you why we praise God for the decision to which you have been led. Your father's heart was set upon being a Minister, but other claims forced him to give

it up. When you were given to them, your father
and mother laid you upon the altar, their first-born,
to be consecrated, if God saw fit, as a Missionary of
the Cross ; and it has been their constant prayer that
you might be prepared, qualified, and led to this very
decision ; and we pray with all our heart that the
Lord may accept your offering, long spare you, and
give you many souls from the Heathen World for
your hire." From that moment, every doubt as to my
path of duty for ever vanished. I saw the hand of
God very visibly, not only preparing me for, but now·
leading me to, the Foreign Mission field.

Well did I know that the sympathy and prayers
of my dear parents were warmly with me in all my
studies and in all my Mission work; but for my
education they could, of course, give me no money
help. All through, on the contrary, it was my pride
and joy to help them, being the eldest in a family
of eleven. First, I assisted them to purchase the
family cow, without whose invaluable aid my ever-
memorable mother never could have reared and fed
her numerous flock; then, I paid for them the house-
rent and the cow's grass on the Bank Hill, till
some of the others grew up and relieved me by
paying these in my stead; and finally, I helped to
pay the school-fees, to provide clothing—in short,
I gave, and gladly, what could possibly be saved
out of my City Mission salary of £40, ultimately
advanced to £45 per annum. Self-educated thus,
and without the help of one shilling from any other

source, readers will easily imagine that I had many
a staggering difficulty to overcome in my long cur-
riculum in Arts, Divinity, and Medicine; but God so
guided me, and blessed all my little arrangements,
that I never incurred one farthing of personal debt.
There was, however, a heavy burden always pressing
upon me, and crushing my spirit from the day I left
my home, which had been thus incurred.

The late owner of the Dalswinton estate allowed, as
a prize, the cottager who had the tidiest house and
most beautiful flower-garden to sit rent free.   For
several years in succession, my old sea-faring grandfather won this prize, partly by his own handy skill,
partly by his wife's joy in flowers.   Unfortunately no
clearance-receipt had been asked or given for these
rents—the proprietor and his cottars treating each
other as friends rather than as men of business.
The new heir, unexpectedly succeeding, found himself in need of money, and threatened prosecution
for such rents as arrears.   The money had to be
borrowed.   A money-lending lawyer gave it at usu-
rious interest, on condition of my father also becoming responsible for interest and principal.   This
burden hung like a millstone around my grandfather's neck till the day of his death; and it then
became suspended round my father's neck alone.
The lawyer, on hearing of my giving up trade and
entering upon study, threatened to prosecute my
father for the capital, unless my name were given
along with his for security.   Every shilling that I or

any of us could save, all through these ten years of my preparatory classes, went to pay off that interest and gradually to reduce the capital; and this burden we managed, amongst us, to extinguish just on the eve of my departure for the South Seas. Indeed, one of the purest joys connected with that time was that I received my first Foreign Mission salary and outfit money in advance, and could send home a sum sufficient to wipe out the last penny of a claim by that money-lender or by any one else against my beloved parents, in connection with the noble struggle they had made in rearing so large a family in thorough Scottish independence. And that joy was hallowed by the knowledge that my other brothers and sisters were now all willing and able to do what I had been doing—for we stuck to each other and to the old folks like burs, and had all things "in common," as a family in Christ— and I knew that never again, howsoever long they might be spared through a peaceful autumn of life, would the dear old father and mother lack any joy or comfort that the willing hands and loving hearts of all their children could singly or unitedly provide. For all this I did praise the Lord. It consoled me, beyond description, in parting from them, probably for ever in this world at least.

The Directors of Glasgow City Mission along with the Great Hamilton Street congregation, had made every effort to find a suitable successor to me in my Green Street work, but in vain. Des-

pairing of success, as no inexperienced worker could
with any hope undertake it, Rev. Mr. Caie, the superintendent, felt moved to appeal to my brother
Walter,—then in a good business situation in the city,
who had been of late closely associated with me
in all my undertakings,—if he would not come to
the rescue, devote himself to the Mission, and prepare for the Holy Ministry. My brother resigned
a good position and excellent prospects in the business world, set himself to carry forward the Green
Street Mission and did so with abundant energy and
manifest blessing, persevered in his studies, despite
a long-continued illness through injury to his foot,
and became an honoured Minister of the Gospel, in
the Reformed Presbyterian Church first of all, and
now in the Free Church of Scotland, at Chapelton,
near Hamilton.

On my brother withdrawing from Green Street, God
provided for the district a devoted young Minister, admirably adapted for the work, Rev. John Edgar, M.A.,
who succeeded in drawing together such a body of
people that they hived off and built a new church in
Landressy Street, which is now, by amalgamation,
known as the Barrowfield Free Church of Glasgow.
For that fruit too, while giving all praise to other devoted workers, we bless God as we trace the history of
our Green Street Mission. Let him that soweth and
him that reapeth rejoice unfeignedly together! The
spirit of the old Green Street workers lives on too,
as I have already said, in the new premises erected

close thereby; and in none more conspicuously than in the son of my staunch patron and friend, another Thomas Binnie, Esq., who in Foundry Boy meetings and otherwise devotes the consecrated leisure of a busy and prosperous life to the direct personal service of his Lord and Master. The blessing of Jehovah God be ever upon that place, and upon all who there seek to win their fellows to the love and service of Jesus Christ!

When I left Glasgow, many of the young men and women of my classes would, if it had been possible, have gone with me, to live and die among the Heathen. Though chiefly working girls and lads in trades and mills, their deep interest led them to unite their pence and sixpences and to buy web after web of calico, print, and woollen stuffs, which they themselves shaped and sewed into dresses for the women, and kilts and pants for men, on the New Hebrides. This continued to be repeated year by year, long after I had left them; and to this day no box from Glasgow goes to the New Hebrides Mission which does not contain article after article from one or other of the old Green Street hands. I do certainly anticipate that, when they and I meet in Glory, those days in which we learned the joy of Christian service in the Green Street Mission Halls will form no unwelcome theme of holy and happy converse!

That able and devoted Minister of the Gospel, Dr. Bates, the Convener of the Heathen Missions,

P. 7

had taken the deepest and most fatherly interest in all our preparations.   But on the morning of our final examinations he was confined to bed with sickness ; yet could not be content without sending his daughter to wait in an adjoining room near the Presbytery House, to learn .the result, and instantly to carry him word.   When she, hurrying home, informed him that we both had passed successfully, and that the day of our ordination as Missionaries to the New Hebrides had been appointed, the apostolic old man praised God for the glad tidings, and said his work was now done, and that he could depart in peace,—having seen two devoted men set apart to preach the Gospel to these dark and b'oody Islands in answer to his prayers and tears for many a day. Thereafter he rapidly sank, and soon fell asleep in Jesus.   He was from the first a very precious friend to me, one of the ablest Ministers our Church ever had, by far the warmest advocate of her Foreign Missions, and altogether a most attractive, whitesouled, and noble specimen of an ambassador for Christ, beseeching men to be reconciled to God.

V.

THE NEW HEBRIDES.

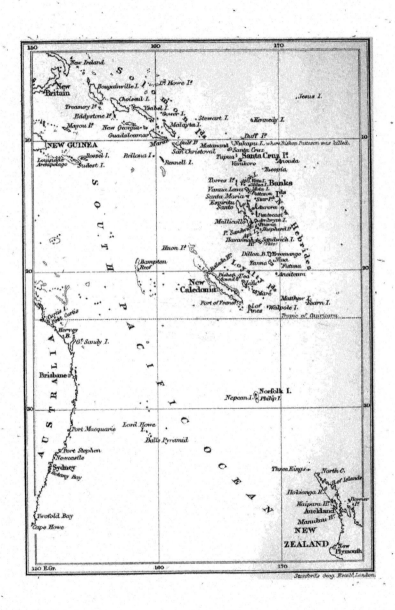

CHAPTER V.

THE NEW HEBRIDES.

License and Ordination.—At Sea.—From Melbourne to Anei-
tyum.—Settlement on Tanna.—Our Mission Stations.—
Diplomatic Chiefs.—Painful First Impressions.—Bloody
Scenes.—The Widow's Doom.

ON the first of December, 1857, the other Mis-
sionary-designate and I were "licensed" as
preachers of the Gospel. Thereafter we spent four
months in visiting and addressing nearly every congregation and Sabbath school in the Reformed Presbyterian Church of Scotland, that the people might
see us and know us, and thereby take a personal
interest in our work. That idea was certainly excellent, and might well be adapted to the larger
Churches, by allocating one Missionary to each pro-
vince or to so many presbyteries, sending him to
address these, and training them to regard him as
their Missionary and his work as theirs. On the
23rd March, 1858, in Dr. Symington's church, Glasgow, in presence of a mighty crowd, and after a
magnificent sermon on "Come over and help us,"
we were solemnly ordained as Ministers of the Gos-

pel, and set apart as Missionaries to the New Hebrides. On the 16th April, 1858, we left the Tail of
the Bank at Greenock, and set sail in the *Clutha*
for the Foreign Mission field.

Our voyage to Melbourne was rather tedious, but
ended prosperously, under Captain Broadfoot, a
kindly, brave-hearted Scot, who did everything that
was possible for our comfort. He himself led the
singing, on board at worship, which was always
charming to me, and was always regularly conducted
—on deck when the weather was fair, below when
it was rough. I was also permitted to conduct Bible
classes amongst the crew and amongst the passengers, at times and places approved of by the
Captain—in which, there was great joy. Nearly
thirty years after, when I returned the second time
to Scotland, a gentleman of good position, and the
father of a large family in the West, saluted me
warmly at the close of one of my meetings, and reminded me that he was my precentor in the Bible
class on board the *Clutha!* He was kind enough
to say that he had never forgotten the scene and
the lessons there.

Arriving at Melbourne, we were welcomed by Rev.
Mr. Moor, Mr. and Mrs. Samuel Wilson, and Mr.
Wright, all Reformed Presbyterians from Geelong.
Mr. Wilson's two children, Jessie and Donald, had
been under our care during the voyage; and my
young wife and I went with them for a few days
on a visit to Geelong, while Mr. Copeland remained

on board the *Clutha* to look after our boxes and to watch for any opportunity of reaching our destination on the Islands. He heard that an American ship, the *Francis P. Sage*, was sailing from Melbourne to Penang; and the Captain agreed to land us on Aneityum, New Hebrides, with our two boats and fifty boxes, for £100. We got on board on the 12th August, but such a gale blew that we did not sail till the 17th. On the *Clutha* all was quiet, and good order prevailed; in the *F. P. Sage* all was noise and profanity. The Captain said he kept his second mate for the purpose of swearing at the men and knocking them about. The voyage was most disagreeable to all of us, but fortunately it lasted only twelve days. On the 29th we were close up to Aneityum; but the Captain refused to land us, even in his boats; some of us suspecting that his men were so badly used, that had they got on shore they would never have returned to him! In any case he had beforehand secured his £100.

He lay off the island till a trader's boat came off to see what we wanted, and by it we sent a note to Dr. Geddie, one of the Missionaries there. Early next morning, Monday, he came off to us in his boat, accompanied by Mr. Mathieson, a newly-arrived Missionary from Nova Scotia; bringing also Captain Anderson in the small mission schooner, the *John Knox*, and a large mission boat called the *Columbia*, well manned with crews of able and willing Natives. Our fifty boxes were soon on board the *John Knox*,

the *Columbia*, and our own boats—all being heavily
loaded and built up, except those that had to be
used in pulling the others ashore. Dr. Geddie, Mr.
Mathieson, Mrs. Paton, and I, were perched among
the boxes on the *John Knox*, and had to hold on
as best we could. On sheering off from the *F. P.
Sage*, one of her davits caught and broke the main-
mast of the little *John Knox* by the deck, and I
saved my wife from being crushed to death by its
fall through managing to swing her instantaneously
aside in an apparently impossible manner. It did
graze Mr. Mathieson, but he was not hurt. The
John Knox, already overloaded, was thus quite disabled; we were about ten miles at sea, and in
imminent danger; but the Captain of the *F. P. Sage*
heartlessly sailed away and left us to struggle with
our fate.

We drifted steadily towards Tanna, an island
of Cannibals, where our goods would have been
plundered and all of us cooked and eaten. Dr.
Geddie's boat and mine had the *John Knox* in
tow; and Mr. Copeland, with a crew of Natives,
was struggling hard with his boat to pull the *Columbia* and her load towards Aneityum. As God
mercifully ordered it, though we had a stiff trade
wind to pull against, we had a comparatively calm
sea; yet we drifted still to leeward, till Dr. Inglis
going round to the harbour in his boat, as he had
heard of our arrival, saw us far at sea, and hastened
to our rescue. All the boats now, with their willing

native crews, got fastened to our schooner, and to
our great joy she began to move ahead. After
pulling for hours and hours, under the scorching
rays of an almost tropical sun, we were all safely
landed on shore at Aneityum about six o'clock in
the evening of August 30th, just four months and
fourteen days since we sailed from Greenock. We
got a hearty welcome from the Missionaries' wives
on the shore, Mrs. Geddie, Mrs. Inglis, and Mrs.
Mathieson, and from all our new friends, the Christian Natives of Aneityum; and the great danger
in which both life and property had been placed
at the close of our voyage, made us praise God all
the more, that He had brought us to this quiet
resting-place, around which lay the Islands of the
New Hebrides, to which our eager hearts had looked
forward, and into which we entered now in the name
of the Lord.

Mr. Copeland, Mrs. Paton, and I went round the
island to Dr. Inglis's Station, where we were most
cordially received and entertained by his dear lady,
and by the Christian Natives there. As he was
making several additions to his house at that time,
we received for the next few weeks our first practical
and valuable training in Mission house-building, as
well as in higher matters. Soon after, a meeting
was called to consult about our settlement, and, by
the advice and with the concurrence of all, Mr. and
Mrs. Mathieson from Nova Scotia were located on
the south side of Tanna, at Umairarekar, and Mrs.

Paton and I at Port Resolution, on the same island.
At first it was agreed that Mr. Copeland should
be placed along with us ; but owing to the weakly
state of Mrs. Mathieson's health, it was afterwards
resolved that, for a time at least, Mr. Copeland
should live at either Station, as might seem most
suitable or most requisite.   Till the close of the
sailing season, his time was spent chiefly in the *John
Knox*, helping Captain Anderson in loading and
disloading the wood and house-building materials
betwixt Aneityum and Tanna ; while I was occupied
chiefly with the house-building and preparatory
arrangements.

Dr. Inglis and a number of his most energetic
Natives accompanied us to Kwamera, Tanna.   There
we purchased a site for Mission House and Church,
and laid a stone foundation, and advanced as far
as practicable the erection of a dwelling for Mr. and
Mrs. Mathieson.   Thence we proceeded to Port
Resolution, Tanna, and similarly purchased a site,
and advanced, to a forward stage, the house which
Mrs. Paton and I were to occupy on our settlement
there.   Lime, for plastering, had to be burned in
kilns from the coral rocks ; and thatch, for roofing
with sugar-cane leaf, had to be prepared by the
Natives at both stations before our return ; for which,
as for all else, a price was duly agreed upon, and
was scrupulously paid.   Unfortunately we learned,
when too late, that both houses were too near the
shore, exposed to unwholesome miasma, and pro-

ductive of the dreaded fever and ague,—the most virulent and insidious enemy to all Europeans in those Southern Seas.

At both Stations, but especially at Port Resolution, we found the Natives in a very excited and unsettled state. Threatened wars kept them in constant terror—war betwixt distant tribes, or adjoining villages, or nearest neighbours. The Chiefs, at both Stations, willingly sold sites for houses, and appeared to desire Missionaries to live amongst them ; but perhaps it was with an eye to the axes, knives, fishhooks, blankets, and clothing, which they got in payment, or hoped for in plunder, rather than from any thirst for the Gospel, as they were all savages and cannibals. They warily declined to promise protection to the Mission families and the Teachers ; but they said they would not themselves do them any harm, though they could not say what the Inland people might do ;—not a bad specimen of diplomacy, leaving an open door for any future emergency, and neither better nor worse than the methods by which the civilized European nations make and break their treaties in peace and in war! Such promises meant and were intended to mean nothing. The Natives, both on Tanna, and on my second home at Aniwa, believed that they had kept their promise if they inflicted no injury with their own hands, even though they had hired others to do so. No Heathen there could be trusted one step beyond what appeared to be his own self-interest for the nonce; and nothing conceivable was too base or cruel to be done, if only it served his turn. The depths of Satan, outlined in the first chapter of the Romans, were uncovered there before our eyes in the daily life of the people, without veil and without excuse.

My first· impressions drove me to the verge of utter dismay. On beholding these Natives in their paint and nakedness and misery, my heart was as full of horror as of pity. Had I given up my much-beloved work and my dear people in Glasgow, with so many delightful associations, to consecrate my life to these degraded creatures? Was it possible to teach them right and wrong, to Christianize, or even to civilize them? But that was only a passing feeling! I soon got as deeply interested in them, and in all that tended to advance them, and to lead them to the knowledge and love of Jesus, as ever I had been in my work at Glasgow. We were surprised and delighted at the remarkable change produced on the natives of Aneityum through the instrumentality of Drs. Geddie and Inglis in so short a time; and we hoped, by prayerful perseverance in the use of similar means, to see the same work of God repeated on Tanna. Besides, the wonderful and blessed work done by Mrs. Inglis and Mrs. Geddie, at their Stations, filled our wives with the buoyant hope of being instruments in the hand of God to produce an equally beneficent change amongst the savage women of Tanna. Mrs. Paton had been left with Mrs. Inglis 'to learn all she could from her of Mission work on the Islands, till I returned with Dr. Inglis from the house-building operations on Tanna; during which period Mr. and Mrs. Mathieson were also being instructed by Dr. and Mrs. Geddie. To the Tannese, Dr. Inglis and I were objects of curiosity and fear; they came crowding to gaze on our wooden and lime-plastered house, they chattered incessantly with each other, and left the scene day after day with undisguised and increasing wonderment. Possibly they thought us rather mad than wise!

Party after party of armed men, going and coming in a state of great excitement, we were informed that war was on foot; but our Aneityumese Teachers were told to assure us that the Harbour people would only act on the defensive, and that no one would molest us at our work. One day two hostile tribes met near our Station; high words arose, and old feuds were revived. The Inland people withdrew; but the Harbour people, false to their promises, flew to arms and rushed past us in pursuit of their enemies. The discharge of muskets in the adjoining bush, and the horrid yells of the savages, soon informed us that they were engaged in deadly fights. Excitement and terror were on every countenance; armed men rushed about in every direction, with feathers in their twisted hair,—with faces painted red, black, and white, and some, one cheek black, the other red, others, the brow white, the chin blue—in fact, any colour and on any part,—the more grotesque and savage-looking, the higher the art! Some of the women ran with their children to places of safety ; but even then we saw other girls and women, on the shore close by, chewing sugar-cane and chaffering and laughing, as if their fathers and brothers had been engaged in a country dance, instead of a bloody conflict. In the afternoon, as the sounds of the muskets and the yelling of the warriors came unpleasantly near to us, Dr. Inglis, leaning against a post for a little while in silent prayer, looked on us and said,—

"The walls of Jerusalem were built in troublous times, and why not the Mission House on Tanna ? But let us rest for this day, and pray for these poor Heathen."

We retired to a native house, that had been temporarily granted to us for rest, and there pled before God for them all. The noise and the discharge of muskets gradually receded, as if the Inland people were retiring ; and towards evening the people around us returned to their villages. We were afterwards informed that five or six men had been shot dead ; that their bodies had been carried by the conquerors from the field of battle, and cooked and eaten that very night by the savages at a boiling spring near the head of the bay, less than a mile from the spot where my house was being built. We had also a more graphic illustration of the surroundings into which we had come, through Dr. Inglis's

Aneityum boy, who accompanied us as cook. When our tea was wanted that evening, the boy could not be found. After a while of great anxiety on our part, he returned, saying,—

"Missi, this is a dark land. The people of this land do dark works. At the boiling spring they have cooked and feasted upon the slain. They have washed the blood into the stream; they have bathed there till all the waters are red. I cannot get water to make your tea. What shall I do?"

Dr. Inglis told him that he must try for water elsewhere, till the rains came and cleansed the polluted stream; and that, meanwhile, instead of tea, we would drink from the cocoa-nut, as they had often done before. The lad was quite relieved. It not a little astonished us, however, to see that his mind regarded their killing and eating each other as a thing scarcely to be noticed, but that it was horrible that they should spoil the water! How much are even our deepest instincts the creatures of mere circumstances! I, if trained like him, would probably have felt like him.

Next evening, as we sat talking about the people and the dark scenes around us, the quiet of the night was broken by a wild wailing cry from the villages around, long-continued and unearthly. We were informed that one of the wounded men, carried home from the battle, had just died; and that they had strangled his widow to death, that her spirit might accompany him to the other world, and be his servant there, as she had been here. Now their dead bodies were laid side by side, ready to be buried in the sea. Our hearts sank to think of all this happening within ear-shot, and that we knew it not! Every new scene, every fresh incident, set more clearly before us the benighted condition and shocking cruelties of these heathen people, and we longed to be able to speak to them of Jesus and the love of God. We eagerly tried to pick up every word of their language, that we might, in their own tongue, unfold to them the knowledge of the true God and the salvation from all these sins through Jesus Christ.

Dr. Inglis and I, with the help of the Natives from Aneityum, having accomplished all that could be done for lack of lime and sawn wood to finish the new Mission House on Tanna, made an agreement with the Natives for knives, calico, and axes, to burn lime and prepare other things for our return We then hastened back to Aneityum, that we might, if possible, get ready for settling on Tanna before the Rainy Season set in. That was rapidly approaching, and it brings with it discomfort and unhealth to Europeans throughout all these Pacific Isles.

VI.

LIFE AND DEATH ON TANNA.

CHAPTER VI.

LIFE AND DEATH ON TANNA.

Our Island Home.—Learning the Language.—A Religion of
Fear.—With or Without a God.—Ideas of the Invisible.—
Gods and Demons.—My Companion Missionary.—Pioneers
in the New Hebrides—Missionaries of Aneityum.—The
Lord's Arrowroot.—Unhealthy Sites.—The Great Bereavement.—Memorial Tributes.—Selwyn and Patteson at a
Tannese Grave.—Her Last Letter.—Last Words.—Presentiment and Mystery.

OUR little missionary ship, the *John Knox*,
having no accommodation for lady passengers,
and little for anybody else, except the discomfort
of lying on deck, we took advantage of a trader
to convey us from Aneityum to Tanna. The captain
kindly offered to take us and about thirty casks
and boxes to Port Resolution for £5, which we gladly
accepted. After a few hours' sailing we were all
safely landed on Tanna on the 5th November, 1858.
Dr. Geddie went for a fortnight to Umairarekar, on
the south side of Tanna, to assist in the settlement
of Mr. and Mrs. Mathieson, and to help in making
their house habitable and comfortable. Mr. Copeland, Mrs. Paton, and I were left at Port Resolution,

to finish the building of our house there, and work our way into the goodwill of the Natives as best we could. On landing there, we found the people to be literally naked and painted savages; they were at least as destitute of clothing as Adam and Eve after the fall, when they sewed fig-leaves for a girdle; and even more so, for the women wore only a tiny apron of grass, in some cases shaped like a skirt or girdle, the men an indescribable affair, like a pouch or bag, and the children absolutely nothing whatever!

At first they came in crowds to look at us, and at everything we did or had. We knew nothing of their language; we could not speak a single word to them, nor they to us. We looked at them, they at us; we smiled, and nodded, and made signs to each other; this was our first meeting and parting. One day I observed two men, the one lifting up one of our articles to the other, and saying,—

"Nunksi nari enu?"

I concluded that he was asking, "What is this?" Instantly, lifting a piece of wood, I said,—

"Nunksi nari enu?"

They smiled and spoke to each other. I understood them to be saying, "He has got hold of our language now." Then they told me their name for the thing which I had pointed to. I found that they understood my question, What is this? or, What is that? and that I could now get from them the name of every visible or tangible thing around us! We carefully noted down every

name they gave us, spelling all phonetically, and
also every strange sound we heard from them;
thereafter, by painstaking comparison of different
circumstances, we tried to ascertain their meanings,
testing our own guess by again cross-questioning the
Natives. One day I saw two males approaching,
when one, who was a stranger, pointed to me with
his finger, and said,—

"Se nangin?"

Concluding that he was asking my name, I pointed
to one of them with my finger, and looking at the
other, inquired,—

"Se nangin?"

They smiled, and gave me their names. We were
now able to get the names of persons and things,
and so our ears got familiarized with the distinctive
sounds of their language; and being always keenly
on the alert, we made extraordinary progress in attempting bits of conversation and in reducing their
speech for the first time to a written form—for the
New Hebrideans had no literature, and not even the
rudiments of an alphabet. I used to hire some of
the more intelligent lads and men to sit and talk
with us, and answer our questions about names and
sounds; but they so often deceived us, and we,
doubtless, misunderstood them so often, that this
course was not satisfactory, till after we had gained
some knowledge of their language and its construction, and they themselves had become interested in
helping us. Amongst our most interested helpers,

and most trustworthy, were two aged chiefs—Nowar and Nouka—in many respects two of Nature's noblest gentlemen, kind at heart to all, and distinguished by a certain native dignity of bearing. But they were both under the leadership of the war-chief Miaki, a kind of devil-king over many villages and tribes. He and his brother were the recognised leaders in all deeds of darkness; they gloried in bloodshedding, and in war, and in cannibalism ; and they could always command a following of desperate men, who lived in or about their own village, and who were prepared to go anywhere and do anything at Miaki's will.

The Tannese had hosts of stone idols, charms, and sacred objects, which they abjectly feared, and in which they devoutly believed. They were given up to countless superstitions, and firmly glued to their dark heathen practices. Their worship was entirely a service of fear, its aim being to propitiate this or that Evil Spirit, to prevent calamity or to secure revenge. They deified their chiefs, like the Romans of old, so that almost every village or tribe had its own sacred man, and some of them had many. They exercised an extraordinary influence for evil, these village or tribal priests, and were believed to have the disposal of life and death through their sacred ceremonies, not only in their own tribe, but over all the Islands. Sacred men and women, wizards and witches, received presents regularly to influence the gods, and to remove sickness, or to cause it by the

Nahak, i.e., incantation over remains of food, or the skin of fruit, such as banana, which the person has eaten, on whom they wish to operate. They also worshipped the spirits of departed ancestors and heroes, through their material idols of wood and stone, but chiefly of stone. They feared these spirits and sought their aid; especially seeking to propitiate those who presided over war and peace, famine and plenty, health and sickness, destruction and prosperity, life and death. Their whole worship was one of slavish fear; and, so far as ever I could learn, they had no idea of a God of mercy or grace.

Let me here give my testimony on a matter of some importance—that among these Islands, if anywhere, men might be found destitute of the faculty of worship, men absolutely without idols, if such men exist under the face of the sky. Everything seemed to favour such a discovery; but the New Hebrides, on the contrary, are full of gods. The Natives, destitute of the knowledge of the true God, are ceaselessly groping after Him, if perchance they may find Him. Not finding Him, and not being able to live without some sort of god, they have made idols of almost everything; trees and groves, rocks and stones, springs and streams, insects and other beasts, men and departed spirits, relics such as hair and finger nails, the heavenly bodies and the volcanoes; in fact, every being and everything within the range of vision or of knowledge has been appealed to by them as God,—clearly proving that the instincts of

Humanity, however degraded, prompt man to worship
and lean upon some Being or Power outside himself,
and greater than himself, in whom he lives and
moves and has his being, and without the knowledge
of whom his soul cannot find its true rest or its
eternal life.   Imperfect acquaintance with the language and customs of certain tribes may easily lead
early discoverers to proclaim that they have no sense
of worship and no idols, because nothing of the kind
is visible on the surface ; but there is a sort of free-
masonry in Heathen Religions ; they have mysterious
customs and symbols, which none, even amongst
themselves, understand, except the priests and sacred
men.   It pays these men to keep their devotees in
the dark—and how much more to deceive a passing
inquirer ! Nor need we hold up our hands in surprise
at this ; it pays also nearer home, to pretend and to
perpetuate a mystery about beads and crucifixes,
holy water and relics—a state of mind not so very far
removed from that of the South Sea islander, not
disproving but rather strongly proving that, whether
savage or civilized, man must either know the true
God, or must find an idol to put in His place.

Further, these very facts—that they did worship,
that they believed in spirits of ancestors and heroes,
and that they cherished many legends regarding
those whom they had never seen, and handed these
down to their children—and the fact that they had
ideas about the invisible world and its inhabitants,
made it not so hard as some might suppose to convey

to their minds, once their language and modes of thought were understood, some clear idea of Jehovah God as the great uncreated Spirit Father, who Himself created and sustains all that is. But it could not be done off-hand, or by a few airy lessons. The whole heart and soul and life had to be put into the enterprise. The idea that man disobeyed God, and was a fallen and sinful creature,—the idea that God, as a Father, so loved man that He sent His only Son Jesus to this earth to seek and to save him,—the idea that this Jesus so lived and died and rose from the dead as to take away man's sin, and make it possible for men to return to God, and to be made into the very likeness of His Son Jesus,—and the idea that this Jesus will at death receive to the mansions of Glory every creature under heaven that loves and tries to follow Him,—these ideas had to be woven into their spiritual consciousness, had to become the very warp and woof of their religion. But it could be done—that we believed because they were men, not beasts; it had been done—that we saw in the converts on Aneityum; and our hearts rose to the task with a quenchless hope!

The Tannese called Heaven by the name Aneai; and we afterwards discovered that this was the name of the highest and most beautifully situated village on the island. Their best bit of Earth was to them the symbol and type of Heaven; their Canaan, too, was a kind of prophecy of another country, even a heavenly Canaan. The fact that they had an Aneai, a promised land, opened their minds naturally to our idea of the promised land of the future, the Aneai of the Gospel hope and faith.   The universal craving to know the greater and more powerful gods, and to have them on their side, led them, whenever we could speak their language, to listen eagerly to all our stories about the Jehovah God and His Son Jesus, and all the mighty works recorded in the Bible. ·But when we began to teach them that, in order to serve this Almighty and living Jehovah God, they must cast aside all their idols and leave off every heathen custom and vice, they rose in anger and cruelty against us, they persecuted every one that was friendly to the Mission, and passed us through the dreadful experiences to be hereafter recorded.   It was the old battle of History ; light had attacked darkness in its very stronghold, and it almost seemed for a season that the light would be finally eclipsed, and that God's Day would never dawn on Tanna !

My companion Missionary, Mr. Copeland, had ·to go to Aneityum and take charge of Dr. Inglis's Station, during the absence of that distinguished Missionary and his devoted wife, while carrying through the press at home the first complete Aneityumese New Testament.   He succeeded admirably in taking up and carrying forward all their work, and gave vital assistance in translating the Old Testament into the language of Aneityum, for his was an exact and scholarly mind.   After their return, he similarly occupied· the Station of Dr. Geddie on another part

of the same island, while he sought re-invigoration in
Nova Scotia on a well-merited furlough. Thereafter,
he was placed on the island of Fotuna; and there, with
Mrs. Copeland, he laboured devotedly and zealously,
till at last she died and his own health gave way to
such an extent as compelled him to retire from the
Mission field. He found congenial employment in
editing, with great acceptance, the Sydney *Presbyterian Witness*, and thereby still furthering the cause
of the Gospel and of Missions.

A glance backwards over the story of the Gospel
in the New Hebrides may help to bring my readers
into touch with the events that are to follow. The
ever-famous names of Williams and Harris are associated with the earliest efforts to introduce Christianity amongst this group of islands in the South
Pacific Seas. John Williams and his young missionary companion Harris, under the auspices of the
London Missionary Society, landed on Erromanga
on the 30th of November, 1839. Instantly, within a
few minutes of their touching land, both were clubbed
to death; and the savages proceeded to cook and
feast upon their bodies. Thus were the New Hebrides
baptized with the blood of martyrs; and Christ thereby told the whole Christian world that He claimed
these Islands as His own. His cross must yet be
lifted up, where the blood of His saints has been
poured forth in His name! The poor Heathen knew
not that they had slain their best friends; but tears
and prayers ascended for them from all Christian

souls, wherever the story of the martyrdom on Erromanga was read or heard.

Again, therefore, in 1842, the London Missionary Society sent out Messrs. Turner and Nisbet to pierce this kingdom of Satan. They placed their standard on this same island of Tanna, the nearest to Erromanga. In less than seven months, however, their persecution by the savages became so dreadful, that we see them in a boat trying to escape by night with bare life. Out on that dangerous sea they would certainly have been lost, but the Ever-Merciful drove them back to land, and sent next morning a trading vessel, which, contrary to custom, called there and just in the nick of time. They, with all goods that could be rescued, were got safely on board, and sailed for Samoa. Say not their plans and prayers were baffled; for God heard and abundantly blessed them there, beyond all their dreams. Dr. Turner has been specially used of God for educating many native teachers and missionaries, and in translating and publishing edition after edition of the Bible, besides giving them many other educational and religious books in their own language; —blessed work, in which, while I am writing these words, he and his gifted wife are still honourably and fruitfully engaged in the holy autumn of their days.

After these things, the London Missionary Society again and again placed Samoan native teachers on one or other island of the New Hebrides; but their unhealthiness, compared with their own happier

Samoa or Rarotonga, so afflicted them with the dreaded ague and fever, besides what they endured from the inhospitable savages themselves, that no effective mission work had been accomplished there till at last the Presbyterian Missionaries were led to enter upon the scene. Christianity had no foothold anywhere on the New Hebrides, unless it were in the memory and the blood of the martyrs of Erromanga.

The Rev. John Geddie and his wife, from Nova Scotia, were landed on Aneityum, the most southerly island of the New Hebrides, in 1848 ; and the Rev. John Inglis and his wife, from Scotland, were landed on the other side of the same island, in 1852. An agent for the London Missionary Society, the Rev. T. Powell, accompanied Dr. Geddie for about a year, to advise as to his settlement and to assist in opening up the work. Marvellous as it may seem, the Natives on Aneityum showed interest in the missionaries from the very first, and listened to their teachings ; so that in a few years Dr. Inglis and Dr. Geddie saw about 3,500 savages throwing away their idols, renouncing their heathen customs, and avowing themselves to be worshippers of the true Jehovah God. Slowly, yet progressively, they unlearned their Heathenism; surely and hopefully they learned Christianity and civilization. In course of time a simple form of family worship was introduced into and observed by every household on the island ; God's blessing was asked on every meal ; peace and public order were secured ; and property was perfectly safe under the sanctifying and civilizing Gospel of Christ. And by-and-by these Missionaries lived to see the whole Bible, which they and Mr. Copeland had so painfully translated, placed in the hands of the Aneityumese by the aid of the British and Foreign Bible Society—that noblest handmaid of every Missionary enterprise. But how was this accomplished? As a boon of charity? Listen!

These poor Aneityumese, having glimpses of this Word of God, determined to have a Holy Bible in their own mother tongue, wherein before no book or page ever had been written in the history of their race. The consecrated brain and hand of their Missionaries kept toiling day and night in translating the book of God ; and the willing hands and feet of the Natives kept toiling through fifteen long but unwearying years, planting and preparing arrowroot to pay the £1,200 required to be laid out in the printing and publishing of the book. Year after year the arrowroot, too sacred to be used for their daily food, was set apart as the Lord's portion ; the Missionaries sent it to Australia and Scotland, where it was sold by private friends, and the whole proceeds consecrated to this purpose. On the completion of the great undertaking by the Bible Society, it was found that the Natives had earned as much as to pay every penny of the outlay ; and their first Bibles went out to them, purchased with the consecrated toils of fifteen years! Some of our friends may think that the sum was large ; but I know, from experience, that if such a difficult job had been carried through the press and so bound by any other printing establishment, the expense would have been greater far. One book of Scripture, printed by me in Melbourne for the Aniwans, under the auspices of the Bible Society too, cost eight shillings per leaf, and that was the cheapest style ; and this the Aniwans also paid for by dedicating their arrowroot to God.

Let those who lightly esteem their Bibles think on those things. Eight shillings for every leaf, or the labour and proceeds of fifteen years for the Bible entire, did not appear to these poor converted savages too much to pay for that Word of God, which had sent to them the Missionaies, which had revealed to them the grace of God in Christ, and which had opened their eyes to the wonders and glories of redeeming love! They had felt, and we had observed, that in all lands and amongst all branches of the human family, the Holy Bible is, wheresoever received and obeyed, the power of God unto salvation ; it had lifted them out of savagery, and set them at the feet of the Lord Jesus. Oh, that the pleasure-seeking men and women of the world could only taste and feel the real joy of those who know and love the true God— a heritage which the world and all that pertains thereto cannot give to them, but which the poorest and humblest followers of Jesus inherit and enjoy !

My first house on Tanna was on the old site occupied by Turner and Nisbet, near the shore for obvious reasons, and only a few feet above tide-mark.

So was that of Mr. Mathieson, handy for materials
and goods being landed, and close to the healthy
breezes of the sea.   Alas! we had to learn by sad
experience, like our brethren in all untried Mission
fields.   The sites proved to be hot-beds for Fever and
Ague, mine especially ; and much of this might have
been escaped by building on the higher ground, and
in the sweep of the refreshing trade-winds.   For all
this, however, no one was to blame; everything
was done for the best, according to the knowledge
then possessed.   Our house was sheltered behind by
an abrupt hill from three to four hundred feet high,
which gave the site a feeling of cosiness.   It was surrounded, and much shaded, by beautiful breadfruit
trees, and very large cocoanut trees; too largely
beautiful, indeed, for they shut out many a healthy
breeze that we sorely needed!   There was a long
swamp all round the head of the bay, and, the
ground at the other end on which our house stood
being scarcely raised perceptibly higher, the malaria
almost constantly enveloped us.   Once, after a smart
attack of the fever, an intelligent Chief said to me,—

"Missi, if you stay here, you will soon die!   No
Tanna-man sleeps so low down as you do, in this
damp weather, or he too would die.   We sleep on
the high ground, and the trade-wind keeps us well.
You must go and sleep on the hill, and then you will
have better health."

I at once resolved to remove my house to higher
ground, at the earliest practicable moment; heavy

though the undertaking would necessarily be, it seemed my only hope of being able to live on the island.

My dear young wife, Mary Ann Robson, and I were landed on Tanna on the 5th November, 1858, in excellent health and full of all tender and holy hopes. On the 12th February, 1859, she was confined of a son; for two days or so both mother and child seemed to prosper, and our island-exile thrilled with joy! But the greatest of sorrows was treading hard upon the heels of that joy! My darling's strength showed no signs of rallying. She had an attack of ague and fever, a few days before her confinement; on the third day or so thereafter, it returned, and attacked her every second day with increasing severity for a fortnight. Diarrhœa ensued, and symptoms of pneumonia, with slight delirium at intervals; and then in a moment, altogether unexpectedly, she died on the 3rd March. To crown my sorrows, and complete my loneliness, the dear baby-boy, whom we had named after her father, Peter Robert Robson, was taken from me after one week's sickness, on the 20th March. Let those who have ever passed through any similar darkness as of midnight feel for me; as for all others, it would be more than vain to try to paint my sorrows!

I knew then, when too late, that our work had been entered on too near the beginning of the Rainy Season. We were both, however, healthy and hearty; and I daily pushed on with the house, making things hourly more comfortable, in the hope that long

P

lives were before us both, to be spent for Jesus in
seeking the salvation of the perishing Heathen. Oh,
the vain yet bitter regrets, that my dear wife had not
been left on Aneityum till after the unhealthy Rainy
Season ! But no one advised this course ; and she,
high-spirited, full of buoyant hope, and afraid of
being left behind me, or of me being left without her
on Tanna, refused to allow the thing to be suggested.
In our mutual inexperience, and with our hearts aglow
for the work of our lives, we incurred this risk which
should never have been incurred ; and I only refer to
the matter thus, in the hope that others may take
warning.

Stunned by that dreadful loss, in entering upon
this field of labour to which the Lord had Himself
so evidently led me, my reason seemed for a time
almost to give way. Ague and fever, too, laid a
depressing and weakening hand upon me, continuously recurring, and reaching oftentimes the very
height of its worst burning stages. But I was never
altogether forsaken. The ever-merciful Lord sustained me, to lay the precious dust of my beloved.
Ones in the same quiet grave, dug for them close by
at the end of the house ; in all of which last offices
my own hands, despite breaking heart, had to take
the principal share ! I built the grave round and
round with coral blocks, and covered the top with
beautiful white coral, broken small as gravel; and
that spot became my sacred and much-frequented
shrine, during all the following months and years

when I laboured on for the salvation of these savage
Islanders amidst difficulties, dangers, and deaths.
Whensoever Tanna turns to the Lord, and is won for
Christ, men in after-days will find the memory of that
spot still green,—where with ceaseless prayers and
tears I claimed that land for God in which I had
"buried my dead" with faith and hope. But for
Jesus, and the fellowship He vouchsafed me there,
I must have gone mad and died beside that lonely
grave.

The organ of the Church to which we belonged, *The
Reformed Presbyterian Magazine,* published the following words of condolence :—" In regard to the death of
Mrs. Paton, one feeling of grief and regret will fill
the hearts of all who knew her. To add a sentence
to the singularly just and graceful tribute Mr. Inglis
pays to the memory of the deceased, would only mar
its pathos and effect. Such language, from one accustomed to weigh carefully every word he pens,
bespeaks at once the rare excellences of her that is
gone, as well as the heavy loss our Mission and our
Church have sustained in her death. Her parents,
who gave her by a double baptism to the Lord, have
this consolation, that her death may exert a more
elevating and sanctifying influence for good, than the
longest life of many ordinary Christians. . Deep sympathy with Mr. Paton will pervade the Church, in the
sore trial with which he has been visited."

Dr. Inglis, my brother Missionary on Aneityum,
wrote to the same Magazine :—" I trust all those who

shed tears of sorrow on account of her early death
will be enabled in the exercise of faith and resignation
to say, 'The Will of the Lord be done ; the Lord gave
and the Lord hath taken away : blessed be the name
of the Lord !' I need not say how deeply we sym-
pathise with her bereaved parents, as well as with
her sorrowing husband. By her death the Mission
has sustained a heavy loss. We were greatly pleased
with Mrs. Paton, during the period of our short intercourse with her. Her mind, naturally vigorous, had
been cultivated by a superior education. She was
full of Missionary spirit, and took a deep interest in
the native women. This was seen further, when she
went to Tanna, where, in less than three months, she
had collected a class of eight females, who came
regularly to her to receive instruction. There was
about her a maturity of thought, a solidity of character, a loftiness of aim and purpose rarely found in
one so young. Trained up in the fear of the Lord
from childhood, like another Mary she had evidently
chosen that good part, which is never taken away
from those possessed of it. When she left this island,
she had to all human appearance a long career of
usefulness and happiness on Earth before her, but the
Lord has appointed otherwise. She has gone, as we
trust, to her rest and her reward. The Lord has said
to her, as He said to David, 'Thou didst well in that
it was in thine heart to build a House for My Name.'
Let us watch and pray, for our Lord cometh as a
thief in the night."

The Mission Synod at Tanna, on April 27th, 1859, passed the following resolution :—" That this meeting deeply and sincerely sympathises with Mr. Paton in the heavy and trying bereavement with which the Lord has seen meet to visit him in the death of his beloved wife and child ; and the Missionaries record their sense of the loss this Mission has sustained, in the early, sudden, and unexpected death of Mrs. Paton. Her earnest Christian character, her devoted Mission-ary spirit, her excellent education, her kind and obliging disposition, and the influence she was fast acquiring over the Natives excited expectations of great future usefulness.   That they express their heart-felt sympathy with the parents and other relatives of the deceased ; that they recommend Mr. Paton to pay a visit to Aneityum for the benefit of his health ; that they commend him to the tender mercies of Him who was sent to comfort all who mourn ; and that they regard this striking dispensa-sation of God's providence as a loud call to them-selves, to be more in earnest in attending to the state of their own souls, and more diligent in pressing the concerns of Eternity on the minds of others."

Soon after her death, the good Bishop Selwyn called at Port Resolution, Tanna, in his Mission ship. He came on shore to visit me, accompanied by the Rev. J. C. Patteson. They had met Mrs. Paton on Aneityum in the previous year soon after our arrival, and, as she was then the picture of perfect health, they also felt her loss very keenly. Standing with me beside the grave of mother and child, I weeping aloud on his one hand, and Patteson—afterwards the Martyr Bishop of Nakupu—sobbing silently on the other, the godly Bishop Selwyn poured out his heart to God amidst sobs and tears, during which he laid his hands on my head, and invoked Heaven's richest consolations and blessings on me and my trying labours. The virtue of that kind of Episcopal consecration I did and do most warmly appreciate! They urged me by many appeals to take a trip with them round the Islands, as my life was daily in great danger from the savages ; they generously offered to convey me direct to Aneityum, or wherever I wished to go, as I greatly needed rest and change. But, with a heart full of gratitude to them, I yet resolved to remain, feeling that I was at the post of duty where God had placed me ; and besides, fearing that if I left once the natives would not let me land again on returning to their island, I determined to hold on as long as possible, though feeling very weak and suffering badly from ague.

Sorrow and love make me linger a little to quote these extracts, printed in the *Reformed Presbyterian Magazine* for January, 1860, from Mrs. Paton's last letter to her friends at home. It is dated from Port Resolution, Tanna, 28th December, 1858.

"MY DEAR FATHER, MOTHER, AND SISTERS,—

"When I wrote last, we were just about to leave Aneityum for Tanna, the sphere of our future labours. One can have no idea of the dark and degraded state of these poor Heathen, unless really living amongst them. Still we trust that the cloud which has so long enveloped Tanna will soon be rolled away, and the light of the Sun of Righteousness irradiate this dark land. We have been here about two months, and so far the people among whom we live appear to be friendly. A numerous priesthood reside in the neighbourhood of the Volcano, from whom we anticipate much opposition, as they know that wherever the Missionary gains a footing among the people, their influence is lost. The Tannese are very avaricious. If one renders the least assistance, he demands a most exorbitant pay; indeed, we can hardly satisfy them. We have a number of male, but very few female visitors, the latter being just slaves to do all the work. The men disfigure their faces with red and black paint, and always carry spears and clubs. At first I was quite shocked with their appearance, but one soon becomes accustomed to such sights. They likewise possess powder and muskets,—guns and tobacco being the chief objects of their ambition. Indeed, such is their degraded condition that, were not the power and grace of God all-sufficient, one might almost despair of ever making any impression on them. All the Natives are in a state of entire nudity, with this exception, that females wear short petticoats made of grass. Young girls are very fond of beads, and sometimes have their necks quite covered with them. They likewise bore holes in the ear, from which they suspend large rolls (circles) of tortoise shell. Two or three little girls come about me, whom I am teaching to sew and sing; but no great good can be accomplished till we master their language. We have picked up a good many words, and I trust, with the blessing of God, will soon be able to speak to them of things pertaining to their everlasting peace.

"Port Resolution is a most beautiful Bay. I have never seen such a lovely spot. Indeed, everything around delights the eye, and 'only man is vile.' Our house is at the head of the Bay, on the foundation of Dr. Turner's, from which he had to fly fifteen years ago. The sea, at full tide, comes within a few yards of the door. Mr. Copeland is staying with us now. During the Rainy Season, he is to be sometimes with us, and at other times with Mr. Mathieson, who is in delicate health. The thermometer averages from 80° to 85°. The Rainy Season having now set in, it is not likely we will have any opportunity of sending or receiving letters for three or four months. I am wearying very much to hear from you. I can hardly realize that nine months have rolled away since I left bonnie Scotia! How many changes will take place before I again revisit it! Both my husband and I are in excellent health, and, though the heat feels oppressive, we like the climate very well. A Happy New Year to you all, and many happy returns! I am writing hurriedly, as a vessel has called, and leaves to-morrow morning. I expect to get all the news when you write, for my interest in and affection for home and home-folks have not in the least abated.

"Now I must conclude; with love to you all, and to all my old companions, believe me ever your loving daughter and sister,

"MARY ANN PATON."

Her last words were,—

"Oh, that my dear mother were here! She is a good woman, my mother, a jewel of a woman."

Then, observing Mr. Copeland near by, she said,—

"Oh, Mr. Copeland, I did not know you were there! You must not think that I regret coming here, and leaving my mother. If I had the same thing to do over again, I would do it with far more pleasure, yes, with all my heart. Oh, no! I do not regret leaving home and friends, though at the time I felt it keenly."

Soon after this, looking up and putting her hand in mine, she said,—

"J. C. wrote to our Janet saying, that young Christians under their first impressions thought they could do anything or make any sacrifice for Jesus, and he asked if she believed it, for he did not think they could, when tested; but Janet wrote back that she believed they could, and (added she with great emphasis) *I believe it is true!*"

In a moment, altogether unexpectedly, she fell asleep in Jesus, with these words on her lips. "Not lost, only gone before to be for ever with the Lord,"—

my heart keeps saying or singing to itself from that hour till now.

Ever since the day of our happy marriage, a strange presentiment possessed my heart that I should lose her soon and suddenly. Perhaps I am not the first who has wrestled through such unworthy forebodings—that that which was so precious and blessed was about to be withdrawn! Our short united life had been cloudless and happy; I felt her loss beyond all conception or description, in that dark land. It was verily difficult to be resigned, left alone, and in sorrowful circumstances; but feeling immovably assured that my God and Father was too wise and loving to err in anything that He does or permits, I looked up to the Lord for help, and struggled on in His work. I do not pretend to see through the mystery of such visitations,—wherein God calls away the young, the promising, and those sorely needed for His service here; but this I do know and feel, that, in the light of such dispensations, it becomes us all to love and serve our blessed Lord Jesus so that we may be ready at His call for death and Eternity.

VII.

MISSION LEAVES FROM TANNA.

CHAPTER VII.

MISSION LEAVES FROM TANNA.

IN the first letter, sent jointly by Mr. Copeland
and me from Tanna to the Church at home, the
following statements are found :—

"We, found the Tannese to be painted Savages,
enveloped in all the superstition and wickedness of
Heathenism. All the men and children go in a state
of nudity. The older women wear grass skirts, and
the young women and girls, grass or leaf aprons
like Eve in Eden. They are exceedingly ignorant,
vicious, and bigoted, and almost void of natural affection. Instead of the inhabitants of Port Resolution

being improved by coming in contact with white men, they are rendered much worse; for they have learned all their vices, but none of their virtues,—if such are possessed by the pioneer traders among such races! The sandalwood Traders are as a class the most godless of men, whose cruelty and wickedness make us ashamed to own them as our countrymen. By them the poor, defenceless Natives are oppressed and robbed on every hand; and if they offer the slightest resistance, they are ruthlessly silenced by the musket or revolver. Few months here pass without some of them being so shot, and, instead of their murderers feeling ashamed, they boast of how they despatch them. Such treatment keeps the Natives always burning under a desire for revenge, so that it is a wonder any white man is allowed to come among them. Indeed, all Traders here are able to maintain their position only by revolvers and rifles; but we hope a better state of affairs is at hand for Tanna."

The novelty of our being among them soon passed away, and they began to show their avarice and deceitfulness in every possible way. The Chiefs united and refused to give us the half of the small piece of land which had been purchased, on which to build our Mission House, and when we attempted to fence in the part they had left to us, they "tabooed" it, *i.e.*, threatened our Teachers and us with death if we proceeded further with the work. This they did by placing certain reeds stuck into the ground here and there around our house, which our Aneityumese servants at once. knew the meaning of, and warned us of our danger; so we left off making the fence, that we might if possible evade all offence. They then divided the few bread-fruit and cocoa-nut trees on the ground amongst themselves, or demanded such payment for these trees as we did not possess, and threatened revenge on us if the trees were injured by any person. They now became so unreasonable and offensive, and our dangers so increased, as to make our residence amongst them extremely trying. At this time a vessel called; I bought from the Captain the payment they demanded; on receiving it, they lifted the Taboo, and for a little season appeared to be friendly again. This was the third payment they had got for that site, and to yield was teaching them a cruel lesson; all this we felt and clearly saw, but they had by some means to be conciliated, if possible, and our lives had to be saved, if that could be done without dishonour to the Christian name.

After these events, a few weeks of dry weather began to tell against the growth of their yams and bananas. The drought was instantly ascribed to us and our God. The Natives far and near were summoned to consider the matter in public assembly. Next day, Nouka, the high chief, and Miaki, the war-chief, his nephew, came to inform us, that two powerful Chiefs had openly declared in that assembly that if the Harbour people did not at once kill us or compel us to leave the island, they would, unless the rain came plentifully in the meantime, summon all the Inland people and murder both our Chiefs and us. The friendly Chiefs said,—

" Pray to your Jehovah God for rain, and· do not go far beyond your door for a time ; we are all in greatest danger, and if war breaks out, we fear we cannot protect you."

But this friendliness was all pretence ; they.themselves, being sacred men, professed to have the power of sending or withholding rain, and tried to. fix the blame of their. discomfiture on us.   The rage of the poor ignorant Heathen was thereby fed against us. The Ever-Merciful, however, again interposed on our behalf. On the following Sabbath, just when we were assembling for worship, rain began to fall, and in great abundance.   The whole inhabitants believed, · apparently, that it was sent to save us in answer to our prayers; so they met again, and resolved to allow us to remain on Tanna.   Alas ! the continuous and heavy rains brought much sickness and fever in their train, and again their sacred men pointed to us as the cause.   Hurricane winds also, blew and injured their fruits and fruit-trees,—another opportunity for our enemies to lay the blame of everything upon the Missionaries and their Jehovah God ! The trial and the danger daily grew of living among a people so dreadfully benighted by superstition, and · so easily swayed by prejudice and passion.

On Sabbath afternoon, the 6th of January, 1860, in a severe gale, we were surprised to see a large

Sydney vessel come to anchor in the Harbour at Port Resolution, right opposite our house. Though wind and sea were both dangerously high, the Captain and all hands, as we were afterwards informed, coolly went to sleep. Gradually, but quite perceptibly, the vessel was allowed to drift as if by deliberate intention, till she struck on the beach at the head of the Bay, and there was soon broken up and became a total wreck. For this also the ignorant Natives gave us credit, as for everything uncommon or disagreeable on Tanna ; but we were ever conscious that our Lord Jesus was near us, and all trials that lead us to cling closer in fellowship with our Saviour are really blessings in disguise. The Captain of that vessel, known to us only as "Big Hays," and his wife, said to be the wife of a man in Sydney who had run away with him, and his like-minded crew became by their shocking conduct a horrible curse to our poor Islanders, and greatly embittered the feeling against us. They were armed with deadly weapons, and did their wicked will amongst our Natives, who durst not attack so large a party of desperate and well-armed men. But they were white people, and so were the Missionaries ; to the savage mind that was enough, and revenge would be taken upon the first white faces, however innocent, who came within their power.

The Natives of Tanna were well-nigh constantly at war amongst themselves, every man doing that which was right in his own eyes, and almost every quarrel ending in an appeal to arms. Besides many battles far inland, one was fought closely around our house, and several .were fought around the Harbour. In these conflicts, many men were bruised with clubs and wounded with arrows, but few lives were lost, considering the savage uproar and frenzy of the scene. In one case, of which we obtained certain informa- · tion, seven men were killed in an engagement, and, according to Tannese custom, the warriors and their friends feasted on them at the close of the fray, the widows of the slain being also strangled to death, and similarly disposed of. Besides those who fell in war, the Natives living in our quarter had killed and·· feasted on eight persons, usually in sacrificial rites.

It is said, that the habitual Cannibal's desire for human flesh becomes so horrible that he has been known to disinter and feast upon those recently buried. Two cases of this revolting barbarism were reported as having occurred amongst the villagers living near us. On another occasion the great chief Nouka took seriously unwell, and his people sacrificed three women for his recovery! All such cruel and horrifying practices, however, they tried to conceal from us ; and many must have perished in this way of whom we, though living at their doors, were never permitted to hear.

Amongst the Heathen, in the New Hebrides, and especially on Tanna, *woman* is the down-trodden slave of man. She is kept working hard, and bears all the heavier burdens, while he walks by her side with musket, club, or spear. If she offends him, he

beats or abuses her at pleasure. A savage gave his
poor wife a severe beating in front of our house and
just before our eyes, while in vain we strove to prevent it. Such scenes were so common that no one
thought of interfering. Even if the woman died in
his hands, or immediately thereafter, neighbours took
little notice, if any at all. And their children were
so little cared for, that my constant wonder was how
any of them survived at all! As soon as they are
able to knock about, they are left practically to care
for themselves; hence the very small affection they
show towards their parents, which results in the aged
who are unable to work being neglected, starved to
death, and sometimes even more directly and vio-
lently destroyed.

A Heathen boy's education consists in being taught
to aim skilfully with the bow, to throw the spear
faultlessly at a mark, to wield powerfully the club
and tomahawk, and to shoot well with musket and
revolver when these can be obtained. He accom-
panies his father and brothers in all the wars and
preparations for war, and is diligently initiated into
all their cruelties and lusts, as the very prerequisite
of his being regarded and acknowledged to be a *man*
and a warrior. The girls have, with their mother and
sisters, to toil and slave in the village plantations, to
prepare all the materials for fencing these around, to
bear every burden, and to be knocked about at will
by the men and boys.

Oh, how sad and degraded is the position of Woman,

where the teaching of Christ is unknown, or disregarded though known! It is the Christ of the Bible, it is His Spirit entering into Humanity, that has lifted Woman, and made her the helpmate and the friend of Man, not his toy or his slave. .

To the best of our observation, the Heathen, though vaguely following some division of the week into seven days, spent the Sabbath on Tanna much the same as their other days were spent. Even when some were led to give up manual labours on that day, they spent it, like too many Christians elsewhere, in visiting friends and in selfish pleasures, on feasting and drinking. After we had been about one year on the island, we had a morning Church Service, attended by about ten Chiefs and as many women and children belonging to them; though, once the Service was over, they paid no more attention to the Lord's Day. On some of the more Northern Islands of the group, the Heathen had a sacred day. Twice, sailing with the *Dayspring*, we cast anchor at an Island, but could not see a single Native till next day, when one who could speak broken English informed us that none of the people had been seen moving about because they were "keeping their Sunday." A number of the Tannese spoke a little English, but they were the worst and most treacherous characters of all. They had imbibed the profane Trader's language and his hatred of Missionaries and their work; and these, added to their own Heathen prejudices, made them the most troublesome and dangerous of men.

After the Sabbath Morning Service we used to walk many miles, visiting all the villages within reach, even before we had got so much of their language as to be able to speak freely to the people. Sometimes we made a circuit amongst them, ten or twelve miles away and as many back again. We tried to talk a little to all who were willing to listen ; and we conducted the Worship of Jehovah, wherever we could find two or three disposed to gather together and to sit or kneel beside us. It was to flesh and blood weary work, and in many ways disheartening—no responsive faces and hearts there to cheer us on and lift us up into fellowship with the Lord! But it helped us to see the people, and to get acquainted with the districts around ; it also secured for us very considerable audiences, except when they were engaged in war.

No real progress could be made in imparting to them spiritual knowledge, till we had attained some familiarity with their language. By finding out, as before recorded, the Tannese for " What is this ? " and "What is his or her name?" we got the names of things and people, and made amazing progress towards mutual intelligence. We soon found out that there were two distinct languages spoken in and around Port Resolution ; but we confined ourselves to that which was understood as far as the other Mission Station ; and, by God's help and great diligence, we were able ere long to speak to them of sin and of salvation through Jesus Christ.

Twelve Aneityumese Teachers were, at this time living on Tanna, but they had no Schools, and no Books in Tannese, for that language had never yet been reduced to forms that could be printed. The work of the Teachers, besides telling to the people around all that they could regarding Christ and the Christian religion, found its highest value in presenting through their own spirit and character a nobler type of life than any that Heathenism could show.

When a Missionary arrives, the Teacher's first duty is to help him in house-building, fencing, and the many manual and other toils required in organizing the new Station, besides accompanying him on the inland journeys, assisting him in regard to the language as far as possible, and in general furthering the cause. But in altogether virgin soil like that of Tanna, the Aneityumese Teacher, or one from any other island, had the language to acquire first of all, not less than the European Missionary, and was therefore of little use except for manual labour, and that too had to be carried on by signs much more than by words. Not only has every island its own tongue, differing widely from and unintelligible to all the others, but even the people on one side of an island could not sometimes understand or converse with the people on the opposite side of the same. This rendered our work in the New Hebrides not only exceptionally difficult, but its progressive movement distressingly slow.

Word had reached Tanna, that, in a quarrel with Sandal-wooders, the Erromangans had murdered

three white men and a number of Natives in their
employment, in revenge for the white men's shame-
fully entreating and murdering the Erromangans.
On Tanna all such news were reported and talked
over, when the Chiefs and their men of war met for
their evening repast—an event that generally wound
up with drinking *Kava*, which first produced intoxi-
cation like whisky and then stupefaction like a
dose of laudanum. Excited by the rumours from
Erromanga, they had drunk more than usual, and
lay about their Village Drinking-Hall in a helpless
host. Enemies from an inland tribe stealthily drew
near, and discharged their muskets amongst them in
the dark, killing one man, and so, according to their
custom, war was known to be declared.

Early next morning, Miaki, the war-chief, despatched his herald to sound the Conch and summon
the people to battle. He made the Harbour and all
the country resound with it for six miles around, and
the savage hordes gathered to the call. Putting our
trust in God, we quietly resolved to attend as usual
to our work and await the result. Excitement and
terror drove the Natives hither and thither. One man
close to us being nearly killed, his friends assembled
in great force, and with clubs and spears, tomahawks
and muskets, drove the offending tribe more than a
mile into the bush. They, in turn, being reinforced,
drove their enemies back again to the beach. There,
seated within hearing distance, they carried on a
grand sort of barbarous-Homeric scolding match,

and exhausted their rage in javelins of reproach. A great relief seemed thereby to ensue, for the rival Chiefs thereon approached our house and entreated me to dress their wounds! I did so, and appealed to them for peace, and got their promise to let that conflict come to an end. Alas, for the passing influence of such appeals,—for I learned shortly after this, on my return from Aneityum, where I had gone for a fortnight to recruit from the effects of an almost three months' continuance of recurring ague and fever, that eight of the Harbour people had been murdered near our house at Port Resolution. The Natives got into a dreadfully unsettled state, each one wondering in terror who would be the next to fall.

About the time of my dear wife's death, our brother Missionary, Mr. Mathieson, also became exceedingly unwell. His delicate frame fast gave way, and brought with it weakness of the mind as well; and he was removed to Aneityum apparently in a dying condition. These sad visitations had a bad effect on the Natives, owing to their wild superstitions about the cause of death and sickness. We had reason to fear that they would even interfere with the precious grave, over which we kept careful watch for a season; but God mercifully restrained them. Unfortunately, however, one of my Aneityumese Teachers who had gone round to Mr. Mathieson's Station took ill and died there, and this rekindled all their prejudices. He, poor fellow, before death said,—

"I will not again return to Port Resolution, or see my dear Missi; but tell him that I die happy, for I love Jesus much, and am going to Jesus!".

Hearing these things, the Natives insolently demanded me to tell them the cause of this death, and of Mr. Mathieson's trouble, and of the other deaths. Other reasoning or explanation being to them useless, I turned the tables, and demanded them to tell me why all this trouble and death had overtaken us in their land, and whether they themselves were not the cause of it all? Strange to say, this simple question turned the whole current of their speculations. They held meeting after meeting to discuss it for several days, and returned the message,—

"We do not blame you, and you must not blame us for causing these troubles and deaths; but we believe that a Bushman must have got hold of portion of something we had eaten, and must have thrown it to the great Evil Spirit in the volcano thereby bringing all these troubles and curses."

Another Chief vindicated himself and others thus:—"Karapanamun, the Auruman or great Evil Spirit of Tanna, whom we all fear and worship, is causing these troubles; for he knows that if we become worshippers of your Jehovah God, we cannot continue to fear him, or present him with the best of everything, as our forefathers have always done; he is angry at you and at us all."

The fear of the deaths and troubles being ascribed

to them silenced their talk against us for a season;
but very little made them either friends or foes, as
the next event will too painfully show.

Nowhat, an old Chief of the highest rank from
Aneityum, who spoke Tannese and was much respected by the Natives all round the south side of
Tanna, came on a visit to our island. After returning home, he became very ill and died in a few days.
The deluded Tannese, hearing of his death, ascribed
it to me and the Worship, and resolved to burn our
house and property, and either murder the whole
Mission party, or compel us to leave the island.
Nowhat's brother was sent from Aneityum to talk to
the Tannese and conciliate them, but unfortunately
he could not speak the language well; and the
Aneityumese Teachers felt their lives to be at this
time in such danger that they durst not accompany
him as interpreters, while I on the other hand did not
understand his language, nor he, mine. Within two
days after landing, he had a severe attack of ague and
fever; and, though the vessel he came in remained
eight days, he was prostrated all the time, so that his
well-intentioned visit did us much harm. The Tannese became furious. This was proof positive, that we
were the cause of all their sickness and death. Inland and all along the weather side of the island, when
far enough away from us, they said that the Natives
were enjoying excellent health. Meeting after meeting was held; exciting speeches were delivered; and
feasts were given, for which it was said that several

women were sacrificed, cooked, and eaten,—such being the bonds by which they entered into covenant with each other for life or death.

On the morning of the following Sabbath, we heard what were said to be the dying shrieks of two woman-sacrifices; but we went not near,—we had no power to save them, and the savages only waited such a chance of sacrificing us too. Soon after, three women came running to the Mission House, and in tears implored us to try and protect them from being killed by their husbands. Alas, we could only plead for them, the Tannese and Aneityumese Teachers warning us that if we even pled we would be instantly murdered, as the men were raging mad with the thirst of blood. At another time, eight inland girls came running to us and sat in front of our house all day, saying they were afraid to go home, as the men were fighting with their women and killing them. At night-fall, however, the poor creatures withdrew, we knew not to what fate.

The inhabitants for miles around united in seeking our destruction, but God put it into even savage hearts to save us. Old Nowar, the Chief under whom we lived, and the Chief next under him, Arkurat, set themselves to rescue us. Along with Manuman and Sirawia they opposed every plan in the public assembly for taking our lives. Some of their people also remained friendly to us, and by the help of our Aneityumese Teachers, warned us of danger and protected our lives. Determined not to be baffled, a

meeting of all our enemies on the island was summoned, and it was publicly resolved that a band of
men be selected and enjoined to kill the whole of
those friendly to the Mission, old Nowar among the
rest, and not only to murder the Mission party, but
also a Trader who had lately landed to live there, that
no one might be left to give information to the white
men or bring punishment on the islanders. Frenzy
of excitement prevailed, and the blood-fiend seemed
to over-ride the whole assembly; when, under an
impulse that surely came from the Lord of Pity, one
great warrior Chief who had hitherto kept silent, rose,
swung aloft a mighty club and smashing it earth-
wards, cried aloud,—

"The man that kills Missi must first kill me,—the
men that kill the Mission Teachers must first kill me
and my people,—for we shall stand by them and
defend them till death."

Instantaneously, another Chief thundered in with
the same declaration ; and the great assembly broke
up in dismay. All the more remarkable was this
deliverance, as these two Chiefs lived nearly four
miles inland, and, as reputed disease makers and
sacred men, were regarded as amongst our bitterest
enemies. It had happened that, a brother of the
former Chief having been wounded in battle, I had
dressed his wounds and he recovered, for which
perhaps he now favoured us. But I do not put very
much value on that consideration ; for too clearly did
our dear Lord Jesus interpose directly on our behalf

that day. I and my defenceless company had spent it in anxious prayers and tears; and our hearts overflowed with gratitude to the Saviour who rescued us from the lions' jaws,

The excitement did not at once subside, men continuing to club and beat the women for the smallest offence. At every opportunity I denounced their conduct and rebuked them severely,—especially one wretch, who beat his wife just in front of our house as well as one of the women who tried to protect her. On the following day, he returned with an armed band, and threatened our lives; but I stood up in front of their weapons, and firmly condemned their conduct, telling that man particularly that his conduct was bad and cowardly. At length his wrath gave way; he grounded his club in a penitent mood, and promised to refrain from such evil ways.

Leaving all consequences to the disposal of my Lord, I determined to make an unflinching stand against wife-beating and widow-strangling, feeling confident that even their natural conscience would be on my side. I accordingly pled with all who were in power to unite and put down these shocking and disgraceful customs. At length, ten Chiefs entered into an agreement not to allow any more beating of wives or strangling of widows, and to forbid all common labour on the Lord's Day; but alas, except for purposes of war or other wickedness, the influence of the Chiefs on Tanna was comparatively small. One Chief boldly declared,—

"If we did not beat our women, they would never work; they would not fear and obey us; but when we have beaten, and killed, and feasted on two or three, the rest are all very quiet and good for a long time to come!"

I tried to show him how cruel it was, besides that it made them unable for work, and that kindness would have a much better effect; but he promptly assured me that Tannese women "could not understand kindness." For the sake of teaching by example, my Aneityumese Teachers and I used to go a mile or two inland on the principal pathway, along with the Teachers' wives, and there, cutting and carrying home a heavy load of firewood for myself and each of the men, while we gave only a small burden to each of the women. Meeting many Tanna-men by the way, I used to explain to them that this was how Christians helped and treated their wives and sisters, and then they loved their husbands and were strong to work at home; and that as men were made stronger, they were intended to bear the heavier burdens, and especially in all labours out of doors. Our habits and practices had thus as much to do as, perhaps more than, all our appeals, in leading them to glimpses of the life to which the Lord Jesus was calling them.

Another war-burst, that caused immense consternation, passed over with only two or three deaths; and I succeeded in obtaining the consent of twenty Chiefs to fight no more except on the defensive,—a covenant

to which, for a considerable time, they strictly adhered, in the midst of fierce provocations. But to
gain any such end, the masses of the people must be
educated to the point of desiring it. The few cannot,
in such circumstances, act up to it, without laying
themselves open to be down-trodden and swept away
by the savages around.

About this time, several men, afraid or ashamed
by day, came to me regularly by night for conversation and instruction. Having seen the doors of the
Mission House made fast and the windows blinded
so that they could not be observed, they continued
with me for many hours, asking all strange questions
about the new Religion and its laws. I remember one
Chief particularly, who came often, saying to me,—

"I would be an Awfuaki man (*i.e.*, a Christian)
were it not that all the rest would laugh at me; that
I could not stand!"

"Almost persuaded":—before you blame him,
remember how many in Christian lands and amid
greater privileges live and die without ever passing
beyond that stage.

The wife of one of those Chiefs died, and he resolved
to imitate a Christian burial. Having purchased
white calico from a Trader, he came to me for some
tape which the Trader could not supply, and told me
that he was going to dress the body as he had seen
my dear wife's dressed and lay her also in a similar
grave. He declined my offer to attend the funeral
and to pray with them, as in that case many of the

villagers would not attend. He wanted all the people
to be present, to see and to hear, as it was the first
funeral of the kind ever celebrated among the Tannese; and my friend Nowar the Chief had promised
to conduct a Service and offer prayer to Jehovah
before all the Heathen. It moved me to many
strange emotions, this Christian burial, conducted by
a Heathen and in the presence of Heathens, with
an appeal to the true and living God by a man as
yet darkly groping among idols and superstitions!
Many were the wondering questions from time to
time addressed to me. The idea of a resurrection
from the dead was that which most keenly interested
these Natives, and called forth all their powers of
inquiry and argument. Thus the waves of hope
and fear swept alternately across our lives; but we
embraced every possible opportunity of telling them
the story of the life and death of Jesus, in the
strong hope that God would spare us yet to
bring the benighted Heathen to the knowledge
of the true salvation, and to love and serve the only
Saviour.

Confessedly, however, it was uphill, weary, and
trying work. For one thing, these Tannese were
terribly dishonest; and when there was any special
sickness, or excitement from any cause, their bad
feeling towards the Worship was displayed by the
more insolent way in which they carried off whatever
they could seize. When I opposed them, the club or
tomahawk, the musket or *kawas* (*i.e.*, killing stone),

being instantly raised, intimated that my life would be taken, if I resisted them. Their skill in stealing on the sly was phenomenal! If an article fell, or was seen on the floor, a Tannaman would neatly cover it with his foot, while looking you frankly in the face, and, having fixed it by his toes or by bending in his great toe like a thumb to hold it, would walk off with it, assuming the most innocent look in the world. In this way, a knife, a pair of scissors, or any smaller article, would at once disappear. Another fellow would deftly stick something out of sight amongst the whip-cord plaits of his hair, another would conceal it underneath his naked arm, while yet another would shamelessly lift what he coveted and openly carry it away.

With most of them, however, the shame was not in the theft, but in doing it so clumsily that they were discovered! Once, after continuous rain and a hot damp atmosphere, when the sun shone out I put my bed-clothes on a rope to dry. I stood at hand watching, as also the wives of two Teachers, for things were mysteriously disappearing almost under our very eyes. Suddenly, Miaki, who with his war-companions had been watching us unobserved, came rushing to me breathless and alone, crying,—

"Missi, come in, quick, quick! I want to tell you something and to get your advice!"

He ran into my house, and I followed; but before he had got into his story, we heard the two women crying out,—

P.   11

"Missi, missi, come quick! Miaki's men are stealing your sheets and blankets!"

I ran at once, but all were gone into the bush,
and with them my sheets and blankets. Miaki for
a moment looked abashed, as I charged him with
deceiving me just to give his men their opportunity.
But he soon rose to the occasion. He wrought himself into a towering rage at them, flourished his huge
club and smashed the bushes all around, shouting
to me,—

"Thus will I smash these fellows, and compel them
to return your clothes."

Perhaps he hoped to move me to intercede for his
men, and to prevent bloodshed, as he knew that I
always did, even to my own loss; but I resisted all
his tricks, and urged him to return these articles at
once if there were any honour or honesty in him
or his men. Of course, he left me but to share
the plunder. He kept out of my way for a considerable time, which showed some small glimmer-
ing of conscience somewhere; and when I tackled
him on the subject, at our first meeting, he declared
he was unable to get the articles back, which of
course showed the lying spirit, amongst them everywhere applauded,—for a lie that succeeded, or seemed
to succeed, was in their esteem a crowning virtue.

One dark night, I heard them amongst my fowls.
These I had purchased from them for knives and
calico; and they now stole them all away, dead
or alive. Had I interfered, they would have gloried

in the chance to club or shoot me in the dark, when
no one could exactly say who had done the deed.
Several of the few goats, which I had for milk, were
also killed or driven away; indeed, all the injury that
was possible was done to me, short of taking away
my life, and that was now frequently attempted.
Having no fires or fireplaces in my Mission House,
such being not required there,—though sometimes a
fire would have been invaluable for drying our bed-
clothes in the Rainy Season,—we had a house near by
in which all our food was cooked, and there, under
lock and key we secured all our cooking utensils,
pots, dishes, etc. One night, that too was broken
into, and everything was stolen. In consternation, I
appealed to the Chief, telling him what had been
done. He also flew into a great rage, and vowed
vengeance on the thieves, saying that he would
compel them to return everything. But, of course,
nothing was returned; the thief could not be found!
I, unable to live without something in which to boil
water, at length offered a blanket to any one that
would bring back my kettle. Miaki himself, after
much professed difficulty, returned it *minus* the lid—
that, he said, probably fishing for a higher bribe,
could not be got at any price, being at the other side
of the island in a tribe over which he had no controll
In the circumstances, I was glad to get kettle *minus*
lid—realizing how life itself may depend on so small
a luxury!

Having no means of redress, and feeling ourselves

entirely at their mercy, we strove quietly to bear all
and to make as little of our trials as possible ; indeed,
we bore them all gladly for Jesus' sake. All through
these sorrows, our assurance deepened rather than
faded, that if God only spared us to lead them to love
and serve the same Lord Jesus, they would soon learn
to treat us as their friend and helper. That, however,
did not do away with the hard facts of my life—being
now entirely alone amongst them, and opposed by
their cruelty at every turn, and deceived by their un-
failing lies.

One morning, the Tannese, rushing towards me in
great excitement, cried,—

" Missi, Missi, there is a God, or a ship on fire, or
something of fear, coming over the sea ! We see no
flames, but it smokes like a volcano. Is it a Spirit,
God, or a ship on fire ? What is it ? what is it ? "

One party after another followed in quick succession, shouting the same questions, in great alarm, to
which I replied,—

" I cannot go at once ; I must dress first in my best
clothes ; it will likely be one of Queen Victoria's Men-
of-war, coming to ask of me if your conduct is good
or bad, if you are stealing my property, or threatening
my life, or how you are using me ? "

They pled with me to go and see it ; but I made
much fuss about dressing and getting ready to meet
the great Chief on the vessel, and would not go with
them. The two principal Chiefs now came running
and asked,—

"Missi, will it be a ship of war?"

I called to them, "I think it will; but I have no time to speak to you now, I must get on my best clothes!"

They said, "Missi, only tell us, will he ask you if we have been stealing your things?"

I answered, "I expect he will."

They asked, "And will you tell him?"

I said, "I must tell him the truth; if he asks, I will tell him."

They then cried out, "Oh, Missi, tell him not! Everything shall be brought back to you at once, and no one will be allowed again to steal from you."

Then said I, "Be quick! Everything must be returned before he comes. Away, away! and let me get ready to meet the great Chief on the Man-of-war."

Hitherto, no thief could ever be found, and no Chief had power to cause anything to be restored to me; but now, in an incredibly brief space of time, one came running to the Mission House with a pot, another with a pan, another with a blanket, others with knives, forks, plates, and all sorts of stolen property. The Chiefs called me to receive these things, but I replied,—

"Lay them all down at the door, bring everything together quickly; I have no time to speak with you!"

I delayed my toilet, enjoying mischievously the magical effect of an approaching vessel that might

bring penalty to thieves.   At last the Chiefs, running
in breathless haste, called out to me,—

"Missi, Missi, do tell us, is the stolen property all
here ? "

Of course I could not tell, but, running out, I looked
on the promiscuous heap of my belongings, and said,—

"I don't see the lid of the kettle there yet!"

One Chief said, "No, Missi, for it is on the other
side of the island ; but tell him not, I have sent for it,
and it will be here to-morrow."

I answered, "I am glad you have brought back so
much ; and now, if you three Chiefs, Nauka, Miaki,
and Nowar, do not run away when he comes, he will
not likely punish you ; but, if you and your people run
away, he will ask me why you are afraid and I will
be forced to tell him!   Keep near me and you are
all safe ; only there must be no more stealing from
me."

They said, "We are in black fear, but we will keep
near you, and our bad conduct to you is done."

The charm and joy of that morning are fresh to me
still, when H.M.S. *Cordelia*, Captain Vernon, steamed
into our lovely Harbour.   The Commander, having
heard rumour of my dangers on Tanna, kindly came
on shore as soon as the ship cast anchor, with two
boats, and a number of his officers and men, so far
armed.   He was dressed in splendid uniform, being a
tall and handsome man, and he and his attendants
made a grand and imposing show.   On seeing Captain
Vernon's boat nearing the shore, and the men glitter-

ing in gold lace and arms, Miaki the Chief left my side on the beach and rushed towards his village. I concluded that he had run for it through terror, but he had other and more civilized intentions in his heathen head! Having obtained, from some trader or visitor in previous days, a soldier's old red coat, he had resolved to rise to the occasion and appear in his best before the Captain and his men. As I was shaking hands with them and welcoming them to Tanna, Miaki returned with the short red coat on, buttoned tightly round his otherwise naked body; and, sur-mounted by his ugly painted face and long whip-cords of twisted hair, it completely spoiled any appearance that he might otherwise have had of savage freedom, and made him look a dirty and insignificant creature.

The Captain was talking to me, his men stood in order near by,—to my eyes, oh how charming a glimpse of Home life!—when Miaki marched up and took his place most consequentially at my side. He felt himself the most important personage in the scene, and with an attempt at haughty dignity he began to survey the visitors. All eyes were fixed on the impudent little man, and the Captain asked,—

"What sort of character is this?"

I replied, "This is Miaki, our great war Chief;" and whispered to the Captain to be on his guard, as this man knew a little English, and might understand or misunderstand just enough to make it afterwards dangerous to me.

The Captain only muttered, "The contemptible creature!"

But such words were far enough beyond Miaki's vocabulary, so he looked on and grinned complacently.

At last he said, "Missi, this great Chief whom Queen Victoria has sent to visit you in her Man-of-war, cannot go over the whole of this island so as to be seen by all our people; and I wish you to ask him if he will stand by a tree, and allow me to put a spear on the ground at his heel, and we will make a nick in it at the top of his head, and the spear will be sent round the island to let all the people see how tall this great man is!"

They were delighted at the good Captain agreeing to their simple request; and that spear was exhibited to thousands, as the vessel, her Commander, officers, and men, were afterwards talked of round and round the island.

Captain Vernon was extremely kind, and offered to do anything in his power for me, thus left alone on the island amongst such savages; but, as my main difficulties were connected with my spiritual work amongst them rousing up their cruel prejudices, I did not see how his kindness could effectually interpose. At his suggestion, however, I sent a general invitation to all the Chiefs within reach, to meet the Captain next morning at my house. True to their instincts of suspicion and fear, they despatched all their women and children to the beach on the opposite

side of the island beyond reach of danger, and next
morning my house was crowded with armed men,
manifestly much afraid. Punctually at the hour
appointed, 10 a.m., the Captain came on shore; and
soon thereafter twenty Chiefs were seated with him
in my house. He very kindly spent about an hour,
giving them wise counsels and warning them against
outrages on strangers, all calculated to secure our
safety and advance the interests of our Mission work.
He then invited all the Chiefs to go on board and see
his vessel. They were taken to see the Armoury, and
the sight of the big guns running so easily on rails
vastly astonished them. He then placed them round
us on deck and showed them two shells discharged
towards the Ocean, at which, as they burst and fell
far off, splash—splashing into the water, the terror of
the Natives visibly increased. But, when he sent a
large ball crashing through a cocoa-nut grove, breaking the trees like straws and cutting its way clear and
swift, they were quite dumb-foundered and pled to be
again set safely on shore. After receiving each some
small gift, however, they were reconciled to the situation, and returned immensely interested in all that
they had seen. Doubtless many a wild romance was
spun by these savage heads, in trying to describe
and hand down to others the wonders of the fire-god
of the sea, and the Captain of the great white Queen.
How easily it all lends itself to the service of poetry
and myth!

About this time also, the London Missionary

Society's ship, the *John Williams*, visited me, having on board the Rev. Messrs. Turner, Inglis, Baker, and Macfarlan. They urged me to go with them on a three weeks' trip round the Islands, as I had lately suffered much from fever and ague, and was greatly reduced by it. But a party of Bush natives had killed one of our Harbour people the week before, and sadly bruised several others with their clubs, and I feared a general war of revenge if I left—for my presence amongst them at least helped to keep the peace. I also was afraid that, if I left, they might not allow me to return to the island,—so I declined once more the pleasure of much-needed change and rest. Further, as the *John Williams* brought me the wood for building a Church which I had bought on Aneityum, the Tannese now plainly saw that, though their conduct had been very bad, and I had suffered much on their island, I had no intention of leaving them or of giving up the work of Jehovah.

Too much, perhaps, had I hoped for from the closely succeeding visits of the good Bishop Selwyn, the gallant Captain Vernon, and the Mission ship *John Williams*. The impressions were undoubtedly good, but evanescent; and things soon went on as they had done before among our benighted Tannese, led by Satan at his will, and impelled to the grossest deeds of heathen darkness. The change by Divine grace, however, we knew to be possible; and for this we laboured and prayed incessantly, fainting not, or if fainting, only to rise again and tackle every duty in the name of the Lord who had placed us there.

Fever and ague had attacked me fourteen times severely, with slighter recurring attacks almost continuously after my first three months on the island, and I now felt the necessity of taking the hint of the Tannese Chief before referred to,—" Sleep on the higher ground." Having also received medical counsel to the same effect, though indeed experience was painfully sufficient testimony, I resolved to remove my house, and began to look about for a suitable site. There rose behind my present site, a hill about three hundred feet high or rather more, surrounded on all sides by a valley, and swept by the breezes of the trade winds, being only separated from the Ocean by a narrow neck of land. On this I had set my heart; there was room for a Mission House and a Church, for which indeed Nature seemed to have adapted it. I proceeded to buy up every claim by the Natives to any portion of the hill, paying each publicly and in turn, so that there might be no trouble afterwards. I then purchased from a Trader the deck planks of a shipwrecked vessel, with which to construct a house of two apartments, a bed-room and a small store-room adjoining it, to which I purposed to transfer and add the old house as soon as I was able.

Just at this juncture, the fever smote me again more severely than ever; my weakness after this attack was so great, that I felt as if I never could rally again. With the help of my faithful Aneityumese Teacher, Abraham, and his wife, however, I made what appeared my last effort to creep, I could not climb, up the hill to get a breath of wholesome air. When about two-thirds up the hill, I became so faint that I concluded I was dying. Lying down on the ground, sloped against the root of a tree to keep me from rolling to the bottom, I took farewell of old Abraham, of my Mission work, and of everything around! In this weak state I lay, watched over by my faithful companion, and fell into a quiet sleep. When consciousness returned, I felt a little stronger, and a faint gleam of hope and life came back to my soul.

Abraham and his devoted wife, Nafatu, lifted me and carried me to the top of the hill. There they laid me on cocoa-nut leaves on the ground, and erected over me a shade or screen of the same; and there the two faithful souls, inspired surely by something diviner even than mere human pity, gave me the cocoa-nut juice to drink and fed me with native food and kept me living—I know not for how long. Consciousness did, however, fully return. The trade wind refreshed me day by day. The Tannese seemed to have given me up for dead; and providentially none of them looked near us for many days. Amazingly my strength returned, and I began planning about my new house on the hill. Afraid again to sleep at the old site, I slept under the tree, and sheltered by the cocoa-nut leaf screen, while preparing my new bedroom.

Here again, but for these faithful souls, the Aneityumese Teacher and his wife, I must have been baffled, and would have died in the effort. The planks of the wreck, and all other articles required they fetched and carried, and it taxed my utmost strength to get them in some way planted together. But' life depended on it. It was at length accomplished ; and after that time I suffered comparatively little from anything like continuous attacks of fever and ague. That noble old soul, Abraham, stood by me as an angel of God in sickness and in danger ; he went at my side wherever I had to go ; he helped me willingly to the last inch of strength in all that I had to do ; and it was perfectly manifest that he was doing all this not from mere human love, but for the sake of Jesus. That man had been a Cannibal in his heathen days, but by the grace of God there he stood verily a new creature in Christ Jesus. Any trust, however sacred or valuable, could be absolutely reposed in him ; and in trial or danger, I was often refreshed by that old Teacher's prayers, as I used to be by the prayers of my saintly father in my childhood's home. No white man could have been a more valuable helper to me in my perilous circumstances, and no person, white or black, could have shown more fearless and chivalrous devotion.

When I have read or heard the shallow objections of irreligious scribblers and talkers, hinting that there was no reality in conversions, and that Mission effort was but waste, oh, how my heart has yearned to plant

them just one week on Tanna, with the "natural"
man all around in the person of Cannibal and Heathen,
and only the one "spiritual" man in the person of
the converted Abraham, nursing them, feeding them,
saving them "for the love of Jesus,"—that I might just
learn how many hours it took to convince them that
Christ in man was a reality after all!   All the scepti-
cism of Europe would hide its head in foolish shame;
and all its doubts would dissolve under one glance of
the new light that Jesus, and Jesus alone, pours from
the converted Cannibal's eye.

Perhaps it may surprise some unsophisticated
reader to learn, though others who know more will
be quite prepared for it, that this removal of our
house, as also Mr. Mathieson's for a similar reason,
was severely criticised by the people who try to
evangelize the world while sitting in easy chairs at
home.   Precious nonsense appeared, for instance, in
the *Nova Scotian Church Magazine*, about my house
being planted on the fighting ground of the Natives,
and thereby courting and provoking hostilities.   As
matter of fact, the hill-top was too narrow to accom-
modate both the Church and my house, and had to
be levelled out for that purpose, and it was besides
surrounded by a deep valley on three sides; but the
arm-chair critics, unwilling to believe in the heathen
hatred of the Gospel, had to invent some reason out
of their own brains to account for my being so persecuted and plundered.   In truth, we were learning
by suffering for the benefit of those who should follow

us to these Islands,—that health could be found only on the higher levels, swept by the breath of the trade winds, and that fever and ague lay in wait near the shore, and especially on the leeward side. Even Mr. Inglis had his house on Aneityum removed also to the higher ground ; and no Missionary since has been located in the fever-beds by the swamp or shore. Life is God's great gift, to be preserved for Him, not thrown away.

VIII.

MORE MISSION LEAVES FROM TANNA.

P

CHAPTER VIII.

MORE MISSION LEAVES FROM TANNA.

The Blood Fiend Unleashed.—In the Camp of the Enemy.—
A Typical South Sea Trader.—Young Rarip's Death.—
The Trader's Retribution.—Worship and War.—Saved
from Strangling.—Wrath Restrained.—Under the Axe.—
The Clubbing of Namuri.—Native Saint and Martyr.—
Bribes Refused.—Widows Saved from Strangling.—The
Sinking of the Well.—Church-Building on Tanna.—Ancient
Stone-God.—Printing First Tannese Book.—A Christian
Captain. —Levelled Muskets.—A French Refugee. —A
Villainous Captain.—Like Master Like Men.—Wrecked on
Purpose.—The Kanaka Traffic.—A Heathen Festival.—
Sacrifices to Idols.—Heathen Dances and Sham Fights.—
Six Native Teachers.—A Homeric Episode.—Victims for
a Cannibal Feast.—The Jaws of Death.—Nahak or
Sorcery.—Killing Me by Nahak.—Nahak Defied.—Pro-
tected by Jehovah.—Almost Persuaded.—Escorted to the
Battlefield.—Praying for Enemies.—Our Canoe on the
Reef.—A Perilous Pilgrimage.—Rocks and Waters.

THE Peace-party, my band of twenty Chiefs
already spoken of, kept all the tribes around
the Harbour acting only on the defensive for a season.
But the Inland people murdered eight Chiefs from a
distance who, after paying a friendly visit to the
Harbour people, were returning to their homes. At

the same time, one of the Inland Chiefs, who had pled with his people to give up war and live at peace with surrounding tribes, was overthrown and murdered by his own men, as also his brother and four wives and two children, and was supplanted by another leader more akin to their wishes and tastes. They proceeded, according to their custom of declaring war, to shoot one of the Harbour men and to break down their fences and plantations. So once again, the blood-fiend was unleashed,—the young men of Tanna being as eager to get up a battle, as young men of the world at home seem eager to get up a concert or a ball.

The Harbour people advised me to remove a mile further away from these warriors; but the Inland tribes sent me word not to desert my house, lest it might be burned and plundered, for that they themselves had no quarrel against me. Early next morning, I, accompanied by Abraham and another Ancityumese, started off to visit the Bush party, and if possible avert the impending war, but without in-forming my Harbour people. About four miles from our Station, we met the Chief of our farthest inland friendly tribe with all his fighting men under arms. Forcing me to disclose our errand, he reluctantly allowed us to pass. Praying to Jesus for guidance and protection, we pressed along the path through the thick bush four miles further still. My two attendants, sinking into silence, betrayed growing fear; and I, after trying to cheer them, had at their most earnest appeal to walk on also in silence, my heart and theirs going up to Jesus in prayer. We passed many deserted villages and plantations, but saw no living person. At last, unexpectedly, we stumbled upon the whole host assembled on the Village Common at a great feast; and at sight of us every man rushed for his weapons of war. Keeping my Teachers close beside me, I walked straight into the midst of them, unarmed of course, and cried as loud as I possibly could in their own tongue,—

" My love to all you men of Tanna! Fear not; I am your friend ; I love you every one, and am come to tell you about Jehovah God and good conduct such as pleases Him !"

An old Chief thereon came and took me by the hand, and, after leading me about among the people, said,—

" Sit down beside me here and talk with me; by-and-by the people will not be afraid."

A few ran off to the bush in terror. Others appeared to be beside themselves with delight. They danced round us frantically, striking the ground and beating a canoe with their clubs, while shouting to each other, " Missi is come! Missi is come!" The confusion grew every moment wilder, and there was a fiendish look about the whole scene. Men and boys rushed thronging around from every quarter, all painted in varied and savage devices, and some with their hair stuck full of fantastic feathers. Women and children peered through the bush, and instantaneously disappeared. Even in that anxious moment, it struck

me that they had many more children amongst them
than the people around the shores, where women and
children are destroyed by the cruelty and vices of
" civilized " visitors!   After spending about an hour,
conversing and answering all questions, they apparently agreed to give up the war, and allowed me
to conduct the Worship amongst them.   They then
made me a present of cocoa-nuts and sugar-cane and
two fowls, which my attendants received from them ;
and I, in return, presented a red shirt to the principal
Chief, and distributed a quantity of fish-hooks and
pieces of red calico amongst the rest.   The leading
men shook hands graciously, and invited us often to
come and see them, for after that visit they would
harm no person connected with our Mission.   Meantime, the Harbour people having learned where we
had gone, had concluded that we would all be killed
and feasted upon.   When we returned, with a present
of food, and informed them what we had heard and
seen, their astonishment was beyond measure ; it
had never been so seen after this manner on Tanna !
The peace continued for more than four weeks, an
uncommonly prolonged truce.   All·hands were busy
at work.   Many yam-plantations were completed, and
all fences were got into excellent condition for a year.

The prejudices and persecutions of Heathens were
a sore enough trial, but sorer and more hopeless was
the wicked and contaminating influence of, alas, my
fellow-countrymen.   One, for instance, a Captain
Winchester, living with a native .woman at the head

of the bay as a trader, a dissipated wretch, though a well-educated man, was angry forsooth at this state of peace! Apparently there was not the usual demand for barter for the fowls, pigs, etc., in which he traded. He developed at once a wonderful interest in their affairs, presented all the Chiefs around with powder, caps, and balls, and lent among them a number of flash-muskets. He urged them not to be afraid of war, as he would supply any amount of ammunition. I remonstrated, but he flatly told me that peace did not suit his purposes! Incited and encouraged thus, these poor Heathen people were goaded into a most unjust war on neighbouring tribes. The Trader immediately demanded a high price for the weapons he had lent; the price of powder, caps, and balls rose exorbitantly with every fresh demand; his yards were crowded with poultry and pigs, which he readily disposed of to passing vessels; and he might have amassed great sums of money but for his vile dissipations. Captain Winchester, now glorying in the war, charged a large hog for a wine-glass full of powder, or three or four balls, or ten gun-caps; he was boastful of his "good luck" in getting rid of all his old muskets and filling his yards with pigs and fowls. Such is the infernal depth, when the misery and ruin of many are thought to be more than atoned for by the wealth and prosperity of a few who trade in their doom!

Miaki the war Chief had a young brother, Rarip by name, about eighteen years of age. When this war began, he came to live with me at the Mission House. After it had raged some time, Miaki forced him to join the fighting men; but he escaped through the bush, and returned to me, saying,—

"Missi, I hate this fighting; it is not good to kill men; I will live with you!"

Again the War Chief came, and forced my dear young Rarip to join the hosts. Of course, I could only plead; I could not prevent him. This time, he placed him at his own side in the midst of his warriors. On coming in sight of the enemy, and hearing their first yells as they rushed from the bush, a bullet pierced young Rarip's breast and he fell dead into the arms of Miaki. The body was carried home to his brother's village, with much wailing, and a messenger ran to tell me that Rarip was dead. On hasting thither, I found him quite dead, and the centre of a tragic ceremonial. Around him, some sitting, others lying on the ground, were assembled all the women and girls, tearing their hair, wounding themselves with split bamboos and broken bottles, dashing themselves headlong to the earth, painting all black their faces, breasts, and arms, and wailing with loud lamentations! Men were also there, knocking their heads against the trees, gashing their bodies with knives till they ran with streaks of blood, and indulging in every kind of savage symbol of grief and anguish. My heart broke to see them, and to think that they knew not to look to our dear Lord Jesus for consolation.

I returned to the Mission House, and brought a white sheet and some tape, in which the body of dear young Rarip was wrapped and prepared for the grave. The Natives appeared to be gratified at this mark of respect; and all agreed that Rarip should have under my direction a Christian burial. The men prepared the grave in a spot selected near to his own house; I read the Word of God; and offered prayer to Jehovah, with a psalm of praise, amidst a scene of weeping and lamentation never to be forgotten; and the thought burned through my very soul —oh, when, when will the Tannese realize what I am now thinking and praying about, the life and immortality brought to light through Jesus?

As the war still raged on, and many more were killed, vengeance threatened the miserable Trader. Miaki attacked him thus,—

"You led us into this war. You deceived us, and we began it. Rarip is dead, and many others. Your life shall yet go for his."

Captain Winchester, heartless as a dog so long as pigs and fowls came to the yard at whatever cost to others' lives, now trembled like a coward for himself. He implored me to let him and his Marè wife sleep at my house for safety; but I refused to allow my Mission to be in any way identified with his crimes. The Natives from other islands, whom he kept and wrought like slaves, he now armed with muskets for his defence; but, having no faith in them protecting or even warning him, he implored me to send one

of my Teachers, to assist his wife in watching till he
snatched a few hours of sleep every day, and, if awake,
he would sell his life as dearly as he could by aid of
musket and revolyer.   The Teachers were both afraid
and disinclined to go ; and I could not honestly ask
them to do so.   His peril and terror became so real
that by night he slept in his boat anchored out in the
centre of the bay, with his arms beside him, and a
crew ready to start off at the approach of danger and
lose everything ; while by day he kept watch on
shore, armed, and also ready to fly.   Thus his miserable existence dragged on, keeping watch alterna-
tively with his wife, till a trading vessel called and
carried him off with all that he had rescued—for
which deliverance we were unfeignedly thankful !
The war, which he had wickedly instigated, lingered
on for three months ; and then, by a present given
secretly to two leading Chiefs, I managed to bring
it to a close.   But feelings of revenge for the slain,
burned fiercely in many breasts ; and young men had
old feuds handed on to them by the recital of their
fathers' deeds of blood.

All through this war, I went to the fighting ground
every Sabbath, and held worship amongst our
Harbour people.   Hundreds assembled around me,
and listened respectfully, but they refused to give up
the war.   One day, I determined to go through the
bush that lay between and speak and pray with the
enemies also.   Our Harbour folks opposed me, and
one leading man said,—

"Missi, pray only for us, and your God will be strong to help us and we will not be afraid! You must not pray with the enemy, lest He may help them too."

After this episode, I made it my duty always to visit both Camps, when I went to the fighting ground, and to have worship with both,—teaching them that Jehovah my God was angry at all such scenes and would not fight for either, that He commanded them to live at peace.

About this time, our Sabbath audiences at the Mission numbered forty or so. Nowar and three or four more, and only they, seemed to love and serve Jesus. They were, however, changeable and doubtful, though they exerted a good influence on their villages, and were generally friendly to us and to the Worship. Events sometimes for a season greatly increased our usefulness. For instance, one of the Sacred Men when fishing on the coral reef was bitten by a poisonous fish. After great agony, he died, and his relatives were preparing to strangle his two wives that their spirits might accompany and serve him in the other world. Usually such tragedies were completed before I ever heard of them. On this occasion, I had called at the village that very day, and succeeded in persuading them to bury him alone—his wives being saved alive at my appeal. Thus the idea got to be talked of, and the horrible custom was being undermined—the strangling of widows!

In connection with such poisonings, I may mention that some of these fishes were deadly poisonous; others were unwholesome, and even poisonous, only at certain seasons; and still others were always nutritious and good. For our own part, we used fish sparingly and cautiously; and the doubtful ones we boiled with a piece of silver in the water. If the silver became discoloured, we regarded the fish as unwholesome; if the silver remained pure, we could risk it.

One morning at daybreak I found my house surrounded by armed men, and a Chief intimated that they had assembled to take my life. Seeing that I was entirely in their hands, I knelt down and gave myself away body and soul to the Lord Jesus, for what seemed the last time on earth. Rising, I went out to them, and began calmly talking about their unkind treatment of me and contrasting it with all my conduct towards them. I also plainly showed them what would be the sad consequences, if they carried out their cruel purpose. At last some of the Chiefs, who had attended the Worship, rose and said,—

"Our conduct has been bad; but now we will fight for you, and kill all those who hate you."

Grasping hold of their leader, I held him fast till he promised never to kill any one on my account, for Jesus taught us to love our enemies and always to return good for evil! During this scene, many of the armed men slunk away into the bush, and those who remained entered into a bond to be friendly and

to protect us. But again their Public Assembly resolved that we should be killed, because, as they said,
they hated Jehovah and the Worship; for it made
them afraid to do as they had always done. If I
would give up visiting the villages, and praying and
talking with them about Jehovah, they intimated
that they would like me to stay and trade with them,
as they liked the Traders but hated the Missionaries!
I told them that the hope of being able to teach
them the Worship of Jehovah alone kept me living
amongst them; that I was there, not for gain or
pleasure, but because I loved them, and pitied their
estate, and sought their good continually by leading
them to know and serve the only true God. One of
the Chiefs, who had lived in Sydney and spoke
English, replied for all the rest,—

"Missi, our fathers loved and worshipped whom
you call the Devil, the Evil Spirit; and we are determined to do the same, for we love the conduct of
our fathers. Missi Turner came here and tried to
break down our worship, but our fathers fought him
and he left us. They fought also Peta, the Samoan
Teacher, and he fled. They fought and killed some
of the Samoan Teachers placed on the other side of
the Harbour, and their companions left. We killed
the last foreigner that lived in Tanna before you
came here. We murdered the Aneityumese Teachers,
and burned down their houses. After each of these
acts, Tanna was good; we all lived like our fathers,
and sickness and death left us. Now, our people are

determined to kill you,, if you do not leave this
island; for you are changing our customs and destroying our worship, and we hate the Jehovah
Worship."

Then, surrounded by a number of men, who had
spent some years in the Colonies, he continued in a
bitter strain to this effect,—

"The people of Sydney belong to your Britain;
they know what is right and wrong as well as you;
and we have ourselves seen them fishing, feasting,
cooking, working, and seeking pleasure on the
Sabbath as on any other day. You say, we do not
here need to cook any food on Sabbaths or to toil
at our ovens, but you yourself cook, for you boil your
kettle on that day! We have seen the people do
all the conduct at Sydney which you call bad, but
which we love. You are but one, they are many;
they are right, and you must be wrong; you are
teaching lies for Worship."

After many such speeches, I answered all the
questions of the people fully, and besides I cross-
questioned my assailants on several subjects, regarding which they grossly contradicted each other,
till the majority of voices cried out,—

"They are lying! Their words are crooked!
Missi knows all the truth about the people of
Sydney!"

Alas, I had to admit that what they reported was
too true regarding the godless multitudes at home
who made the Sabbath a day of pleasure, but not

regarding Jehovah's servants. By this time, they were willing to remain quiet, and allowed me to talk of spiritual things and of the blessings that the Sabbath and the Bible brought to all other lands, and to conduct in their presence and hearing the Worship of Jehovah

But my enemies seldom slackened their hateful designs against my life, however calmed or baffled for the moment. Within a few days of the above events, when Natives in large numbers were assembled at my house, a man furiously rushed on me with his axe; but a Kaserumini Chief snatched a spade with which I had been working, and dexterously defended me from instant death. Life in such circumstances led me to cling very near to the Lord Jesus; I knew not, for one brief hour, when or how attack might be made; and yet, with my trembling hand clasped in the hand once nailed on Calvary, and now swaying the sceptre of the Universe, calmness and peace and resignation abode in my soul.

Next day, a wild Chief followed me about for four hours with his loaded musket, and, though often directed towards me, God restrained his hand. I spoke kindly to him, and attended to my work as if he had not been there, fully persuaded that my God had placed me there, and would protect me till my allotted task was finished. Looking up in unceasing prayer to our dear Lord Jesus, I left all in His hands, and felt immortal till my work was done. Trials and hairbreadth escapes strengthened

my faith, and seemed only to nerve me for more to
follow ; and they did tread swiftly upon each other's
heels. Without that abiding consciousness of the
presence and power of my dear Lord and Saviour,
nothing else in all the world could have preserved
me from losing my reason and perishing miserably.
His words, " Lo, I am with you alway, even unto the
end of the world," became to me so real that it would
not have startled me to behold Him, as Stephen did,.
gazing down upon the scene. I felt His supporting
power, as did St. Paul, when he cried, " I can do all
things through Christ which strengtheneth me." It
is the sober truth, and it comes back to me sweetly
after twenty years, that I had my nearest and dearest
glimpses of the face and smile of my blessed Lord in
those dread moments when musket, club, or spear
was being levelled at my life. Oh the bliss of living
and enduring, as seeing " Him who is invisible ! "

One evening, I awoke three times to hear a Chief
and his men trying to force the door of my house.
Though armed with muskets, they had some sense
of doing wrong, and were wholesomely afraid of a
little retriever dog which had often stood betwixt me
and death. God restrained them again ; and next
morning the report went all round the Harbour, that
those who tried to shoot me were "smitten weak
with fear," and that shooting would not do. A plan
was therefore deliberately set on foot to fire the
premises, and club us if we attempted to escape.
But our Aneityumese Teacher heard of it, and God

helped us to frustrate their designs. When they knew that their plots were revealed to us, they seemed to lose faith in themselves, and cast about to circumvent us in some more secret way. Their evil was overruled for good.

Namuri, one of my Aneityumese Teachers, was placed at our nearest village. There he had built a house for himself and his wife, and there he led amongst the Heathen a pure and humble Christian life. Almost every morning, he came and reported on the state of affairs to me. Without books or a school, he yet instructed the Natives in Divine things, conducted the Worship, and taught them much by his good example. His influence was increasing, when one morning a Sacred Man threw at him the kawas, or killing stone, a deadly weapon, like a scythe stone in shape and thickness, usually round but sometimes angular, and from eighteen to twenty inches long. They throw it from a great distance and with fatal precision. The Teacher, with great agility, warded his head and received the deep cut from it in his left hand, reserving his right hand to guard against the club that was certain to follow swiftly. The Priest sprang upon him with his club and with savage yells. He evaded, yet also received, many blows; and, rushing out of their hands, actually reached the Mission House, bleeding, fainting, and pursued by howling murderers. I had been anxiously expecting him, and hearing the noise I ran out with all possible speed.

P.

On seeing me, he sank down by a tree, and cried,—

"Missi, Missi, quick! and escape for your life! They are coming to kill you; they say, they must kill us all to-day, and they have begun with me; for they hate Jehovah and the Worship!"

I hastened to the good Teacher where he lay; I bound up, washed, and dressed his wounds; and God, by the mystery of His own working, kept the infuriated Tannese watching at bay. Gradually they began to disappear into the bush, and we conveyed the dear Teacher to the Mission House. In three or four weeks, he so far recovered by careful nursing that he was able to walk about again. Some petitioned for him to return to the village; but I insisted, as a preliminary, that the Harbour Chiefs should unitedly punish him who had abused the Teacher; and this to test them, for he had only carried out their own wishes,—Nowar excepted, and perhaps one or two others. They made a pretence of atoning by presenting the Teacher with a pig and some yams as a peace-offering; but I said,—

"No! such bad conduct must be punished, or we would leave their island by the first opportunity."

Now that Sacred Man, a Chief too, had gone on fighting with other tribes, till his followers had all died or been slain; and, after three weeks' palaver, the other Chiefs seized him, tied him with a rope, and sent me word to come and see him punished, as they did not want us after all to leave the island.

I had to go, for fear of more bloody work, and after talk with them, followed by many fair promises, he was loosed.

All appearing friendly for some time, and willing to listen and learn, the Teacher earnestly desired to return to his post. I pled with him to remain at the Mission House till we felt more assured, but he replied,—

"Missi, when I see them thirsting for my blood, I just see myself when the Missionary first came to my island. I desired to murder him, as they now desire to kill me. Had he stayed away for such danger, I would have remained Heathen; but he came, and continued coming to teach us, till, by the grace of God, I was changed to what I am. Now the same God that changed me to this, can change these poor Tannese to love and serve Him. I cannot stay away from them; but I will sleep at the Mission House, and do all I can by day to bring them to Jesus."

It was not in me to keep such a man, under such motives, from what he felt to be his post of duty. He returned to his village work, and for several weeks things appeared most encouraging. The inhabitants showed growing interest in us and our work, and less fear of the pretensions of their heathen Priest, which, alas! fed his jealousy and anger. One morning during worship, when the good Teacher knelt in prayer, the same savage Priest sprang upon him with his great club and left him for dead, wounded and bleeding and unconscious. The people fled and left him in his blood, afraid of being mixed up with the murder. The Teacher, recovering a little, crawled to the Mission House, and reached it about mid-day in a dying condition. On seeing him, I ran to meet him, but he fell near the Teacher's house, saying,—

"Missi, I am dying ꜱ They will kill you also. Escape for your life."

Trying to console him, I sat down beside him, dressing his wounds and nursing him. He was quite resigned ; he was looking up to Jesus, and rejoicing that he would soon be with Him in Glory. His pain and suffering were great, but he bore all very quietly, as he said and kept saying, "For the sake of Jesus ! For Jesu's sake !" He was constantly praying for his persecutors,—

"O Lord Jesus, forgive them, for they know not what they are doing. Oh, take not away all Thy servants from Tanna! Take not away Thy Worship from this dark island! O God, bring all the Tannese to love and follow Jesus !"

To him, Jesus was all and in all; and there were no bands in his death. He passed from us, in the assured hope of entering into the Glory of his Lord. Humble though he may appear in the world's esteem, I knew that a great man had fallen there in the service of Christ, and that he would take rank in the glorious Army of the Martyrs. I made for him a coffin, and dug his grave near the Mission

House. With prayers, and many tears, we consigned his remains to the dust in the certainty of a happy resurrection. Even one such convert was surely a triumphant reward for Dr. and Mrs. Geddie, whom God had honoured in bringing him to Jesus. May they have many like him for their crown of joy and rejoicing in the great day!

Immediately after this, a number of Chiefs and followers called on me at the Mission House, professing great friendliness, and said,—

"Mr. Turner gave our fathers great quantities of calico, axes, and knives, and they became his friends. If you would give the people some just now they would be pleased. They would stop fighting against the Worship."

I retorted, "How was it then, if they were pleased, that they persecuted Messrs. Turner and Nisbet till they had to leave the island? Your conduct is deceitful and bad. I never will reward you for bad actions and for murder! No present will be given by me."

They withdrew sullenly, and seemed deeply disappointed and offended.

On one occasion, when a Chief had died, the Harbour people were all being assembled to strangle his widow. One of my Aneityumese Teachers, hearing of it, hastened to tell me. I ran to the village, and with much persuasion, saved her life. A few weeks thereafter she gave birth to a young chieftain, who prospered well. If our Harbour people told the truth, the widows of all who fell in war were saved by our pleading. Immediately after the foregoing incident, a Sacred Man was dying, and a crowd of people were assembled awaiting the event in order to strangle his three wives. I spoke to them of the horrid wickedness of such conduct. I further reasoned with them, that God had made us male and female, the sexes so balanced, that for every man that had three or a dozen wives, as many men generally had none, and that this caused great jealousy and quarrelling. I showed them further, that these widows being spared would make happy and useful wives for other kind and loving husbands. After the Worship, I appealed to the Chief and he replied,—

"Missi, it was a practice introduced to Tanna from the island of Aneityum. It was not the custom of our fathers here to strangle widows. And, as the Aneityumese have given it up since they became worshippers of Jehovah, it is good that we now should give it up on Tanna too."

Thus these three widows were saved; and we had great hope in Christ that the ghastly practice would soon disappear from Tanna.

An incident of this time created great wonder amongst the Natives; namely, the Sinking of a Well. We had, heretofore, a boiling spring to drink from, the water of which literally required in that climate days to cool down; we had also, a stagnant pool at the lower end of a swamp in which the Natives

habitually bathed, the only available fresh water
bath! Beyond that, no drinking water could be had
for six or seven miles. I managed to sink a well,
near the Mission House, and got about twelve feet
deep a good supply of excellent fresh water, though,
strange to say, the surface of the well rose and
fell regularly with every tide! This became the
universal supply for us and for the Natives all round
the Harbour and for miles inland. Hundreds of
Natives from all parts of Tanna flocked to examine
this greatest wonder they had ever seen—rain rising
up out of the earth. I built it round with a kind of
stone brought in my boat from the other side of the
bay; and for many years it was the only fresh water
supply for the Natives all around. Some years later
a native Chief sank a well about a mile nearer the
entrance to the Harbour at his own village, and built
it round with the bricks that I had purchased for
house-building; these he grabbed and thus appropriated! Many a vessel, calling at the Harbour, was
glad to get her casks refilled at my well, and all were
apparently more friendly because of it; but the Sinking of this Well produced no such revolution as on
Aniwa,—to be hereafter related.

For fully three months, all our available time, with
all the native help which I could hire, was spent in
erecting a building to serve for Church and School.
It was fifty feet long, by twenty-one feet six inches
broad. The studs were three feet apart, and all
fixed by tenon and mortise into upper and lower wall

plates.   The beautiful roof of iron, wood, and sugar-
cane leaf, was supported by three massive pillars of
wood, sunk deeply into the ground.   The roof extended about three feet over the wall plates, both to
form a verandah and to carry the rain-drop free beyond the walls.   It was made of sugar-cane leaf and
cocoa-nut leaves all around.   The floor was laid with
white coral, broken small, and covered with cocoa-nut
leaf mats, such as those on which the Natives sat.
Indeed, it was as comfortable a House of Prayer as
any man need wish for in the tropics, though having
only open spaces for doors and windows !   I bought
the heavy wood for it on Aneityum—price, fifty pairs
of native trousers ; and these again were the gift of
my Bible Class in Glasgow, all cut and sewed by
their own hands. . I gave also one hundred and
thirty yards of cloth, along with other things, for
other needful wood.

My Tannese people at first opposed the erection
of a Church.   They did not wish Jehovah to secure
a House on their island.   On the opening day, only
five men, three women, and three children were
present, besides our Aneityumese Teachers.   But
after the morning service, on that day, I visited ten
villages, and had worship in each.   The people were
generally shy and unfriendly.   They said that we
were the cause of the prevailing sickness and fever.
They had no idea of any sickness or death being
natural, but believed that all such events were caused
by some one *nahaking*, *i.e.*, bewitching them.   Hence

their incessant feuds; and many were murdered in blind revenge.

As we were preparing a foundation for the Church, a huge and singular-looking round stone was dug up, at sight of which the Tannese stood aghast. The eldest Chief said,—

"Missi, that stone was either brought there by Karapanamun (the Evil Spirit), or hid there by our great Chief who is dead. That is the Stone God to which our forefathers offered human sacrifices; these holes held the blood of the victim 'till drunk up by the Spirit. The Spirit of that stone eats up men and women and drinks their blood, as our fathers taught us. We are in greatest fear!".

A Sacred Man claimed possession, and was exceedingly desirous to carry it off; but I managed to keep it, and did everything in my power to show them the absurdity of these foolish notions. Idolatry had not, indeed, yet fallen throughout Tanna, but one cruel idol, at least, had to give way for the erection of God's House on that benighted land.

An ever-memorable event was the printing of my first book in Tannese. Thomas Binnie, Esq., Glasgow, gave me a printing press and a font of type. Printing was one of the things I had never tried, but having now prepared a booklet in Tannese, I got my press into order, and began fingering the type. But book-printing turned out to be for me a much more difficult affair than house-building had been. Yet by dogged perseverance I succeeded at last. My

biggest difficulty was how to arrange the pages pro
perly! After many failures, I folded a piece of paper
into the number of leaves wanted, cut the corners,
folding them back, and numbering as they would be
when correctly placed in the book; then folding all
back without cutting up the sheet, I found now by
these numbers how to arrange the pages in the frame
or case for printing, as indicated on each side. And
do you think me foolish, when I confess that I
shouted in an ecstasy of joy when the first sheet
came from the press all correct? It was about one
o'clock in the morning. I was the only white man
then on the island, and all the Natives had been fast
asleep for hours! Yet I literally pitched my hat into
the air, and danced like a schoolboy round and round
that printing-press; till I began to think, Am I losing
my reason? Would it not be liker a Missionary to
be upon my knees, adoring God for this first portion
of His blessed Word ever printed in this new language? Friend, bear with me, and believe me, that
was as true worship as ever was David's dancing
before the Ark of his God! Nor think that I did
not, over that first sheet of God's Word ever printed
in the Tannese tongue, go upon my knees too, and
then, and every day since, plead with the mighty
Lord to carry the light and joy of His own Holy
Bible into every dark heart and benighted home on
Tanna! But the Tannese had a superstitious dread
of books, and especially of God's Book. I afterwards
heard that Dr. Turner had printed a small primer in

Tannese, translated by the help of the Samoan Teachers ; but this I never saw till near the close of my work on Tanna. Dr. Geddie sent me a copy, but it was more Samoan than Tannese, especially in its spelling, and I could make little or nothing of it.

Shortly after this, I was greatly refreshed by the visit of an American whaler, the *Camden Packet,* under Captain Allan. He, his chief officer, and many of his double company of seamen, were decided Christians—a great contrast to most of the Traders that had called at Port Resolution. The Captain cordially invited me on board to preach and conduct a religious service. That evening I enjoyed exceedingly—wells in the desert! The Captain introduced me, saying,—

"This is my ship's company. My first officer and most of my men are real Christians, trying to love and serve Jesus Christ. We have been three years out on this voyage, and are very happy with each other. You would never hear or see worse on board of this vessel than you see now. And God has given us gratifying success."

He afterwards told me that he had a very valuable cargo of sperm oil on board, the vessel being nearly filled up with it. He was eager to leave supplies, or do something for me, but I needed nothing that he could give. His mate, on examining my boat, found a hole in her, and several planks split and bulged in, as I had gone down on a reef with her when out on Mission work, and narrowly escaped drowning. Next

morning, the Captain, of his own accord, set his car-
penter to repair the boat, and left it as good as new.
Not one farthing of recompense would any of them
take from me; their own Christian love rewarded
them, in the circumstances. I had been longing for
a chance to send it to Sydney for repairs, and felt
deeply thankful for such unexpected and generous
aid. The Captain would not admit that the delay
was any loss to him,—his boats spending the day in
purchasing cocoa-nuts and provisions from the Natives for his own ship. Oh, how the Christlike spirit
knits together all true followers of Christ! What
other earthly or human tie could have so bound that
stranger to me? In the heart of Christ we met as
brothers.

Dangers again darkened round me. One day,
while toiling away at my house, the war Chief, his
brother, and a large party of armed men surrounded
the plot where I was working. They all had muskets, besides their own native weapons. They
watched me for some time in silence, and then every
man levelled a musket straight at my head. Escape
was impossible. Speech would only have increased
my danger. My eyesight came and went for a few
moments. I prayed to my Lord Jesus, either Himself to protect me, or to take me home to His Glory.
I tried to keep working on at my task, as if no one
was near me. In that moment, as never before, the
words came to me,—" Whatsoever ye shall ask in
My name, I will do it; " and I knew that I was safe.

Retiring a little from their first position, no word
having been spoken, they took up the same attitude
somewhat farther off, and seemed to be urging one
another to fire the first shot.   But my dear Lord restrained them once again, and they withdrew, leaving
me with a new cause for trusting Him with all that
concerned me for Time and Eternity. · Perils seemed,
however, to enclose me `on every hand, and my life
was frequently attempted.   I had to move about
more cautiously than ever, some days scarcely daring
to appear outside my Mission premises.   For I have
ever most firmly believed, and do believe, that only
when we use every lawful and possible means for ·the
preservation of our life, which is God's second greatest gift to man (His Son being the first), can we
expect God to protect us, or have we·the right to
plead His precious promises.

The vessel of one calling himself Prince de Jean
Beuve, a French refugee, who had become a natural-
ized American, visited Port Resolution.   He said,
he had to escape from his own country for political
offences. .His large and beautiful ship was fitted up,
· and armed like a Man-of-war.   She was manned
chiefly by slaves, whom he ruled with an iron hand.
What a contrast to Captain Allan's whaler !   Yet he
· also was very sympathetic and kind to me.   Having
heard rumour of my trials and dangers, he came on
shore, as soon as his ship cast anchor, with a body
of armed men.   He was effusively polite, with all
a Frenchman's gush and gesticulation, and offered

to do anything possible for me. He would take me to Aneityum or Sydney or wherever I wished. The ship was his own ; he was sailing chiefly for pleasure, and he had called at our Islands to see if sufficient trade could be opened up to justify his laying on a line of steamers to call here in their transit. He urged me, I believe sincerely, to give him the pleasure of taking me and my belongings to some place of safety. But I was restrained from leaving, through the fear that I would never be permitted to return, and that Christ's work would suffer. In the still burning hope of being able to lead the Tannese to love and serve Jesus, I declined with much gratitude his genuine kindness. He looked truly sorry to leave me in the circumstances wherein I was placed. After two hours on shore, he returned to his ship towards evening.

Knowing that the Tannese were threatening to burn my former house, which I wished to remove to higher ground and add to the room I now occupied on the hill, I took advantage of the presence of the Prince's vessel, and set my Aneityumese Teachers and some friendly Natives to prepare for the task ; but unfortunately, I forgot to send word to the Frenchman regarding my plans and aims. We removed the sugar-cane leaf thatch from the roof of the house, and began burning it on cleared ground, so that I might be able to save the heavy wood which could not be replaced on Tanna. Our French friend, on seeing the flames rising up furiously, at once loaded his heavy guns, and prepared his men for action. Under great excitement, he came ashore with a large number of armed men, leaving the rest on board ready at a given signal to protect them with shot and shell. Leaving one-half of those brought on shore to guard the boats, he came running towards my house, followed by the other half, wet with perspiration, and crying,—

"Fer are dey? fer are dey? De scoundrels! I vill do for dem, and protect you. I sall punish dem, de scoundrels!"

He was so excited, he could scarcely compose himself to hear my explanations, which, when understood, he laughed at heartily. He again urged me to leave in his vessel; he could not bear me to lead such a life amongst savages. I explained to him my reasons for not leaving the island, but these he seemed unable to understand. He put his men through drill on shore, and left them under officers, ready for action at a moment's warning, saying they would all be the better for a day on shore. He wished to take pot luck with me at our Mission House of one room for all purposes! My humble dinner and tea must have been anything but a treat for him, but he seemed to relish the deliverance for once from all the conventionalisms of the world. Before he left, he sent of his own accord for all the Chiefs within reach, and warned them that if they hurt me or took my life, he would return with his Man-of-war and punish them, by killing themselves and firing their villages; and that a British Man-of-war would also come and set their island on fire. They promised all possible good conduct, being undoubtedly put into great terror. The kind-hearted Frenchman left, with profuse expressions of admiration for my courage and of pity for my lot. No doubt he thought me a foolish dreamer of dreams.

A miserable contrast befell us in the bad impression produced by the conduct of one of Captain T——'s vessels in the Sydney sandal-wood trade. Whale-boats had been sent out with Mr. Copeland and myself from Glasgow, as part of the necessary equipment of every Missionary on these Islands. Mine being rather large and heavy, I had sold it to one of T——'s captains; but the other had also been left to my care. After having used my boat for about twelve months—the best boat in that trade only being expected to last two years—the Captain called on Mr. Copeland, and got a note from him to me regarding the sale of his boat too. He declared, when calling on me, that Mr. Copeland had authorized him to get his boat from me in exchange for mine, which he had now been using for a year. I asked for the letter, and found it to be authority for me to sell his boat for cash only and at the same price as mine. Captain V—— then raged at me and stormed, declaring that he would return my old boat, and take the other in defiance of me. Swearing dreadfully, he made for his ship, and returned with a large party of men whom he had picked up amongst the Islands. Collecting also a company of Tannese, and offering them tobacco, he broke down the fence, burst into the boat-house, and began to draw out the boat. Here I reached the spot, and sternly opposed them. He swore and foamed at me, and before the natives knocked and pulled me about, even kicking at me, though I evaded his blows. Standing by, I said in Tannese,—

"You are helping that man to steal my boat; he is stealing it as you see."

On hearing this, the Tannese ran away, and his own party alone could not do it. In great wrath, he went off again to his vessel, and brought on shore as much tobacco as could be held in a large handkerchief tied by the four corners; but even for that, our own Natives refused to help him. He offered it then to a crowd of Inland savages, gathered at the head of the bay, who, regardless of my remonstrances, launched the boat, he raging at and all but striking me. Instead of returning, however, the other boat to the house, he merely set it adrift from his vessel, and it was carried on to the reef, where it remained fast, and was knocked about by the waves. After his vessel left, I, with much difficulty, got it off and brought it to the boat-house. Imagine, when such was their tyrannical treatment of a Missionary and a British fellow-subject, how they would act towards these poor native Islanders.

By the earliest opportunity, I wrote all the facts of the case to his employer, Captain T—— of Sydney.

P. 14

but got not even a reply, while Captain V—— continued in their trade, a scourge to these Islands, and a dishonour to his country and to humanity. Unfriendly Tannese now said,—

"When a white man from his own country can so pull and knock the Missionary about and steal his boat and chain without being punished for it, we also may do as we please!"

I hesitate not to record my conviction that that man's conduct had a very bad effect, emboldening them in acts of dishonesty and in attempts upon my life, till the Mission Station was ultimately broken up. After I had to escape from Tanna, with bare life in my hand, one of the same Captain's vessels called at Port Resolution and gave the Natives about three pounds weight of useless tobacco, purchasable at Sydney for less than one shilling per pound, to allow them to take away my boat, with oars, sails, mast, and all other belongings. They also purchased all the plunder from my house. Both boats were so large and so strongly built, that by adding a plank or two they turned them into small-decked schooners, admirably suited for the sandal-wood traffic round the shores, while larger vessels lay at safe anchorage to receive what they collected. Once, when Dr. Inglis and I met in Sydney, we called on Captain T—— and stated the whole case, asking reasonable payment at least for the boats. He admitted that the boats had been taken and were in his service, and agreed to pay us for the boats if we would repay the

large sum invested therein by his Captains. Calling
one of his clerks, he instructed him to trace in the
office record how much had been paid to the Tannese
for the Missionary's boat.

The young man innocently returned the reply,
"Three pounds of tobacco."

In anger, he said, "I understood that a larger
value had been given!"

The clerk assured him, "That is the only record."

Captain T——, after discussing the worth of the
boat as being about £80, agreed to give us £60, but
in writing out the cheque, threw down the pen and
shouted, "I'll see you —— first!"

Offering £50, to which we agreed, he again resiled,
and declared he would not give a penny above £30.

We appealed to him to regard this as a debt of
honour, and to cease haggling over the price, as he
well knew how we had been wronged in the matter.

Finally we left him declaring, "I am building
similar boats just now at £25 apiece; I will send you
one of them, and you may either take that or want!"

We left, glad to get away on any terms from such
a character; and, though next year he did send
one of his promised boats for me to Aneityum, yet
the conduct of his degraded servants engaged in the
sandal-wood trade had a great share in the guilt of
breaking up and ruining our Mission. Thousands
upon thousands were made by it yearly, so long as
it lasted; but it was a trade steeped in human blood
and indescribable vice, nor could God's blessing rest

on them and their ill-gotten gains. Oh, how often
did we pray at that time to be delivered from the
hands of unreasonable and wicked men!   Sandal-
wood traders murdered many of the Islanders when
robbing them of their wood, and the Islanders murdered many of them and their servants in revenge.
White men, engaged in the trade, also shot dead and
murdered each other in vicious and drunken quarrels,
and not a few put end to their own lives.   I have
scarcely known one of them who did not come to ruin
and poverty ; the money that came even to the ship-
owners was a conspicuous curse.   Fools there made
a mock at sin, thinking that no one cared for these
poor savages, but their sin did find them out, and
God made good in their experience His own irrepeal-
able law, " The wages of sin is death."

Ships, highly insured, were said to be sent into our
Island trade to be deliberately wrecked.   One Sabbath evening, towards dark, the notorious Captain
H——, in command of a large ship, allowed her to ·
drift ashore and be wrecked without any apparent
effort to save her.   Next morning, the whole company
were wading about in the water and pretending to
have lost everything!   The Captain, put in prison
when he returned to Sydney for running away with
another man's wife and property, imposed on Mr.
Copeland and myself, getting all the biscuits, flour,
and blankets we could spare for his destitute and
shipwrecked company.   We discovered afterwards
that she was lying on a beautiful bank of sand, only

a few yards from the shore, and that everything contained in her could be easily rescued without danger
to life or limb! What we parted with was almost
necessary for our life and health; of course he gave
us an order on Captain T—— for everything, but not
one farthing was ever repaid. At first he made a
pretence of paying the Natives for food received; but
afterwards, an armed band went inland night by night
and robbed and plundered whatever came to hand.
The Natives, seeing the food of their children ruthlessly stolen, were shot down without mercy when
they dared to interfere; and the life of every white
man was marked for speedy revenge. Glad were
we when a vessel called, and carried away these white
heathen Savages.

The same Captain T—— also began the shocking
Kanaka labour-traffic to the Colonies, after the sandal-
wood trade was exhausted, which has since destroyed
so many thousands of the Natives in what was
nothing less than Colonial slavery, and has largely
depopulated the Islands either directly or indirectly.
And yet he wrote, and published in Sydney, a pam-
phlet declaring that he and his sandal-wooders and
Kanaka-labour collectors had done more to civilize
the Islanders than all our Mission efforts combined.
Civilize them, indeed! By spreading disease and
vice, misery and death amongst them, even at the
best; at the worst, slaving many of them till they
perished at their toils, shooting down others under
one or other guilty pretence, and positively sweeping

thousands into an untimely grave. A common cry on their lips was,—

" Let them perish and let the white men occupy these Isles."

It was such conduct as this, that made the Islanders suspect all foreigners and hate the white man and seek revenge in robbery and murder. One Trader, for instance, a sandal-wooder and collector of Kanakas, living at Port Resolution, abominably ill-used a party of Natives. They determined in revenge to plunder his store. The cellar was un-derneath his house, and he himself slept above the trap-door by which alone it could be entered. Night and day he was guarded by armed men, Natives of adjoining islands, and all approaches to his premises were watched by savage dogs that gave timely warning. He felt himself secure. But the Tannese actually constructed a tunnel underground from the bush, through which they rolled away to-bacco, ammunition, etc, and nearly emptied his cellar ! My heart bled to see men so capable and clever thus brutally abused and demoralized and swept away. By the Gospel, and the civilization which it brings, they were capable of learning anything and being trained to a useful and even noble manhood. But all influence that ever I witnessed from these Traders was degrading, and dead against the work of our Missions.

The Chief, Nowar Noukamara, usually known as Nowar, was my best and most-to-be-trusted friend.

He was one of the nine or ten who were most favourable to the Mission work, attending the Worship ·pretty regularly, conducting it also in their own houses and villages, and making generally a somewhat unstable profession of Christianity. One or more of them often accompanied me on Sabbath, when going to conduct the Worship at inland villages, and sometimes they protected me from personal injury. This Nowar influenced the Harbour Chiefs and their people for eight or ten miles around to get up a great feast in favour of the Worship of Jehovah. All were personally and specially invited, and it was the largest Assembly of any kind that I ever witnessed on the Islands.

When all was ready, Nowar sent a party of Chiefs to escort me and my Aneityumese Teachers to the feast. Fourteen Chiefs, in turn, made speeches to the assembled multitude ; the drift of all being, that war and fighting be given up on Tanna,—that no more people be killed by nahak, for witchcraft and sorcery were lies,—that Sacred Men no longer profess to make wind and rain, famine and plenty, disease and death,—that the dark heathen talk of Tanna should cease, that all here present should adopt the Worship of Jehovah as taught to them by the Missionary and the Aneityumese,—and that all the banished Tribes should be invited to their own lands to live in peace! These strange speeches did not draw forth a single opposing voice. Doubtless these men were in earnest, and had there been one master mind to rule and

mould them, their regeneration had dawned. Though
for the moment a feeling of friendliness prevailed,
the Tannese were unstable as water and easily swayed·
one way or the other. They are born talkers, and
can and will speechify on all occasions, but most of it
means nothing, bears no fruit.·

After these speeches, a scene followed which gradually assumed shape as an idolatrous ceremonial and
greatly horrified me. It was in connection with the
immense quantity of food that had been prepared for
the feast, especially pigs and fowls. A great heap had
been piled up for each Tribe represented, and a handsome portion also set apart for the Missionary and
his Teachers. The ceremony was this, as nearly as
I could follow it. One hundred or so of the leading
men marched into the large cleared space in the centre
of the assembled multitudes, and stood there facing
each· other in equal lines, with a man at either end
closing up the passage between. At the middle they
stood eight or ten feet apart, gradually nearing till
they almost met at either end. Amid tremendous
silence for a few moments all stood hushed; then
every man kneeled on his right knee, extended his
right hand, and bent forward till his face nearly
touched the ground. Thereon the man at the one
end began muttering something, his voice rising ever
louder as he rose to his feet, when it ended in a fearful yell as he stood erect. Next the two long lines of
men, all in a body, went through the same ceremonial,
rising gradually to their feet, with mutterings deepen-

ing into a howl, and heightening into a yell as they
stood erect.   Finally, the man at the other end went
through the same hideous forms.   All this was thrice
deliberately repeated, each time with growing frenzy.
And then, all standing on their feet, they united as
with one voice in what sounded like music running
mad up and down the scale, closing with a long,
deep-toned, hollow howl as of souls in pain.   With
smiles of joy, the men then all shook hands with
each other.   Nowar and another Chief briefly spoke,
and the food was then divided and exchanged, a
principal man of each Tribe standing by to receive
and watch his portion.

At this stage, Nowar and Nerwangi, as leaders,
addressed the Teachers and the Missionary to this
effect :—

"This feast is held to move all the Chiefs and
People here to give up fighting, to become friends,
and to worship your Jehovah God.   We wish you to
remain, and to teach us all good conduct.   As an
evidence of our sincerity, and of our love, we have
prepared this pile of food for you."

In reply, I addressed the whole multitude, saying
how pleased I was with their speeches and with the
resolutions and promises which they all had made.   I
further urged them to stick fast by these, and that
grand fruits would arise to their island, to themselves
and to their children.

Having finished a brief address, I then walked forward to the very middle of the circle, and laid down

before them a bundle of stripes of red calico and pieces of white calico, a number of fish-hooks, knives, etc. etc., requesting the two Chiefs to divide my offering of goodwill among the Tribes assembled, and also the pile of food presented to us, as a token of my love and friendship to them all.

Their insisting upon me taking their present of food, laid upon me an unpleasant and dangerous necessity of explaining my refusal. I again thanked them very warmly, and explained that, as they had in my presence given away all their food to an Idol God and asked his blessing on it as a sacrifice, even to Karapa-namun, the great Evil Spirit, my people and I durst not and could not eat of it, for that would be to have fellowship with their Idols and to dishonour Jehovah God. Christians could acknowledge only the one true and living God, and ask His blessing on their food, and offer it and themselves in thanksgiving unto Him, but unto no cruel or evil Spirit. Yet I explained to them how much I thanked them, and how I loved them just as much as if we had eaten all their gifts, and how it would please us to see them all, along with my own gifts, divided amongst their Tribes.

Not without some doubt, and under considerable trial, did I take this apparently unfriendly attitude. But I feared to seem even to approve of any act of devil-worship, or to confirm them in it, being there to discourage all such scenes, and to lead them to acknowledge only the true God. I felt as if guilty and as if the hat were rising from my head, when I heard

them imprecating and appeasing their God, without
being able to show them the God of Love and the
better way into His presence through Jesus Christ.
My opportunity to do so arose over the refusal of the
food offered unto Idols, and I told them of the claims
of Jehovah, the jealous God, who would not share His
worship with any other. But all the time I felt this
qualm,—that it were better to eat food with men who
acknowledged some God and asked his blessing than
with those white Heathens at home, who asked the
blessing of no God, nor thanked Him, in this worse
than the dog which licks the hand that feeds it!
Nowar and Nerwangi explained in great orations what
I meant, and how I wished all to be divided amongst
the assembled Tribes to show my love. With this, all
seemed highly satisfied.

Heathen dances were now entered upon, their
paint and feathers and ornaments adding to the wild-
ness of the scene. The men seemed to dance in an
inside ring, and the women in an outside ring, at a
considerable distance from each other. Music was
supplied by singing and clapping of hands. The order
was perfect, and the figures highly intricate. But I
have never been able to associate dancing with things
lovely and of good report! After the dancing, all
retired to the bush, and a kind of sham fight followed
on the public cleared ground. A host of painted
savages rushed in and took possession with songs and
shoutings. From the bush, on the opposite side, the
chanting of women was heard in the distance, louder

and louder as they approached. Snatching from a burning fire flaming sticks, they rushed on the men with these, beating them and throwing burning pieces of wood among them, till with deafening yells amongst themselves and amidst shouts of laughter from the crowd, they drove them from the space, and danced thereon and sang a song of victory. The dancing and fighting, the naked painted figures, and the constant yells and shoutings gave one a weird, sensation, and suggested strange ideas of Hell broken loose.

The final scene approached, when the men assisted their women to fill all the allotted food into baskets, to be carried home and eaten there ; for the different Tribes do not sit down together and eat to-gether as we would do ; their coming together is for the purpose of exchanging and dividing the food presented. And now they broke into friendly confusion, and freely walked about mingling with each other; and a kind of savage rehearsal of Jonathan and David took place. They stripped themselves of their fantastic dresses, their handsomely woven and twisted grass skirts, leaf skirts, grass and leaf aprons ; they gave away, or exchanged all these, and their ornaments and bows and arrows, besides their less romantic calico and print dresses more recently acquired. The effusion and ceremonial of the gifts and exchanges seemed to betoken a loving people ; and so they were for the feast—but that laid not aside a single deadly feud, and streams of blood and cries of hate would soon efface all traces of this day.

I had now six Stations, opened up and ministered
to by Aneityumese Teachers, at the leading villages
along the coast, and forming links in a chain towards
the other Mission Establishment on Tanna.   And
there were villages prepared to receive as many
more.   These Teachers had all been cannibals once,
yet, with one exception, they proved themselves to
the best of my judgment to be a band of faithful
and devoted followers of Christ.   Their names were
Abraham, Kowari, Nomuri, Nerwa, Lazarus, and
Eoufati.   I visited them periodically and frequently,
encouraging and guiding them, as well as trying to
interest the villagers in their teaching and work.
But, whenever war broke out they had all to return
to the Mission House, and sleep there for safety by
night, visiting their Stations, if practicable, by the
light of day.   My poor dear Teachers, too, had to bear
persecutions for Jesu's sake, as the following incident
will sorrowfully prove.

A native woman, with some murderous purpose in
her heart, pretended great friendship to the excellent
wife of one of my fellow-labourers.   She was specially
effusive in bringing to her dishes of food from time
to time.   Having thus gained confidence, she caught
a little black fish of those parts, known to be deadly
poisonous, and baked it up in a mess for the unsus-
pecting Teacher's wife.   On returning, she boasted of
what she had done, and thereon a friendly neighbour
rushed off to warn the other, but arrived just to learn
that the fatal meal had been taken.   Beyond all reach

of human skill, this unknown martyr for Christ died soon after in great agony, and doubtless received her Master's reward.·

In helping to open up new Stations, those dear native Teachers often bore the greatest hardships and indignities with a noble self-denial and positively wonderful patience. Nothing known to men under Heaven could have produced their new character and disposition, except only the grace of God in Christ Jesus. Though still marred·by many of the faults of Heathenism, they were at the roots of their being literally new creatures, trying, according to their best light, to live for and to please their new Master, Jesus Christ. This shone out very conspicuously in these two apostolic souls, Abraham and Kowari, as leaders among all the devoted band.

Let me recall another occasion, on which· I prevented a war. Early one morning, the savage yells of warring Tribes woke me from sleep. They had broken into a quarrel about a woman, and were fiercely engaged with their clubs. According to my custom, I rushed in amongst them, and, not without much difficulty, was blessed in separating them before deadly wounds had been given or received. On this occasion, the Chiefs of both Tribes, being very friendly to me, drove their people back from each other at my earnest appeals. Sitting down at length within earshot, they had it out in a wild scolding match, a contest of lung and tongue. Meanwhile I rested on a canoe midway betwixt them, in the hope

of averting a renewal of hostilities. By-and-by an
old Sacred Man, a Chief called Sapa, with some
touch of savage comedy in his breast, volunteered an
episode which restored good humour to the scene.
Leaping up, he came dancing and singing towards
me, and there, to the amusement of all, re-enacted the
quarrel, and mimicked rather cleverly my attempt at
separating the combatants. Smashing at the canoe
with his club, he yelled and knocked down imaginary
enemies ; then, rushing first at one párty and then at
the other, he represented me as appealing and ges-
ticulating and pushing them afar from each other, till
he became quite exhausted. Thereon he came and
planted himself in great glee beside me, and looked
around as if to say,—"You must laugh, for I have
played." At this very juncture, a loud cry of " Sail
O !" broke upon our ears, and all parties leapt to
their feet, and prepared for a new sensation ; for in
those climes, everything—war itself—is a smaller
interest than a vessel from the Great Unknown
World sailing into your Harbour.

Not many days thereafter, a very horrible trans-
action occurred. Before daybreak, I heard shot after
shot quickly discharged in the Harbour. One of my
Teachers came running, and cried,—

" Missi, six or seven men have been shot déad this
morning for a great feast. It is to reconcile Tribes
that have been at war, and to allow a banished Tribe
to return in peace."

I learned that the leading men had in council

agreed upon this sacrifice, but the name of each
victim was kept a secret till the last moment. The
torture of suspense and uncertainty seemed to be
borne by all as part of their appointed lot, nor did
they prepare as if suspecting any dread assault.
Before daylight, the Sacred Men allocated a murderer
to the door of each house where a victim slept. A
signal shot was fired ; all rushed to their doors, and
the doomed ones were shot and clubbed to death,
as they attempted to escape. Their bodies were
then borne to a sacred tree, and hung up there by the
hands for a time, as an offering to the Gods. Being
taken down, they were carried ceremoniously and
laid out on the shore near my house, placed under a
special guard.

Information had reached me that my Teachers and
I were also destined victims for this same feast, and
sure enough we espied a band of armed men, the
killers, despatched towards our premises. Instantaneously I had the Teachers and their wives and myself securely locked into the Mission House ; and, cut
off from all human hope, we set ourselves to pray to
our dear Lord Jesus, either Himself to protect us or
to take us to His glory. All through that morning
and forenoon we heard them tramp-tramping round
our house, whispering to each other, and hovering
near window and door. They knew that there were
a double-barrelled fowling-piece and a revolver on the
premises, though they never had seen me use them,
and that may, under God, have held them back in

dread. But such a thought did not enter our souls even in that awful time. I had gone to save, and not to destroy. It would be easier for me at any time to die than to kill one of them. Our safety lay in our appeal to that blessed Lord who had placed us there, and to whom all power had been given in Heaven and on Earth. He that was with us was more than all that could be against us. This is strength; this is peace :—to feel, in entering on every day, that all its duties and trials have been committed to the Lord Jesus,—that, come what may, He will use us for His own glory and our real good!

All through that dreadful morning, and far into the afternoon, we thus abode together, feeling conscious that we were united to this dear Lord Jesus, and we had sweet communion with Him, meditating on the wonders of His person and the hopes and glories of His kingdom. Oh, that all my readers may learn something of this in their own experience of the Lord! I can wish them nothing more precious. Towards sundown, constrained by the Invisible One, they withdrew from our Mission House, and left us once more in peace. They bore away the slain to be cooked, and distributed amongst the Tribes, and eaten in their feast of reconciliation; a covenant sealed in blood, and soon, alas, to be buried in blood again! For many days thereafter, we had to take unusual care, and not unduly expose ourselves to danger; for dark characters were seen prowling about in the bush near at hand, and we

P. 15

knew that our life was the prize. We took what
care we could, and God the Lord did the rest, or
rather He did all—for His wisdom guided us, and
His power baffled them.

Shortly thereafter, war was again declared by the
Inland people attacking our Harbour people. It was
an old quarrel ; and the war was renewed and continued, long after the cause thereof had passed away.
Going amongst them every day, I did my utmost to
stop hostilities, setting the evils of war before them,
and pleading with the leading men to renounce it.
Thereon arose a characteristic incident of Island and
Heathen life. One day I held a Service in the village
where morning after morning their Tribes assembled,
and declared that if they would believe in and follow the Jehovah God, He would deliver them from
all their enemies and lead them into a happy life.
There were present three Sacred Men, Chiefs, of
whom the whole population lived in terror,—brothers
or cousins, heroes of traditional feats, professors of
sorcery, and claiming the power of life and death,
health and sickness, rain and drought, according to
their will. On hearing me, these three stood up and
declared they did not believe in Jehovah, nor did
they need His help, for they had the power to kill my
life by Nahak (*i.e.*, sorcery or witchcraft), if only they
could get possession of any piece of the fruit or food
that I had eaten. This was an essential condition of
their black art ; hence the peel of a banana or an
orange, and every broken scrap of food, is gathered

up by the Natives, lest it should fall into the hands of the Sacred Men, and be used for Nahak. This superstition was the cause of most of the bloodshed and terror upon Tanna ; and being thus challenged, I asked God's help, and determined to strike a blow against it. A woman was standing near with a bunch of native fruit in her hand, like our plums, called quonquore. I asked her to be pleased to give me some ; and she, holding out a bunch, said,—

"Take freely what you will !"

Calling the attention of all the Assembly to what I was doing, I took three fruits from the bunch, and taking a bite out of each, I gave them one after another to the three Sacred Men, and deliberately said in the hearing of all,—

"You have seen me eat of this fruit, you have seen me give the remainder to your Sacred Men ; they have said they can kill me by Nahak, but I challenge them to do it if they can, without arrow or spear, club or musket, for I deny that they have any power against me or against any one by their Sorcery."

The challenge was accepted ; the Natives looked terror-struck at the position in which I was placed ! The ceremony of Nahak was usually performed in secret,—the Tannese fleeing in dread, as Europeans would from the touch of the plague ; but I lingered and eagerly watched their ritual. As the three Chiefs arose, and drew near to one of the Sacred Trees, to begin their ceremonial, the Natives fled in terror, crying,—

"Missi, away! Alas, Missi!"

But I held on at my post of observation. Amidst wavings and incantations, they rolled up the pieces of the fruit from which I had eaten, in certain leaves of this Sacred Tree into a shape like a waxen candle; then they kindled a sacred fire near the root, and continued their mutterings, gradually burning a little more and a little more of the candle-shaped things, wheeling them round their heads, blowing upon them with their breaths, waving them in the air, and glancing wildly at me as if expecting my sudden destruction. Wondering whether after all they did not believe their own lie, for they seemed to be in dead earnest, I, more eager than ever to break the chains of such vile superstition, urged them again and again, crying,—

"Be quick! Stir up your Gods to help you! I am not killed yet; I am perfectly well!"

At last they stood up and said,—

"We must delay till we have called all our Sacred Men. We will kill Missi before his next Sabbath comes round. Let all watch, for he will soon die and that without fail."

I replied, "Very good! I challenge all your Priests to unite and kill me by Sorcery or Nahak. If on Sabbath next I come again to your village in health, you will all admit that your Gods have no power over me, and that I am protected by the true and living Jehovah God!"

For every day throughout the remainder of that

week, the 'Conchs were sounded, and over that side
of the island all their Sacred Men were at work
trying to kill me by their arts.   Now and again
messengers arrived from every quarter of the island,
inquiring anxiously after my health, and wondering
if I was not feeling sick, and great excitement prevailed amongst the poor deluded idolaters.

Sabbath dawned upon me peacefully, and I went
to that village in more than my usual health and
strength.   Large numbers assembled, and when I
appeared they looked at each other in terror, as if
it could not really be I, myself, still spared and well.
Entering into the public ground, I saluted them to
this effect,—

"My love to you all, my friends !   I have come
again to talk to you about the Jehovah God and
His Worship."

The three Sacred Men, on being asked, admitted
that they had tried to kill me by Nahak, but had
failed ; and on being questioned, why they had
failed, they gave the acute and subtle reply, that
I also was myself a Sacred Man, and that my God
being the stronger had protected me from their Gods.
Addressing the multitude, I answered thus,—

"Yea, truly ; my Jehovah God is stronger than
your Gods.   He protected me, and helped me ; for
He is the only living and true God, the only God
that can hear or answer any prayer from the children of men.   Your Gods cannot hear prayers, but
my God can and will hear and answer you, if you

will give heart and life to Him, and love and serve Him only. This is my God, and He is also your friend if you will hear and follow His voice."

Having said this, I sat down on the trunk of a fallen tree, and addressed them,—

"Come and sit down all around me, and I will talk to you about the love and mercy of my God, and teach you how to worship and please Him."

Two of the Sacred Men then sat down, and all the people gathered round and seated themselves very quietly. I tried to present to them ideas of sin, and of salvation through Jesus Christ, as revealed to us in the Holy Scriptures.

The third Sacred Man, the highest in rank, a man of great stature and uncommon strength, had meantime gone off for his warrior's spear, and returned brandishing it in the air and poising it at me. I said to the people,—

"Of course he can kill me with his spear, but he undertook to kill me by Nahak or Sorcery, and promised not to use against me any weapons of war; and if you let him kill me now, you will kill your friend, one who lives among you and only tries to do you good, as you all know so well. I know that if you kill me thus, my God will be angry and will punish you."

Thereon I seated myself calmly in the midst of the crowd, while he leaped about in rage, scolding his brothers and all who were present for listening to me. The other Sacred Men, however, took my side,

and, as many of the people also were friendly to
me and stood closely packed around me, he did not
throw his spear. To allay the tumult and obviate
further bloodshed, I offered to leave with my Teachers
at once, and, in doing so, I ardently pled with them
to live at peace. Though we got safely home, that
old Sacred Man seemed still to hunger after my blood.
For weeks thereafter, go where I would, he would
suddenly appear on the path behind me, poising in
his right hand that same Goliath spear. God only
kept it from being thrown, and I, using every lawful
precaution, had all the same to attend to my work,
as if no enemy were there, leaving all other results
in the hands of Jesus. This whole incident did,
doubtless, shake the prejudices of many as to Sorcery;
but few even of converted Natives ever get entirely
clear of the dread of Nahak.

If not truly converted, the two Priests were fast
friends of mine from that day, as also another leading
man in the same district. They also received an
Aneityumese Teacher to their village, protecting and
showing kindness to him; one of the Sacred Men
who could speak his language lived almost constantly
with him, and some young people were allowed daily
to attend our School. These two and a number of
others began to wear a kilt, and some a shirt also.
Three of them especially, if not Christians, appeared
to be not far from the Kingdom of God, and did all
that was in their power to protect and to assist me.
A few began to pray to Jehovah in their houses,

offering a kind of rude family worship, and breathing out such prayers and desires as I had taught them for the knowledge of the true God and only Saviour. And these, as my companions, accompanied me from place to place when I visited their district.

But let us return to the war. Many Chiefs and villages were now involved in it; and a large part of the bush over the country between had been consumed by fire, to prevent surprises. Yet, our Harbour people being assembled one night for consultation, a number of the Inland warriors crept near unobserved and discharged a volley of muskets amongst them. Several were shot dead, and in the darkness and confusion the enemy got clear away. Revenge and self-preservation now united our people as one man, and every man assembled for action on the borders of the hostile Tribes. I again visited them on the fighting ground. As I was seen approaching, the two old Priests, my friends, came to receive and escort me, protected by their clubs and muskets,—the one blind of an eye lost in war marching before me, and the other behind me with poised spear and mighty club. Seating me in a central position, they assembled all the warriors, except the watchmen, and these savage men listened attentively to my message, and bowed quietly during prayer. God only knows what may be the fruit in some dark benighted soul! The whole host of them ceased firing, till the two friendly Priests had again conveyed me safely beyond the reach of danger.

Going among them frequently thus, they treated me with exceptional kindness, till one Sabbath I determined to go over and talk with the enemy also, in the hope of getting this sad war put an end to. Our people were sternly opposed to this, not for fear of my safety, but lest I prayed for the enemy and my God might help them in the war. But my two friends, the old Priests, persuaded them to let me go, and to cease their shooting till my return. They had an idea to buy, in this way, my intercession with Jehovah exclusively on their behalf; but I explained to them as on former occasions, that I was there for the good of all alike, that I loved them all and sought to lead them to give up war and bad conduct, for my God would hear and bless only those who feared and loved and obeyed Him. I had a long interview with the enemies also, arguing against the evils of war, and urging them to give it up. They were so far friendly; they allowed me to have worship amongst them, and I returned in safety before another musket was discharged on either side. The war still went on, though more languidly; but after a time the leaders entered into a kind of truce, and peace reigned for a season.

The other Mission Station, on the south-west side of Tanna, had to be visited by me from time to time. Mr. and Mrs. Mathieson, there, were both in a weak state of health, having a tendency to consumption. On this account they visited Aneityum several times. They were earnestly devoted to their work, and were

successful so far as health and the time allowed to
them permitted. At this juncture, a message reached
me that they were without European food, and a request to send them a little flour if possible. The war
made the journey overland impossible. A strong wind
and a high sea round the coast rendered it impractic-
able for my boat to go. The danger to life from the
enemy was so great, that I could not hire a crew.
I pled therefore with Nowar and Manuman, and
a few leading men to take one of their best canoes,
and themselves to accompany me. I had a large
flat-bottomed pot with a close-fitting lid, and that
I pressed full of flour ; and, tying the lid firmly down,
I fastened it right in the centre of the canoe, and as
far above water-mark as possible. All else that was
required we tied around our own persons. Sea and
land being as they were, it was a perilous undertaking, which only dire necessity could have justified.
They were all good swimmers, but as I could not
swim the strongest man was placed behind me, to
seize me and swim ashore, if a crash came.

Creeping round near the shore all the way, we had
to keep just outside the great breakers on the coral
reef, and were all drenched through and through with
the foam of an angry surf. We arrived, however,
in safety within two miles of our destination, where
lived the friends of my canoe's company, but where
a very dangerous sea was breaking on the reef.
Here they all gave in, and protested that no further
could they go ; and truly their toil all the way with

the paddles had been severe. I appealed to them,
that the canoe would for certain be smashed if they
tried to get on shore, that the provisions would be
lost, and some of us probably drowned. But they
turned to the shore, and remained for some time
thus, watching the sea. At last their Captain cried,—

"Missi, hold on ! There's a smaller wave coming ;
we'll ride in now."

My heart rose to the Lord in trembling prayer !
The wave came rolling on ; every paddle with all
their united strength struck into the sea ; and next
moment our canoe was flying like a sea-gull on the
crest of the wave towards the shore. Another instant, and the wave had broken on the reef with a
mighty roar, and rushed passed us hissing in clouds
of foam. My company were next seen swimming
wildly about in the sea, Manuman, the one-eyed
Sacred Man, alone holding on by the canoe, nearly
full of water, with me still clinging to the seat of it,
and the very next wave likely to devour us. In des-
peration, I sprang for the reef, and ran for a man
half-wading, half-swimming to reach us ; and God so
ordered it, that just as the next wave broke against
the silvery rock of coral, the man caught me and
partly swam with me through its surf, partly carried
me till I was set safely ashore. Praising God, I
looked up and saw all the others nearly as safe as
myself, except Manuman, my friend, who was still
holding on by the canoe in the face of wind and sea,
and bringing it with him. Others ran and swam to

his help. The paddles were picked up amid the
surf. A powerful fellow came towards me with the
pot of flour on his head, uninjured by water. The
Chief who held on by the canoe got severely cut
about the feet, and had been badly bruised and
knocked about; but all the rest escaped without
further harm, and everything that we had was saved.
Amongst friends, at last, they resolved to await
a favourable wind and tide to return to their own
homes. Singing in my heart unto God, I hired a
man to carry the pot of flour, and soon arrived at
the Mission Station.

Supplying the wants of our dear friends, Mr. and
Mrs. Mathieson, whom we found as well as could
be expected, we had to prepare, after a few hours
of rest, to return to our own Station by walking
overland through the night. I durst not remain
longer away, lest my own house should be plundered
and broken into. Though weak in health, my fellow-
Missionaries were both full of hope, and zealous in
their work, and this somewhat strange visit was a
pleasant blink amidst our darkness. Before I had
gone far on my return journey, the sun went down,
and no Native could be hired to accompany me.
They all told me that I would for certain be killed
by the way. But I knew that it would be quite
dark before I reached the hostile districts, and that
the Heathen are great cowards in the dark and never
leave their villages at night in the darkness, except
in companies for fishing and such-like tasks. I skirted

along the sea-shore as fast as I could, walking and running alternately ; and, when I got within hearing of voices, I slunk back into the bush till they had safely passed, and then groped my way back near the shore, that being my only guide to find a path.

Having made half the journey, I came to a dangerous path, almost perpendicular, up a great rock round the base of which the sea roared deep. With my heart lifted up to Jesus, I succeeded in climbing it, cautiously grasping roots, and resting by bushes, till I reached safely to the top. There, to avoid a village, I had to keep crawling slowly along the bush near the sea, on the top of that great ledge of rock ; a feat I could never have accomplished even in daylight without the excitement, but I felt that I was supported and guided in all that life or death journey by my dear Lord Jesus. I had to leave the shore, and follow up the bank of a very deep ravine to a place shallow enough for one to cross, and then through the bush away for the shore again. By holding too much to the right, I missed the point where I intended to reach it. Small fires were now visible through the bush ; I heard the voices of the people talking in one of our most heathen villages.

Quietly drawing back, I now knew where I was, and easily found my way towards the shore ; but on reaching the Great Rock, I could not in the darkness find the path down again. I groped about till I was tired. I feared that I might stumble over and be killed; or, if I delayed till daylight, that the savages would kill me. I knew that one part of the rock was steep-sloping, with little growth or none thereon, and I searched about to find it, resolved to commend myself to Jesus and slide down thereby that I might again reach the shore and escape for my life. Thinking I had found this spot, I hurled down several stones and listened for their splash that I might judge whether it would be safe. But the distance was too far for me to hear or judge. At high tide the sea there was deep; but at low tide I could wade out of it and be safe. The darkness made it impossible for me to see anything. I let go my umbrella, shoving it down with considerable force, but neither did it send me back any news.

Feeling sure, however, that this was the place I sought, and knowing that to await the daylight would be certain death, I prayed to my Lord Jesus for help and protection, and resolved to let myself go. First, I fastened all my clothes as tightly as I could, so as not to catch on anything; then I lay down at the top on my back, feet foremost, holding my head downwards on my breast to keep it from striking on the rock; then, after one cry to my Saviour, having let myself down as far as possible by a branch, I at last let go, throwing my arms forward and trying to keep my feet well up. A giddy swirl, as if flying through the air, took possession of me; a few moments seemed an age; I rushed quickly down, and felt no obstruction till my feet struck into the sea below. Adoring and praising my dear Lord Jesus, who had ordered it so, I regained my feet; it was low tide, I had received no injury, I found my umbrella, and, wading through, I found the shore path easier and lighter than the bush had been. The very darkness was my safety, preventing the Natives from rambling about. I saw no person to speak to, till I reached a village quite near to my own house, fifteen or twenty miles from where I had started; here I left the sea path and promised young men some fish-hooks to guide me the nearest way through the bush to my Mission Station, which they gladly and heartily did. I ran a narrow risk in approaching them; they thought me an enemy, and I arrested their muskets only by a loud cry,—

"I am Missi! Don't shoot; my love to you, my friends!"

Praising God for His preserving care, I reached home, and had a long refreshing sleep. The Natives, on hearing next day how I had come all the way in the dark, exclaimed,—

"Surely any of us would have been killed! Your Jehovah God alone thus protects you and brings you safely home."

With all my heart, I said, "Yes! and He will be your protector and helper too, if only you will obey and trust in Him."

Certainly that night put my faith to the test. Had it not been the assurance that I was engaged in His service, and that in every path of duty He would carry me through or dispose of me therein for His glory, I could never have undertaken either journey. St. Paul's words are true to-day and for ever,—" I can do all things through Christ which strengtheneth me."

IX.

DEEPENING SHADOWS.

CHAPTER IX.

DEEPENING SHADOWS.

I N September, 1860, I had the very great pleasure
of welcoming, as fellow-labourers to Tanna, the
Rev. S. F. Johnston and his wife, two able and
pious young Missionaries from Nova Scotia. Having

visited the whole group of the New Hebrides, they preferred to cast their lot on Tanna. During the Rainy Season, and till they had acquired a little of the language, and some preparation had been made of a Station for themselves, I gladly received them as my guests. The company was very sweet to me! I gave them about fourteen Tannese words to be committed to memory every day, and conversed with them, using the words already acquired; so that they made very rapid progress, and almost immediately were of some service in the Mission work. No man could have desired better companions in the ministry of the Gospel.

About this time I had a never-to-be-forgotten illustration of the infernal spirit that possessed some of the Traders towards these poor Natives. One morning, three or four vessels entered our Harbour and cast anchor off Port Resolution. The Captains called on me; and one of them, with manifest delight, exclaimed,—

"'We know how to bring down your proud Tannese now! We'll humble them before you!"

I answered, "Surely you don't mean to attack and destroy these poor people?"

He answered, not abashed but rejoicing, "We have sent the measles to humble them! That kills them by the score! Four young men have been landed at different ports, ill with measles, and these will soon thin their ranks."

Shocked above measure, I protested solemnly and

denounced their conduct and spirit; but my remonstrances only called forth the shameless declaration,—

"Our watchword is,—Sweep these creatures away
and let white men occupy the soil!"

Their malice was further illustrated thus: they
induced Kepuku, a young Chief, to go off to one
of their vessels, promising him a present. He was
the friend and chief supporter of Mr. Mathieson and
of his work. Having got him on board, they confined him in the hold amongst Natives lying ill with
measles. They gave him no food for about four-
and-twenty hours; and then, without the promised
present, they put him ashore far from his own
home. Though weak and excited, he scrambled
back to his Tribe in great exhaustion and terror. He
informed the Missionary that they had put him down
amongst sick people, red and hot with fever, and
that he feared their sickness was upon him. I am
ashamed to say that these Sandal-wood and other
Traders were our own degraded countrymen; and
that they deliberately gloried in thus destroying the
poor Heathen. A more fiendish spirit could scarcely
be imagined, but most of them were horrible drunkards, and their traffic of every kind amongst these
Islands was, generally speaking, steeped in human
blood.

The measles, thus introduced, became amongst our
islanders the most deadly plague. It spread fearfully,
and was accompanied by sore throat and diarrhœa.

In some villages, man, woman, and child were stricken, and none could give food or water to the rest. The misery, suffering, and terror were unexampled, the living being afraid sometimes even to bury the dead. Thirteen of my own Mission party died of this disease; and, so terror-stricken were the few who survived, that when the little Mission schooner *John Knox* returned to Tanna, they all packed up and returned to their own Aneityum, except my own dear old Abraham.

At first, thinking that all were on the wing, he also had packed his things, and was standing beside the others ready to leave with them. I drew near to him, and said,—

"Abraham, they are all going; are you also going to leave me here alone on Tanna, to fight the battles of the Lord?"

He asked, "Missi, will you remain?"

I replied, "Yes; but, Abraham, the danger to life is now so great that I dare not plead with you to remain, for we may both be slain. Still, I cannot leave the Lord's work now."

The noble old Chief looked at the box and his bundles, and, musing, said,—

"Missi, our danger is very great now."

I answered, "Yes; I once thought you would not leave me alone to it; but, as the vessel is going to your own land, I cannot ask you to remain and face it with me!"

He again said, "Missi, would you like me to remain

alone with you, seeing my wife is dead and in her grave here?"

I replied, "Yes, I would like you to remain; but, considering the circumstances in which we will be left alone, I cannot plead with you to do so."

He answered, "Then, Missi, I remain with you of my own free choice, and with all my heart. We will live and die together in the work of the Lord. I will never leave you while you are spared on Tanna."

So saying, and with a light that gave the fore-gleam of a martyr's glory to his dark face, he shouldered his box and bundles back to his own house; and thereafter, Abraham was my dear companion and constant friend, and my fellow-sufferer in all that remains still to be related of our Mission life on Tanna.

Before this plague of measles was brought amongst us, Mr. Johnston and I had sailed round in the *John Knox* to Black Beach on the opposite side of Tanna and prepared the way for settling Teachers there. And they were placed soon after by Mr. Copeland and myself with encouraging hopes of success, and with the prospect of erecting there a Station for Mr. and Mrs. Johnston. But this dreadful imported epidemic blasted all our dreams. Mr. Johnston and his wife devoted themselves, from the very first, and assisted me in every way to alleviate the dread sufferings of the Natives. We carried medicine, food, and even water, to the sur-

rounding villages every day, few of themselves being
able to render us much assistance. Nearly all who
took our medicine and followed instructions as to.
food, etc., recovered; but vast numbers of them
would listen to no counsels, and rushed into experi-
ments which made the attack fatal all around. When
the trouble was at its height, for instance, they would
plunge into the sea, and seek relief; they found it
in almost instant death. Others would dig a hole
into the earth, the length of the body and about
two feet deep; therein they laid themselves down,
the cold earth feeling agreeable to their fevered skins;
and when the earth around them grew heated, they
got friends to dig a few inches deeper, again and
again, seeking a cooler and cooler couch. In this
ghastly effort many of them died, literally in their
own graves, and were buried where they lay! It
need not be surprising, though we did everything in
our power to relieve and save them, that the Natives
associated us with the white men who had 'so dreadfully afflicted them, and that their blind thirst for
revenge did not draw fine distinctions between the
Traders and the Missionaries. Both were whites—
that was enough.

The 1st January, 1861, was a New Year's Day
ever to be remembered. Mr. and Mrs. Johnston,
Abraham and I, had spent nearly the whole time in
a kind of solemn yet happy festival. Anew in a holy
covenant before God, we unitedly consecrated our
lives and our all to the Lord Jesus, giving ourselves

away to His blessed service for the conversion of the
Heathen on the New Hebrides. After evening family
worship, Mr. and Mrs. Johnston left my room to go
to their own house, only some ten feet distant ; but
he returned to inform me that there were two men
at the window, armed with huge clubs, and having
black painted faces. Going out to them and asking
them what they wanted, they replied,—

" Medicine for a sick boy."

With difficulty, I persuaded them to come in and
get it. At once, it flashed upon me, from their agitation and their disguise of paint, that they had come
to murder us. Mr. Johnston had also accompanied
us into the house. · Keeping my eye constantly fixed
on them, I prepared the medicine and offered it.
They refused to receive it, and each man grasped his
killing stone. I faced them firmly and said,—

" You see that Mr. Johnston is now leaving, and
you too must leave this room for to-night. To-
morrow, you can bring the boy or come for the
medicine."

Seizing their clubs, as if for action, they showed
unwillingness to withdraw, but I walked deliberately
forward and made as if to push them out, when both
turned and began to leave.

Mr. Johnston had gone in front of them and was
safely out. But he bent down to lift a little kitten
that had escaped at the open door ; and at that
moment one of the savages, jerking in behind, aimed
a blow with his huge club, in avoiding which Mr.

Johnston fell with a scream to the ground. Both men sprang towards him, but our two faithful dogs ferociously leapt in their faces and saved his life. Rushing out, but not fully aware of what had occurred, I saw Mr. Johnston trying to raise himself, and heard him cry,—

"Take care! these men have tried to kill me, and they will kill you!"

Facing them sternly I demanded,—

"What is it that you want? He does not understand your language. What do you want? Speak with me."

Both men, thereon, raised their great clubs and made to strike me; but quick as lightning these two dogs sprang at their faces and baffled their blows. One dog was badly bruised, and the ground received the other blow that would have launched me into Eternity. The best dog was a little crossbred retriever, with terrier's blood in him, splendid for warning of the approaching dangers, and which had already been the means of saving my life several times. Seeing how matters stood, I now hounded both dogs furiously upon them and the two savages fled. I shouted after them,—

"Remember, Jehovah God sees you and will punish you for trying to murder His servants!"

In their flight, a large body of men, who had come eight or ten miles to assist in the murder and plunder, came slipping here and there from the bush and joined them fleeing too. Verily, "the

wicked flee, when no man pursueth." David's experience and assurance came home to us, that
evening, as very real:—"God is our refuge and
our strength . . . therefore we will not fear."
But, after the danger was all past, I had always a
strange feeling of fear, more perhaps from the
thought that I had been on the verge of Eternity
and so near the great White Throne than from any
slavish fear. During the crisis, I felt·generally calm,
and firm of soul, standing erect and with my whole
weight on the promise, "Lo! I am with you alway."
Precious promise! How often I adore Jesus for it,
and rejoice in it! Blessed be His name.·

I, now accustomed to such scenes on Tanna, retired
to rest and slept soundly; but my dear fellow-
labourer, as I afterwards learned, could not sleep for
one moment. His pallor and excitement continued
next day, indeed for several days; and after that,
though he was naturally lively and cheerful, I never
saw him smile again. He told me next morning,—

"I can only keep saying to myself, Already on the
verge of Eternity! How have I spent my time?
What good have I done? What zeal for souls have
I shown? Scarcely entered on the work of my life,
and so near death! O my friend, I never realized
what death means, till last night!" So saying, he
covered his face with both hands, and left me to
hide himself in his own room. For that morning,
1st January, 1861, the following entry was found in

his Journal :—"To-day, with a heavy heart and a feeling of dread, I know not why, I set out on my accustomed wanderings amongst the sick. I hastened back to get the Teacher and carry Mr. Paton to the scene of distress. I carried a bucket of water in one hand and medicine in the other; and so we spent a portion of this day endeavouring to alleviate their sufferings, and our work had a happy effect also on the minds of others." In another entry, on 22nd December he wrote :—"Measles are making fearful havoc amongst the poor Tannese. As we pass through the villages, mournful scenes meet the eye; young and old prostrated on the ground, showing all these painful symptoms which accompany loathsome and malignant diseases. In some villages few are left able to prepare food, or to carry drink to the suffering and dying. How pitiful to see the sufferers destitute of every comfort, attention, and remedy that would ameliorate their suffering or remove their disease! As I think of the tender manner in which we are nursed in sickness, the many remedies employed to give relief, with the comforts and attention bestowed upon us, my heart sickens, and I say, Oh my ingratitude and the ingratitude of Christian people! How little we value our Christian birth, education, and privileges, etc."

Having, as above recorded, consecrated our lives anew to God on the first day of January, I was, up till the sixteenth of the month, accompanied by Mr. Johnston and sometimes also by Mrs. Johnston on my rounds in the villages amongst the sick, and they greatly helped me. But by an unhappy accident, I was laid aside when most sorely needed. When adzing a tree for house-building, I observed that Mahanan the war Chief's brother had been keeping too near me and that he carried a tomahawk in his hand; and, in trying both to do my work and to keep an eye on him, I struck my ankle severely with the adze. He moved off quickly, saying,—" I did not do that," but doubtless rejoicing at what had happened. The bone was badly hurt, and several of the blood-vessels cut. Dressing it as well as I could, and keeping it constantly soaked in cold water, I had to exercise the greatest care. In this condition, amidst great sufferings, I was sometimes carried to the villages to administer medicine to the sick, and to plead and pray with the dying.

On such occasions, in this mode of transit even, the conversations that I had with dear Mr. Johnston were most solemn and greatly refreshing. He had, however, scarcely ever slept since the first of January, and during the night of the sixteenth he sent for my bottle of laudanum. Being severely attacked with ague and fever, I could not go to him, but sent the bottle, specifying the proper quantity for a dose, but that he quite understood already. He took a dose for himself, and gave one also to his wife, as she too suffered from sleeplessness. This he repeated three nights in succession, and both of them obtained a long, sound, and refreshing sleep.

He came to my bedside, where I lay in the ague-fever, and said with great animation, amongst other things,—

"I have had such a blessed sleep, and feel so refreshed! What kindness in God to provide such remedies for suffering man!"

At midday his dear wife came to me crying,—

"Mr. Johnston has fallen asleep, so deep that 1 cannot awake him."

My fever had reached the worst stage, but I struggled to my feet, got to his bedside, and found him in a state of coma, with his teeth fixed in tetanus. With great difficulty we succeeded in slightly rousing him ; with a knife, spoon, and pieces of wood, we forced his teeth open, so as to administer an emetic with good effects, and also other needful medicines. For twelve hours, we had to keep him awake by repeated cold dash in his face, by ammonia, and by vigorously moving him about. He then began to speak freely; and next day he rose and walked about a little. For the two following days, he was sometimes better and sometimes worse ; but we managed to keep him up till the morning of the 21st, when he again fell into a state of coma from which we failed to rouse him. At two o'clock in the afternoon, he fell asleep, another martyr for the testimony of Jesus in those dark and trying Isles, leaving his young wife in indescribable sorrow, which she strove to bear with Christian resignation. Having made his coffin and dug his grave, we two alone at

sunset laid him to rest beside my own dear wife and
child, close by the Mission House.

In Mrs. Johnston's account, in a letter to friends
regarding his death, she says :—

"Next morning, the 17th, he rose quite well. He
slept well the night before from having taken a dose
of laudanum. He also gave some to me, as I had
been ill all the day, having slept little for two or three
nights. . . . Two men helped Mr. Paton to his
bedside, as I found him lying very low in fever, yet
he waited on Mr. Johnston affectionately. For some
time, while he was in Mr. Paton's hands, I could
scarcely keep myself up at all. We thought it was
from the laudanum I had taken. I had to throw
myself down every few minutes. . . . For some
weeks after, I was almost constantly bedfast. I ate
little ; still I felt no pain, but very stupid. . .
At times, we have services with the Natives. For a
week past, we have scarcely gone to bed without
fears. One night, our house was surrounded with
crowds of armed men, ready at any moment to break
in upon us for our lives. We have had to sit in the
house for days past, with the doors locked, to prevent
any of the savages from entering ; for every party
seems to be united against us now. The great
sickness that prevails amongst them is the cause of
this rage. They say, we made the disease, and we
must be killed for it ; that they never died off in this
way before the religion came amongst them, etc., etc."

Mrs. Johnston recovered gradually, returned by the

first opportunity to Aneityum, and for nearly three years taught the girls' School at Dr. Geddie's Station. Thereafter she was married to my dear friend the Rev. Joseph Copeland, and spent with him the remainder of her life on Fotuna, working devotedly in the service of the Mission, seeking the salvation of the Heathen.

The death of Mr. Johnston was a heavy loss. From his landing on Tanna, he appeared to enjoy excellent health, and was always very active, bright, and happy, till after that attack by the savages with their clubs on New Year's Day. From that night, he never again was the same. He never admitted that he had got a blow, but I fear his nervous system must have been unhinged by the shock and horror of the scene. He was genuinely lamented by all who knew him. Our intercourse on Tanna was very sweet, and I missed him exceedingly. Not lost to me, however; only gone before!

Another tragedy followed, with, however, much of the light of Heaven amid its blackness, in the story of Kowia, a Tannese Chief of the highest rank. Going to Aneityum in youth, he had there become a true Christian. He married an Aneityumese Christian woman, with whom he lived very happily and had two beautiful children. Some time before the measles reached our island, he returned to live with me as a Teacher and to help forward our work on Tanna. He proved himself to be a decided Christian; he was a real Chief amongst them, dignified in his whole conduct, and every way a valuable helper to me. Everything was tried by his own people to induce him to leave me and to renounce the Worship, offering him every honour and bribe in their power. Failing these, they threatened to take away all his lands, and to deprive him of Chieftainship, but he answered,—

"Take all! I shall still stand by Missi and the Worship of Jehovah."

From threats, they passed to galling insults, all which he bore patiently for Jesu's sake. But one day, a party of his people came and sold some fowls, and an impudent fellow lifted them after they had been bought and offered to sell them again to me. Kowia shouted,—

"Don't purchase these, Missi; I have just bought them for you, and paid for them!"

Thereon the fellow began to mock at him. Kowia, gazing round on all present and then on me, rose like a lion awaking out of sleep, and with flashing eyes exclaimed,—

"Missi, they think that because I am now a Christian I have become a coward! a woman! to bear every abuse and insult they can heap upon me. But I will show them for once that I am no coward, that I am still their Chief, and that Christianity does not take away but gives us courage and nerve."

Springing at one man, he wrenched in a moment the mighty club from his hands, and swinging it in air above his head like a toy, he cried,—

"Come any of you, come all against your Chief!

P, 17

My Jehovah God makes my heart and arms strong. He will help me in this battle as He helps me in other things, for He inspires me to show you that Christians are no cowards, though they are men of peace. Come on, and you will yet know that I am Kowia your Chief."

All fled as he approached them ; and he cried,—

" Where are the cowards now ? " and handed back to the warrior his club. After this they left him at peace.

He lived at the Mission House, with his wife and children, and was a great help and comfort to Abraham and myself. He was allowed to go more freely and fearlessly amongst the people, than any of the rest of our Mission staff. The ague and fever on me at Mr. Johnston's death, so increased and reduced me to such weakness that I had become insensible, while Abraham and Kowia alone attended to me. On returning to consciousness, I heard as in a dream Kowia lamenting over me, and pleading that I might recover, so as to hear and speak with him before he died. Opening my eyes and looking at him, I heard him say,—

" Missi, all our Aneityumese are sick. Missi Johnston is dead. You are very sick, and I am weak and dying. Alas, when I too am dead, who will climb the trees and get you a cocoa-nut to drink? And who will bathe your lips and brow ? ". Here he broke down into deep and long weeping, and then resumed,—" Missi, the Tanna men hate us all on

account of the Worship of Jehovah ; and I now fear
He is going to take away all His servants from this
land, and leave my people to the Evil One and his
service !" I was too weak to speak, so he went on,
bursting into a soliloquy of prayer : " O Lord Jesus,
Missi Johnston is dead ; Thou hast taken him away
from this land. Missi Johnston the woman and Missi
Paton are very ill ; I am sick, and Thy servants
the Aneityumese are all sick and dying. O Lord,
our Father in Heaven, art Thou going to take away
all Thy servants, and Thy Worship from this dark
land ? What meanest Thou to do, O Lord ? The
Tannese hate Thee and Thy Worship and Thy
servants, but surely, O Lord, Thou canst not forsake
Tanna and leave our people to die in the darkness ! ·
Oh, make the hearts of this people soft to Thy Word
and sweet to Thy Worship ; teach them to fear and
love Jesus ; and oh, restore and spare Missi, dear
Missi Paton, that Tanna may be saved ! "

Touched to the very fountains of my life by such
prayers, from a man once a Cannibal, I began under
the breath of God's blessing to revive.

A few days thereafter, Kowia came again to me,
and rousing me out of sleep, cried,—

"Missi, I am very weak ; I am dying. I come to
bid you farewell, and go away to die. I am nearing
death now, and I will soon see Jesus."

I spoke what words of consolation and cheer I
could muster, but he answered,—

"Missi, since you became ill my dear wife and children are dead and buried. Most of our Aneityumese are dead, and I am dying. If I remain on the hill, and die here at the Mission House, there are none left to help Abraham to carry me down to the grave where my wife and children are laid. I wish to lie beside them, that we may rise together in the Great Day when Jesus comes. I am happy, looking unto Jesus! One thing only deeply grieves me now; I fear God is taking us all away from Tanna, and will leave my poor people dark and benighted as before, for they hate Jesus and the Worship of Jehovah. O Missi, pray for them, and pray for me once more before I go!"

He knelt down at my side, and we prayed for each other and for Tanna. I then urged him to remain at the Mission House, but he replied,—

"O Missi, you do not know how near to death I am! I am just going, and will soon be with Jesus, and see my wife and children now. While a little strength is left, I will lean on Abraham's arm, and go down to the graves of my dear ones and fall asleep there, and Abraham will dig a quiet bed and lay me beside them. Farewell, Missi, I am very near death now; we will meet again in Jesus and with Jesus!"

With many tears he dragged himself away; and my heart-strings seemed all tied round that noble simple soul, and felt like breaking one by one as he left me there on my bed of fever all alone. Abraham sustained him, tottering to the place of

graves ; there he lay down, and immediately gave
up the ghost and slept in Jesus ; and there the faithful Abraham buried him beside his wife and children.
Thus died a man who had been a cannibal Chief, but
by the grace of God and the love of Jesus changed,
transfigured into a character of light and beauty.
What think ye of this, ye scoffers at Missions? What
think ye of this, ye sceptics as to the reality of conversion? He died, as he had lived since Jesus came
to his heart ; without a fear as to death, with an
ever-brightening assurance as to salvation and glory
through the blood of the Lamb of God, that blood
which had cleansed him from all his sins, and had
delivered him from their power. I lost, in losing
him, one of my best friends and most courageous
helpers ; but I knew, that day, and I know now, that
there is one soul at least from Tanna to sing the
glories of Jesus in Heaven—and, oh, the rapture when
I meet him there !

Before leaving this terrible plague of measles, I
may record my belief that it swept away, with the
accompanying sore throat and diarrhœa, a third of the
entire population of Tanna ; nay, in certain localities
more than a third perished. The living declared
themselves unable to bury the dead, and great want
and suffering ensued. The Teacher and his wife and
child, placed by us at Black Beach, were also taken
away ; and his companion, the other Teacher there,
embraced the first opportunity to leave along with
his wife for his own island, else his life would have

been taken in revenge. Yet, from all accounts afterwards received, I do not think the measles were more fatal on Tanna than on the other Islands of the group. They appear to have carried off even a larger proportion on Aniwa, the future scene of my many sorrows but of greater triumphs.

A new incentive was added to the already cruel superstitions of the Natives. The Sandal-wooders, our degraded fellow-countrymen, in order to divert attention from themselves, stirred the Natives with the wild faith that the Missionaries and the Worship had brought all this sickness, and that our lives should be taken in revenge. Some Captains, on calling with their ships, made a pretence of refusing to trade with the Natives as long as I was permitted to live on the island. One Trader offered to come on shore and live amongst the Tannese, and supply them with tobacco and powder, and caps and balls, on condition that the Missionary and Abraham were got out of the way! He knew that these were their greatest wants, and that they eagerly desired these things, but he refused to make any sales to them, till we were murdered or driven away. This was fuel to their savage hate, and drove them mad with revenge, and added countless troubles to our lot.

Hurricane and tempest also fought against us at that time. On the 3rd, and again on the 10th March, 1861, we had severe and destructive storms. They tore up and smashed breadfruit, chestnut, cocoa-nut, and all kinds of fruit trees. The ground was strewn thick with half-ripe and wasted fruits. Yam plantations and bananas were riven to pieces, and fences and houses lay piled in a common ruin. My Mission House was also greatly injured; and the Church, on which I had spent many weeks of labour, was nearly levelled with the ground. Trees of forty years' growth were broken like straws, or lifted by the roots and blown away. At the other Station, all Mr. Mathieson's premises except one bedroom were swept off in the breath of the hurricane. The sea rose alarmingly and its waves rolled far inland, causing terrible destruction. Had not the merciful Lord left one bedroom at my Station and one at Mr. Mathieson's partly habitable, I know not what in the circumstances we could have done. Men of fifty years declared that never such a tempest had shaken their Islands. Canoes were shivered on the coral rocks, and Villages were left with nothing but ruins to mark where they had been. Though rain poured in torrents, I had to keep near my fallen house for hours and hours to prevent the Natives from carrying away everything I had in this world; and after the second storm, all my earthly belongings had to be secured in the one still-standing room.

Following upon this came another spate of thirst for our blood, which was increased in the following manner. Miaki the war Chief had an infant son, who had just died. They told us that four men were slain at the same time, that their spirits might serve and accompany him in the other world; and that our death also was again resolved upon. For four days they surrounded our diminished premises. We locked ourselves all up in that single bedroom, and armed savages kept prowling about to take our lives. What but the restraining pity of the Lord kept them from breaking in upon us? They killed our fowls. They cut down and destroyed all our remaining bananas. They broke down the fence around the plantation, and tried to burn it, but failed. They speared and killed some of the few goats—my sole supply of milk. We were helpless, and kept breathing out our souls in prayer; and God did preserve us, but, oh, what a trying time!

The horror grew, when shortly thereafter we learned that our people near the Harbour had killed four men and presented their bodies to certain Chiefs who feasted on them; and that they in return had given large fat hogs to our people, one for each of ten bodies which our people had formerly presented to them. Within a few months, thirteen or fourteen persons, nearly all refugees or prisoners of war, were reported to us as killed and feasted upon. We generally heard nothing of these murders till all was over, but in any case, I would have been helpless against their bloodthirst, even had I exposed myself to their savage enmity. They sent two dead bodies to our nearest village, where still we conducted Worship every Sabbath when we durst appear amongst them; but our people refused to receive them, saying, "Now we know that it is wrong to kill and eat our fellow-creatures." A Chief from another village, being present, eagerly received them and carried them off to a great feast for which he was preparing.

At this juncture, our friendly Chief Nowar seemed to become afraid. His life also had been threatened ; and our life had been often attempted of late. Society around was all in turmoil, and Nowar urged us all to leave and take refuge in Aneityum till these dangers blew past, and he himself would accompany us. I refused, however, to leave. Indeed, there was no immediate means of escape, except my boat,— which would have been almost madness in an open sea voyage of fifty miles, with only Nowar and the Teachers, all inexperienced hands. Nowar, being angry and afraid, took his revenge by laying aside his shirt and kilt, returning to his heathen nakedness and paint, attending the meetings of the savages, and absenting himself from the Sabbath Worship. But after about three weeks he resumed the Christian garments, and, feeling that the danger had for the time passed over, he returned to us as friendly as ever. Poor Nowar! if he only knew what thousands of Christians at home do every day just to save their skins ; and then if he only knew how hardly these Christians can speak against Heathen converts!

My first baptism on Tanna was that of a Teacher's child. About fifty persons were present, and Miaki the war Chief was there also. Alas, that child died in the plague of measles, and of course the Worship was blamed. Deaths, hurricanes, all seemed to be turned against us. A thunderstorm came in the wake of the last hurricane. A man and a woman were killed. Not far from my house, the hill was struck, a large mass was dislodged from its shoulder and hurled into the valley below. This was the manifest token to them that the Gods were angry and that we were the cause! God's grace alone kept us from sinking, and the hope of yet seeing them delivered from their Heathenism, and brought to love and serve Jesus Christ. For that everything could be borne; and I knew that this was the post of duty, for it was the Lord undoubtedly that placed me there.

One day, about this time, I heard an unusual bleating amongst my few remaining goats, as if they were being killed or tortured. I rushed to the goat-house, and found myself instantly surrounded by a band of armed men. The snare had caught me, their weapons were raised, and I expected next instant to die. But God moved me to talk to them firmly and kindly; I warned them of their sin and its punishment; I showed them that only my love and pity led me to remain there seeking their good, and that if they killed me they killed their best friend. I further assured them that I was not afraid to die, for at death my Saviour would take me to be with Himself in Heaven, and to be far happier than I had ever been on Earth; and that my only desire to live was to make them all as happy, by teaching them to love and serve my Lord Jesus. I then lifted up my hands and eyes to the Heavens, and prayed aloud for

Jesus to bless all my dear Tannese, and either to protect me or to take me home to Glory as He saw to be for the best. One after another they slipped away from me, and Jesus restrained them once again. Did ever mother run more quickly to protect her crying child in danger's hour, than the Lord Jesus hastens to answer believing prayer, and send help to His servants in His own good time and way, so far as it shall be for His glory and their good? A woman may forget her child, yet will not I forget thee, saith the Lord. Oh, that all my readers knew and felt this, as in those days and ever since I have felt that His promise is a reality, and that He is with His servants to support and bless them even unto the end of the world!

May, 1861, brought with it a sorrowful and tragic event, which fell as the very shadow of doom across our path ; I mean the martyrdom of the Gordons on Erromanga. Rev. G. N. Gordon was a native of Prince Edward Island, Nova Scotia, and was born in 1822. He was educated at the Free Church College, Halifax, and placed as Missionary on Erromanga, in June, 1857. Much troubled and opposed by the Sandal-wooders, he had yet acquired the language and was making progress by inroads on Heathenism. A considerable number of young men and women embraced the Christian Faith, lived at the Mission House, and devotedly helped him and his excellent wife in all their work. But the hurricanes and the measles, already referred to, caused great mortality in Erromanga also ; and the degraded Traders, who had introduced the plague, in order to save themselves from revenge, stimulated the super-stitions of the Heathen, and charged the Missionaries with causing sickness and all other calamities. The Sandal-wooders hated him for fearlessly denouncing and exposing their hideous atrocities.

When Mr. Copeland and I placed the Native Teachers at Black Beach, Tanna, we ran across to Erromanga in the *John Knox*, taking a harmonium to Mrs. Gordon, just come to their order from Sydney. When it was opened out at the Mission House, and Mrs. Gordon began playing on it and singing sweet hymns, the native women were in ecstasies. They at once proposed to go off to the bush and cut each a burden of long grass, to thatch the printing-office which Mr. Gordon was building in order to print the Scriptures in their own tongue, if only Mrs. Gordon would play to them at night and teach them to sing God's praises. They joyfully did so, and then spent a happy evening singing those hymns. Next day being Sabbath, we had a delight-ful season there, about thirty attending Church and listening eagerly. The young men and women, living at the Mission House, were being trained to become Teachers. They were reading a small book in their own language, telling them the story of Joseph ; and the work every way seemed most hopeful. The Mission House had been removed a mile or so up a hill, partly for Mrs. Gordon's health, and partly to escape the annoying and contaminating influence of the Sandal-wooders on his Christian Natives.

On 20th May, 1861, he was still working at the roofing of the printing-office, and had sent his lads to bring each a load of the long grass to finish the thatching. Meantime, a party of Erromangans from a district called Bunk-Hill, under a Chief named Lovu, had been watching him. They had been to the Mission House inquiring, and they had seen him send away his Christian lads. They then hid in the bush, and sent two of their men to the Missionary to ask for calico. On a piece of wood he wrote a note to Mrs. Gordon to give them two yards each. They asked him to go with them to the Mission House, as they needed medicine for a sick boy, and Lovu their Chief wanted to see him. He tied up in a napkin a meal of food, which had been brought to him but not eaten, and started to go with them. He requested the native Narubulet to go on before, with his companion; but they insisted upon his going in front. In crossing a streamlet, which I visited shortly afterwards, his foot slipped. A blow was aimed at him with a tomahawk which he caught; the other man struck, but his weapon was also caught. One of the tomahawks was then wrenched out of his grasp. Next moment, a blow on the spine laid the dear Missionary low, and a second on the neck almost severed the head from the body. The other Natives then rushed from their ambush, and slashed him to pieces, and began dancing round him with frantic shoutings. Mrs. Gordon, hearing the noise, came out and stood in front of the Mission House, looking in the direction of her husband's working place and wondering what had happened. Ouben, one of the party, who had run towards the Station the moment that Mr. Gordon fell, now approached her. A merciful clump of trees had hid from her eyes all that had occurred, and she said to Ouben,—

"What's the cause of that noise?"

He replied, "Oh, nothing! only the boys amusing themselves!"

Saying, "Where are the boys?" she turned round.

Ouben slipped stealthily behind her, sank his tomahawk into her back, and with another blow almost severed her head!

Such was the fate of those two devoted servants of the Lord; loving in their lives, and in their deaths scarcely divided—their spirits, in the crown of martyrdom, entered Glory together, to be welcomed by Williams and Harris, whose blood was shed on the same dark isle for the name and cause of Jesus. They had laboured four years on Erromanga, amidst trials and dangers manifold, and had not been without tokens of blessing in the Lord's work. Never more earnest and devoted Missionaries lived or died in the Heathen field. Other accounts, indeed, have been published, and another was reported to me by Mr. Gordon's Christian lads; but the above combines faithfully the principal facts in the story. One young Christian lad from a distance saw Mr. Gordon

murdered ; and a woman saw Mrs. Gordon fall.
The above facts are vouched for by a Mr. Milne,
one of the few respectable Sandal-wooders, who
was there at the time, and helped the Christian
Natives to bury the remains, which he says were
painfully mutilated.

Some severe criticisms, of course, were written and
published by those angelic creatures who judge all
things from their own safe and easy distance. Mr.
Gordon's lack of prudence was sorely blamed, forsooth! One would so like to see these people just for
one week in such trying circumstances. As my near
fellow-labourer and dearest friend, I know what was
the whole spirit of the man's life, his watchful care, his
ceaseless anxiety to do everything that in his judgment was for God's glory and the prosperity of the
Mission, and my estimate of him and of his action to
the last fills me with supreme regard to his memory.
The Rev. Dr. Inglis of Aneityum, best qualified of
all men living to form an opinion, wrote :—

"Mr. Gordon was a strong, bold, fearless, energetic,
self-denying, and laborious Missionary ; eager, earnest, and unwearied in seeking the salvation of the
Heathen. . . . Even if Mr. Gordon was to blame
for any imprudence, no blame of this kind could be
attached to Mrs. Gordon. Hers was a weak, gentle,
loving spirit; quiet and uncomplaining, prudent,
earnest, and devoted to Christ. She was esteemed
and beloved by all who knew her."

My Amen follows, soft and deep, on all that he has

written ; and I add, Mr. Gordon was doing what any
faithful and devoted Missionary would in all proba-
bility for the Master's sake in similar circumstances
have done.   Those who charge him with imprudence
would, doubtless, grievously blame Stephen for bringing that stoning upon himself, which he could so
easily have escaped !

Mr. Gordon, in his last letter to me, of date 15th
February, 1861, says :—

"MY DEAR BROTHER,—

"I have news of the best and of the worst
character to communicate.   A young man died in
December, in the Lord, as we believe.   We are still
preserved in health at our work by the God of all
grace, whose power alone could have preserved us in
all our troubles, which have come upon us by the
measles *per* the *Blue Bell.*   Ah, this is a season which
we will not soon forget.   Some settlements are nearly
depopulated, and the principal Chiefs are nearly all
dead !   And oh, the indescribable fiendish hatred
that exists against us !   There is quite a famine here.
The distress is awful, and the cry of mourning per-
petual.   A few on both sides of the Island who did not
flee from the Worship of God are living, which is now
greatly impressing some and exciting the enmity of
others.   I cannot now write of perils.   We feel very
anxious to hear from you.   If you have to flee, Aneityum of course is the nearest and best place to which
you can go.   Confidence in us is being restored. Mana,

a native Teacher, remains with us for safety from the fury of his enemies. I cannot visit as usual. The persecution cannot be much worse on Tanna. I hope the worst is past. Mrs. G. unites in love to you, and to Mr. and Mrs. Johnston. In great haste,

"I remain, dear Brother, Yours truly,

"G. N. GORDON."

Let every reader, in view of this epistle, like a voice from the World Unseen, judge of the spirit of the man of God who penned it, and of the causes that were even then at work and were bringing about his sorrowful death. Cruel superstition, measles, and the malignant influences of the godless Traders,— these on Erromanga, as elsewhere, were the forces at work that brought hatred and murder in their train.

Immediately thereafter, a Sandal-wood Trader brought in his boat a party of Erromangans by night to Tanna. They assembled our Harbour Chiefs and people, and urged them to kill us and Mr. and Mrs. Mathieson and the Teachers, or allow them to do so, as they had killed Mr. and Mrs. Gordon. Then they proposed to go to Aneityum and kill the Missionaries there, as the Aneityumese Natives had burned their Church, and thus they would sweep away the Worship and the servants of Jehovah from all the New Hebrides. Our Chiefs, however, refused, restrained by the Merciful One, and the Erromangans returned to their own island in a sulky mood. Notwithstanding this refusal, as if they wished to reserve the murder and

plunder for themselves, our Mission House was next
day thronged with armed men, some from Inland,
others from Mr. Mathieson's Station. They loudly
praised the Erromangans! The leaders said again
and again in my hearing,—

"The men of Erromanga killed Missi Williams
long ago. We killed the Rarotongan and Samoan
Teachers. We fought Missi Turner and Missi Nisbet,
and drove them from our island. We killed the
Aneityumese Teachers on Aniwa, and one of Missi
Paton's Teachers too. We killed several white men,
and no Man-of-war punished us. Let us talk over
this, about killing Missi Paton and the Aneityumese,
till we see if any Man-of-war comes to punish the
Erromangans. If not, let us unite, let us kill these
Missionaries, let us drive the worship of Jehovah from
our land!"

An Inland Chief said or rather shouted in my
hearing,—

"My love to the Erromangans! They are strong
and brave men, the Erromangans. They have killed
their Missi and his wife, while we only talk about
it. They have destroyed the Worship and driven
away Jehovah!"

I stood amongst them and protested,—

"God will yet punish the Erromangans for such
wicked deeds. God has heard all your bad talk, and
will punish it in His own time and way."

But they shouted me down, amidst great excitement, with the cry,—

"Our love to the Erromangans! Our love to the Erromangans!"

After I left them, Abraham heard them say,—

"Miaki is lazy. Let us meet in every village, and talk with each other. Let us all agree to kill Missi and the Aneityumese for the first of our Chiefs that dies."

On Tanna, as on Erromanga, the Natives have no idea of death coming to any one naturally, or sickness or any disease; everything comes by Nahak, or sorcery. When one person grows sick or dies, they meet to talk over it and find out who has bewitched or killed him, and this ends in fixing upon some individual upon whom they take revenge, or whom they murder outright. Thus many wars arise on Tanna, for the friends or the tribe of the murdered man generally seek a counter-revenge; and so the blood-fiend is let loose over all the island, and from island to island throughout the whole of the New Hebrides.

The night after the visit of the Erromangan boat, and the sad news of Mr. and Mrs. Gordon's death the Tannese met on their village dancing-grounds and held high festival in praise of the Erromangans. Our best friend, old Nowar, the Chief, who had worn shirt and kilt for some time and had come regularly to the Worship, relapsed once more; he painted his face, threw off his clothing, resumed his bow and arrows, and his tomahawk, of which he boasted that it had killed very many men and at least one woman! On my shaming him for professing to worship Jehovah and 'yet uniting with the Heathen in rejoicing over the murder of His servants on Erromanga, he replied to this effect,—

"Truly, Missi, they have done well. If the people of Erromanga are severely punished for this by the Man-of-war, we will all hear of it; and our people will then fear to kill you and the other Missionaries, so as to destroy the Worship of Jehovah. Now, they say, the Erromangans killed Missi Williams and the Samoan, Rarotongan, and Aneityumese Teachers, besides other white men, and no Man-of-war has punished either them or us. If they are not punished for what has been done on Erromanga, nothing else can keep them here from killing you and me and all who worship at the Mission House!"

I answered,—"Nowar, let us all be strong to love and serve Jehovah Jesus. If it be for our good and His glory, He will protect us; if not, He will take us to be with Himself. We will not be killed by their bad talk. Besides, what avails it to us, when dead and gone, if even a Man-of-war should come and punish our murderers?"

He shrugged his shoulders, answering,—"Missi, by-and-by you will see. Mind, I tell you the truth. I know our Tannese people. How is it that Jehovah did not protect the Gordons and the Erromangan worshippers? If the Erromangans are not punished, neither will our Tannese be punished, though they murder all Jehovah's people!"

I felt for Nowar's struggling faith, just trembling
on the verge of cannibalism yet, and knowing so little
of the true Jehovah. .

Groups of Natives assembled suspiciously near us
and sat whispering together. They urged old Abraham to return to Aneityum by the very first
opportunity, as our lives were certain to be taken,
but he replied,—

" I will not leave Missi."

Abraham and I were thrown much into each other's
company, and he stood by me in every danger. We
conducted family prayers alternately ; and that evening he said during the prayer in Tannese, in which
language alone we understood each other,—

"O Lord, our Heavenly Father, they have murdered
Thy servants on Erromanga. They have banished
the Aneityumese from dark Tanna. And now they
want to kill Missi Paton and me! Our great King,
protect us, and make their hearts soft and sweet to
Thy Worship. Or, if they are permitted to kill us,
do not Thou hate us, but wash us in the blood of
Thy dear Son Jesus Christ. He came down to Earth
and shed His blood for sinners; through Him forgive us our sins and take us to Heaven—that good
place where Missi Gordon the man and Missi Gordon the woman and all Thy dear servants now are
singing Thy praise and seeing Thy face. Our Lord,
our hearts are pained just now, and we weep over
the death of Thy dear servants; but make our
hearts good and strong for Thy cause, and take

Thou away all our fears.   Make us two and all Thy
servants strong for Thee and for Thy Worship; and
if they kill us two, let us die together in Thy good
work, like Thy servants Missi Gordon the man and
Missi Gordon the woman."

·In this manner his great simple soul poured itself
out to God, and my heart melted within me as it had
never done under any prayer poured from the lips of
cultured Christian men!

Under the strain of these events, Miaki came to
our house, and attacked me in hearing of his men
to this effect :—

"You and the Worship are the cause of all the
sickness and death now taking place on Tanna!
The Erromanga men killed Missi Gordon the man
and also the woman, and they are all well long ago.
The Worship is killing us all; and the Inland people
will kill us for keeping you and the Worship here;
for we love the conduct of Tanna, but we hate the
Worship.   We must kill you and it, and we shall all
be well again."

I tried to reason firmly and kindly with them,
showing them that their own conduct was destroying
them, and that our presence and the Worship could
only be a blessing to them in every way, if only they
would accept of it and give up their evil ways.   I
referred to a poor girl, whom Miaki and his men
had stolen and abused, that they knew such conduct
to be bad, and that God would certainly punish them
for it.

He replied, "Such is the conduct of Tanna. Our fathers loved and followed it, we love and follow it, and if the Worship condemns it, we will kill you and destroy the Worship."

I said, "The Word of the Holy God condemns all bad conduct, and I must obey my God in trying to lead you to give it up, and to love and serve His Son Jesus our Saviour. If I refuse to obey my God, He will punish me."

He replied, "Missi, we like many wives to attend us and to do our work. Three of my wives are dead and three are yet alive. The Worship killed them and my children. We hate it. It will kill us all."

I answered, "Miaki, is it good for you to have so many wives, and many of your men to have none? Who waits on them? Who works for them? They cannot get a wife, and so, having to work for themselves, they are led to hate you and all the Chiefs who have more wives than one. You do not love your wives, else you would not slave them and beat them as you do."

But he declared that his heart was good, that his conduct was good, and that he hated the teaching of the Worship. He had a party of men staying with him from the other side of the island, and he sent back a present of four large fat hogs to their Chiefs, with a message as to the killing of the Mathiesons. If that were done, his hands would be strengthened in dealing with us.

Satan seemed to fill that man's heart. He incited his people to steal everything from us, and to annoy us in every conceivable way. They killed one of my precious watch-dogs, and feasted upon it. So sad was the condition of Tanna, that if a man were desperate enough in wickedness, if he killed a number of men and tyrannized over others, he was dignified with the name and rank of a Chief. This was the secret of Miaki's influence, and of his being surrounded by the outlaws and refugees, not only of his own but even other islands. It was all founded upon terror and upheld by cruelty. The Sacred Man, for instance, who murdered my Teacher, and a young man who threw three spears at me, which by God's help I avoided, were both praised and honoured for their deeds. But the moment they were laid aside by measles and unable to retaliate, their flatterers turned upon them and declared that they were punished for their bad conduct against Jehovah and His servants and His Worship!

To know what was best to be done, in such trying circumstances, was an abiding perplexity. To have left altogether, when so surrounded by perils and enemies, at first seemed the wisest course, and was the repeated advice of many friends. But again, I had acquired the language, and had gained a considerable influence amongst the Natives, and there were a number warmly attached both to myself and to the Worship. To have left would have been to lose all, which to me was heart-rending; therefore,

risking all with Jesus, I held on while the hope of
being spared longer had not absolutely and entirely
vanished. God only knows how deep and genuine were
my pity and affection for the poor Tannese, labouring
and longing to bring them from their dark idolatry
and heathenism to love and serve and please Jesus
Christ as their God and Saviour. True, some of the
awfully wise people wrote, as in the case of Mr.
Gordon, much nonsense about us and the Tanna
Mission. They knew, of course, that I was to blame,
and they from safe distances could see that I was not
in the path of duty!

Perhaps, to people less omnisciently sure, the following quotation from a letter of the late A. Clark,
Esq., J.P., Auckland, New Zealand, will show what
Bishop Selwyn thought of my standing fast on Tanna
at the post of duty, and he knew what he was
writing about. He says,—

"In addition, Bishop Selwyn told us that he had
seen the Commodore (Seymour), who told him that
at Tanna the Natives were in a very insulting and
hostile state of mind; so much so that he felt it his
duty to offer Mr. Paton a passage in his ship to
Auckland or some other place of safety. He said,
'Talk of bravery! talk of heroism! The man who
leads a forlorn hope is a coward in comparison with
him, who, on Tanna, thus alone, without a sustaining
look or cheering word from one of his own race,
regards it as his duty to hold on in the face of such
dangers. We read of the soldier, found after the

lapse of ages among the ruins of Herculaneum, who stood firm at his post amid the fiery rain destroying all around him, thus manifesting the rigidity of the discipline amongst those armies of ancient Rome which conquered the World. Mr. Paton was subjected to no such iron law. He might, with honour, when offered to him, have sought a temporary asylum in Auckland, where he would have been heartily received. But he was moved by higher considerations. He chose to remain, and God knows whether at this moment he is in the land of the living!' When the bishop told us that he declined leaving Tanna by H.M.S. *Pelorus*, he added, 'And I like him all the better for so doing!'"

For my part I feel quite confident that, in like circumstances, that noble Bishop of God would have done the same. I, born in the bosom of the Scottish Covenant, descended from those who suffered persecution for Christ's honour, would have been unworthy of them and of my Lord had I deserted my post for danger only. Yet not to me, but to the Lord who sustained me, be all the praise and the glory! On his next visit to these Islands, the good Bishop brought a box of Mission goods to me in his ship, besides £90 for our work from Mr. Clark and friends in Auckland. His interest in us and our work was deep and genuine, and was unmarred on either side by any consciousness of ecclesiastical distinctions. We were one in Christ, and, when next we meet again in the glory of our Lord, Bishop and

Presbyter will be eternally one in that blessed fellow-ship.

The following incident illustrates the depth of native superstition. One morning two Inland Chiefs came running to the Mission House, breathless, and covered with perspiration. One of them held up a handful of half-rotten tracts, crying,—

"Missi, is this a part of God's Word, the sacred Book of Jehovah? or is it the work, the words, the book of man?"

I examined them and replied, "These are the work, the words, and the book of man, not of Jehovah."

He questioned me again: "Missi, are you certain that it is not the Word of Jehovah?"

I replied, "It is only man's work and man's book."

He continued then, "Missi, some years ago, Kaipai, a sacred Chief, and certain Tannese, went on a visit to Aneityum, and Missi Geddie gave him these books. On his return, when he showed them to the Tannese, the people were all so afraid of them, for they thought they were the sacred Books of Jehovah, that they met for consultation and agreed solemnly to bury them. Yesterday, some person in digging had disinterred them, and at once our Inland people said that our dead Chief had buried a part of Jehovah's Word, which made Him angry, and that He had therefore caused the Chief's death and the plague of measles, etc. Therefore they were now assembled to kill the dead Chief's son and daughter in revenge!

But, before that should be done, I persuaded them to
send these books, to inquire of you if this be part of
Jehovah's Book, and if the burying of it caused all
these diseases and deaths."

I assured him that these books never caused either
sickness or death to any human being; and that
none of us can cause sickness or death by sorcery;
that burying these Tracts did not make Jehovah
angry, nor cause evil to any creature. "You your-
selves know," I said, "the very ships that brought
the measles and caused the deaths; and you killed
some of the young men who were landed sick with
the disease."

The Inland Chief declared, "Missi, I am quite
satisfied; no person shall be put to death over these
books now."

They went off, but immediately returned, saying,
"Missi, have you any books like these to show to us?
And will you show us the sacred Book of Jehovah
beside them?"

I showed them a Bible, and then a handful of
Tracts with pictures like those they had brought;
and I offered them the Bible and specimens of these
Tracts, that they might show both to the people assembled. The Tracts they received, but the Bible
they refused to touch. They satisfied the Inland
people and prevented bloodshed; but oh, what a
depth of superstition to be raised out of! and how
easily life might be sacrificed at every turn!

On another occasion I had the joy of saving the

lives of Sandal-wood Traders, to whom neither I nor the Mission owed anything, except for Christ's sake. The *Blue Bell* cast anchor in the Harbour on a beautiful morning, and the Captain and Mate immediately came on shore. They had letters for me; but, on landing, they were instantly surrounded by the Chiefs and people, who formed a ring about them on the beach and called for me to come. The two white men stood in the midst, with many weapons pointed at them, and death if they dared to move. They shouted to me,—

"This is one of the Vessels which brought the measles. You and they made the sickness, and destroyed our people. Now, if you do not leave with this vessel, we will kill you all."

Of course, their intention was to frighten me on board just as I was, and leave my premises for plunder! I protested,—

"I will not leave you; I cannot leave you in this way; and if you murder these men or me, Jehovah will punish you. I am here for your good; and you know how kind I have been to you all, in giving you medicine, knives, axes, blankets, and clothing. You also know well that I have never done ill to one human being, but have constantly sought your good. I will not and cannot leave you thus."

In great wrath they cried, "Then will we kill you and this Captain and Mate."

I kept reasoning with them against such conduct, standing firmly before them and saying, "If you do kill me, Jehovah will punish you; the other men in that vessel will punish you before they sail; and a Man-of-war will come and burn your villages and canoes and fruit trees."

I urged the two men to try and get into their boat as quickly as possible, in silence, while I kept arguing with the Natives. The letters which they had for me, the savages forbade me to take into my hands, lest thereby some other foreign disease should come to their island. Miaki exclaimed in great wrath that my medicine had killed them all; but I replied,—

"My medicine with God's blessing saved many lives. You know well that all who followed my rules recovered from the measles, except only one man, and are living still. Now, you seek to kill me for saving your lives and the lives of, your people!"

I appealed to Yorian, another Chief, if the medicine had not saved his life when he appeared to be dying, which he admitted to be the truth. The men had now slipped into their boat and were preparing to leave. Miaki shouted,—

"Let them go! Don't kill them to-day." Then he called to the Captain, "Come on shore and trade with us to-morrow."

Next day they foolishly came on shore and began to trade. Natives surrounded the boat with clubs and tomahawks. But Miaki's heart failed him when about to strike; and he called out,—

"Missi said that, if we kill them, a Man-of-war will come and take revenge on us."

In the altercation that followed, the men thrust the boat into deep water and forced it out of the grasp of the savages; but they caught the Captain's large Newfoundland dog and kept it prisoner. As a compensation for this disappointment, Miaki urged that my life and Abraham's be at once taken, but again Nowar's firm opposition and God's goodness rescued us from the jaws of the lion. The *Blue Bell* left next morning, and the dog remained behind, as no one from the vessel would venture ashore.

Revenge for the murder of the four men killed to accompany Miaki's child, threatened to originate another war; but the Chiefs for eight miles around met, and, after much speechifying, agreed that as they were all weak for war, owing to the measles and the want of food through the hurricanes, they should delay it till they all grew stronger. Nowar was, however, greatly excited, and informed me that Miaki had urged the people of an inland district to shoot Nowar and Abraham and me, and he pled with us again to take him and flee to Aneityum,— impossible except by canoe, and perhaps impossible even so. That night and the following night they tried to break into my house. On one occasion my valuable dog was let out, and cleared them away. Next night I shouted at them from inside, when they thought me asleep, and they decamped again. Indeed, our continuous danger caused me now oftentimes to sleep with my clothes on, that I might start at a moment's warning. My faithful dog would give a sharp bark and awake me. At other, times, she would leap up and pull at the clothes till I awoke, and then she turned her head quietly and indicated by a wondrous instinct where the danger lay. God made them fear this precious creature, and often used her in saving our lives. Soon after this six Inland Chiefs came to see me. We had a long talk on the evils of war, and the blessings of the Worship of Jehovah. I gave each a knife and a fork and a tin plate, and they promised to oppose the war which Miaki was forcing on. A man came also with a severe gash in his hand, which a fish had given him; I dressed it, and he went away very grateful and spread everywhere the news of healing, a kind of Gospel which he and they could most readily appreciate.

Another incident made them well-disposed for a season; namely, the use of a fishing-net. Seeing that the Natives had so little food—there being, in fact, a famine after the hurricane—I engaged an inland Tribe to make a net forty feet long and very broad. Strange to say, the Inland people who live far from the sea make the best fishing materials, which again they sell to the Harbour people for the axes, knives, blankets, and other articles obtained from calling vessels. They also make the killing-stones, and trade with them amongst the shore people all round the island. This *kawas* or killing-stone is made of blue whinstone, eighteen to twenty-four inches long, an inch and a half across, perfectly straight, and

hewn as round and neat as any English tradesman
could have done it, exactly like a large scythe-stone,
such as they use on the harvest fields in Scotland.
The kawas seems to be peculiar to Tanna, at least
I have not seen it on any other island. The Natives,
with pieces of very hard heavy wood of the same
size and shape, are taught to throw it from infancy at
a given mark; in warfare, it is thrown first; where it
strikes it stuns or kills, and then they spring forward
with their large double-handed heavy club. Every
man and boy carries his killing-stone and other
weapons, even when moving about peaceably in his
own village, war being, in fact, the only regular occu-
pation for men!

Well, these same Inland people, the sort of arti-
sans of the island, being mostly the women and the
girls, manufactured for me this huge fishing-net.
The cord was twisted from the fibre made out of
the bark of their own trees, and prepared with
immense toil and care; and not without touches
of skill and taste, when woven and knotted and
intertwined. This net I secured, and lent about
three days each to every village all round the Harbour and near it. One night I saw them carrying
home a large hog, which they had got from an Inland
Chief for a portion of the fish which they had taken.
I thought it right to cause them to return the net to
the Mission House every Saturday evening, that they
might not be tempted to use it on Sabbath. It
was a great help to them, and the Harbour yielded

them much wholesome food in lieu of what the hurricane had destroyed.

When, about this time, the *John Knox* came to anchor in the bay, a Native was caught in the act of stealing from her. Angry at being discovered, he and his friends came to shoot me, pretending that it was because the *John Knox* knew they were in want of food and had not brought them a load of Taro from Aneityum. Taro is a plant of the genus *Arum*, the *Æsculentum*, or *Colocasia Æsculenta*, well known all through Polynesia. The Natives spread it in a very simple way. Cutting off the leaves, with a very little of the old bulb still attached, they fix these in the ground, and have the new Taro about a year after that. It is of several kinds and of a great variety of colours—white, yellow, blue, etc. It grows best in ground irrigated by streams of pure water, or in shallow, swampy ground, over which the water runs. The dry-ground Taro is small and inferior compared to the water-grown roots. Nutritious and pleasant, not unlike the texture of cheese when laid in slices on the table, in size and appearance like a Swedish turnip, it can be either boiled or baked. Hurricanes may destroy all other native food, but the Taro lies uninjured below the water; hence on islands, where it will grow, it forms one of the most permanent and valuable of all their crops.

Our people also demanded that the *John Knox* should bring them kava and tobacco. Kava is the plant, *Piper Methysticum*, from which they make a highly intoxicating drink. The girls and boys first chew it, and spit the juice into a basin; there it is mixed with water, and then strained through a fibrous cloth-like texture, which they get from the top of the cocoa-nut trees, where it surrounds the young nuts, and drops off with them when they are ripe. This they freely drink; it does not make them violent, but stupefies them and induces sleep like opium. A portion is always poured out to their Gods; and the dregs in every mouth after drinking are always spit out with the exclamation, "That's for you, Kumesam!" It is sometimes offered and partaken of with very great ceremony; but its general use is as a soporific by the men, regularly after the evening meal. Women and children are not allowed to drink it. Many men have been attacked and murdered at night, when lying enfeebled and enfolded by kava. That, indeed, is their common mode of taking revenge and of declaring war. These angry men, who came to me about the *John Knox*, tried to smash in my window and kill my faithful dog; but I reasoned firmly and kindly with them, and they at last withdrew.

At that time, though my life was daily attempted, a dear lad, named Katasian, was coming six miles regularly to the Worship and to receive frequent instruction. One day, when engaged in teaching him, I caught a man stealing the blind from my window. On trying to prevent him, he aimed his great club at me, but I seized the heavy end of it with both my

hands as it swung past my head, and held on with
all my might. What a prayer went up from me to
God at that dread moment! The man, astonished
and abashed at my kind words and appeal, slunk
away and left me in peace.

I had planted a few Yams, of the genus *Dioscoria;*
a most valuable article of food, nearly as precious
as potatoes were to the poor in Ireland, and used
very much in the same way. Years after, when I
went to Melbourne, I took one from Aniwa, by no
means the largest, weighing seventy-two pounds, and
another, forty-two. The things, however, that I
planted on Tanna the Natives stole and carried away,
making themselves extremely troublesome. But
God never took away from me the consciousness that
it was still right for me to be kind and forgiving, and
to hope that I might lead them to love and imitate
Jesus.

For a season thereafter, the friendly feeling grew
on every side. The Natives prepared, for payment,
an excellent foundation for a new Church, by level-
ling down the hill near to my Mission House. Any
number of men offered to work for calico, knives,
axes, etc. All the fences were renewed, and the
Mission premises began to look nice once more, at
least, in my eyes. My work became encouraging,
and I had many opportunities of talking with them
about the Worship and Jehovah. This state of matters displeased Miaki and his men; and one day,
having been engaged thus, I rushed back only in

time to extinguish a fire which they had kindled under the verandah and close to the door of my house. Our watch had to be unrelaxing. A cousin of Miaki's, for instance, sold me a fish as good for food which he knew to be poisonous, but Nowar saw in time and warned me of its deadly character. Miaki then threatened to shoot any of the Inland people who came to work or to receive instruction, yet larger numbers came than before, but they came fully armed! Nouka, the high Chief of the Harbour, Miaki's uncle, came and sat beside us often, and said,—

"Miaki breaks my heart! He deceives Missi. He hates the Worship of Jehovah."

For some time, Nouka and his wife and daughter —a handsome girl, his only child—and Miaki's principal wife and her two sons, and nine Chiefs attended Worship regularly at the Mission House, on Sabbaths and on the afternoon of every Wednesday. In all, about sixty persons somewhat regularly waited on our ministrations at this time; and amidst all perils I was encouraged, and my heart was full of hope. Yet one evening, when feeling more consoled and hopeful than ever before, a musket was discharged at my very door, and I was constrained to realize that we were in the midst of death. Father, our times are in Thy hand.

As my work became more encouraging, I urgently applied to the Missionaries on Aneityum for more Teachers, but none could be found willing to return to

Tanna. . The plague of measles had almost demoralized them. Even on Aneityum, where they
had medicine and would follow the Missionaries' advice, no fewer than eleven hundred had been cut off;
and the mortality was very much greater on such
islands as Tanna, Aniwa, etc., where they were still
Heathen, and either had not or would not follow
medical counsels. Of my Teachers and their wives
ten were swept away in the epidemic, and the few
that were left were so disheartened that they escaped
to their own land at the first opportunity, as before
recorded, excepting only dear old faithful Abraham.
But I need not wonder; smaller perils deter God's
people at home from many a call of duty.

. In my Mission School, I offered as a prize a red
shirt for the first Chief who knew the whole Alphabet
without a mistake. It was won by an Inakaki Chief,
who was once a terror to the whole community.
Afterwards, when trying to teach the A B C to
others, he proceeded in something like this graphic
style :—

"A is a man's legs with the body cut off; B is
like two eyes; C is a three-quarters moon; D is
like one eye; E is a man with one club under his
feet and another over his head; F is a man with a
large club and a smaller one," etc., etc.; L was like a
man's foot; Q was the talk of the dove, etc. Then he
would say, "Remember these things; you will soon
get hold of the letters and be able to read. I have
taught my little child, who can scarcely walk, the

names of them all. They are not hard to hold, but soft and easy. You will soon learn to read the book, if you try it with all your heart!"

But Miaki was still our evil genius, and every incident seemed to be used by him for one settled pur-· pose of hate. A Kaserumini Chief, for instance, and seven men took away a young girl in a canoe to Aniwa, to be sold to friends there for tobacco leaf,· which the Aniwans cultivated extensively. They also prepared to take revenge there for a child's death, killed in their belief by the sorcery of an Aniwan. When within sight of the shore, the canoes were upset and all were said to have been devoured by sharks, excepting only one canoe out of six. This one returned to Tanna and reported that there were two white Traders living on Aniwa, that they had plenty of ammunition and tobacco, but that they would not come to Tanna as long as a Missionary lived there. Under this fresh incitement, a party of Miaki's men came to my house, praising the Erromangans for the murder of their Missionaries and threatening me.

Even the friendly Nowar said, " Miaki will make a great wind and sink any Man-of-war that comes here. We will take the Man-of-war and kill all that are on board. If you and Abraham do not leave us we will kill you both, for we must have the Traders and the powder."

Just as they were assuming a threatening attitude, other Natives came running with the cry, " Missi, the

John Knox is coming into the Harbour, and two great ships of fire, Men-of-war behind her, coming very fast!"

I retorted upon Nowar and the hostile company, "Now is your time! Make all possible haste! Let Miaki raise his great wind now; get all your men ready; I will tell them that you mean to fight, and you will find them always ready!"

Miaki's men fled away in unconcealed terror; but Nowar came to me and said, "Missi, I know that my talk is all lies, but if I speak the truth, they will kill me!"

I answered, " Trust in Jehovah, the same God who sent these vessels now, to protect us from being murdered."

But Nowar always wavered.

And now from all parts of the island those who were most friendly flocked to us. They were clamorous to have Miaki and some others of our enemies punished by the Man-of-war in presence of the Natives ; and then they would be strong to speak in our defence and to lead the Tannese to worship Jehovah.

Commodore Seymour, Captain Hume, and Dr. Geddie came on shore. After inquiring into everything, the Commodore urged me to leave at once, and very kindly offered to remove me to Aneityum, or Auckland, or any place of safety that I preferred. Again, however, I hesitated to leave my dear benighted Tannese, knowing that both Stations would be instantly broken up, that all the influence gained would be thrown away, that the Church would lose all that had been expended, and above all, that those friendly to us would be left to persecution and destruction. For a long time I had seldom taken off my clothes at night, needing to be constantly on the alert to start at a moment's notice; yet, while hope burned within my soul I could not withdraw, so I resolved to risk all with my dear Lord Jesus, and remained at my post. At my request, however, they met and talked with all the leaders who could be assembled at the Mission House. The Natives declared frankly that they liked me but did not like the Worship. The Commodore reminded them that they had invited me to land among them, and had pledged their word more than once to protect me; he argued with them that as they had no fault to find with me, but only with the Worship, which could do them only good, they must bind themselves to protect my life. Miaki and others promised and gave him their hands to do so. Lathella, an Aneityumese Chief, who was with Dr. Geddie, interpreted for him and them, Dr. Geddie explaining fully to Lathella in Aneityumese what the Commodore said in English, and Lathella explaining all to the Tannese in their own tongue.

At last old Nouka spoke out for all and said, "Captain Paddan and all the Traders tell us that the Worship causes all our sickness and death. They will not trade with us, nor sell us tobacco, pipes,

powder, balls, caps, and muskets, till we kill our Missi
like the Erromangans, but after that they will send
a Trader to live among us and give us plenty of all
these things.   We love Missi.   But when the Traders
tell us that the Worship makes us sick, and when
they bribe us with tobacco and powder to kill him or
drive him away, some believe them and our hearts do
bad conduct to Missi.   Let Missi remain here, and
we will try to do good conduct to Missi ; but you
must tell Queen 'Toria of her people's bad treatment
of us, and that she must prevent her Traders from
killing us with their measles, and from telling us lies
to make us do bad conduct to Missi!   If they come
to us and talk as before, our hearts are very dark and
may again lead us to bad conduct to Missi."

After this little parley, the Commodore invited us
all on board, along with the Chiefs.   They saw about
three hundred brave marines ranked up on deck, and
heard a great cannon discharged.   For all such efforts
to impress them and open their eyes, I felt pro-
foundly grateful; but too clearly I knew and saw
that only the grace of God could lastingly change
them !

They were soon back to their old arguments, and
were heard saying to one another, "If no punishment
is inflicted on the Erromangans for murdering the
Missi there, we fear the bad conduct of the Tannese
will continue."

No punishment was inflicted at Erromanga, and
the Tannese were soon as bold and wicked as

ever. For instance, while the Man-of-war lay in the Harbour, Nowar kept himself closely concealed ; but no sooner had she sailed than the cowardly fellow came out, laughing at the others, and protesting that he was under no promise and was free to act as .he pleased ! Yet in the hour of danger he generally proved· to be our friend ; such was his vacillating character. Nor was Miaki very seriously impressed. Mr. Mathieson shortly thereafter sent his boat round to me, being again short of European food. On his crew leaving her to deliver their message to me, some of Miaki's men at once jumped into the boat and started off round the island in search of kava. I went to Miaki, to ask that the boat might be brought back soon, but on seeing me he ran for his club and aimed to strike me. I managed to seize it, and to hold on, pleading with God and talking with Miaki, till by the interference of some friendly Natives his wrath was assuaged a little. Returning home, I sent food overland to keep them going till the boat returned, which she did in about eight days. Thus light and shadow ·pursued each other, the light brightening for a moment, but upon the whole the shadows deepening.

X.

FAREWELL SCENES.

CHAPTER X.

FAREWELL SCENES.

A TIME of great excitement amongst the Natives now prevailed. War, war, nothing but war was spoken of! Preparations for war were being made in all the villages far and near.   Fear sat on every face, and armed bands kept watching each other, as if uncertain where the war was to begin or by whom.   All work was suspended, and that war spirit was let loose which rouses the worst passions of human nature. Again we found ourselves the centre of conflict, one party set for killing us or driving us away; the other wishing to retain us, while all old bitter grievances were also dragged into their speeches.

Miaki and Nouka said, "If you will keep Missi and his Worship, take him with you to your own land, for we will not have him to live at the Harbour."

Ian, the great Inland Chief, rose in wrath and said, " On whose land does the Missi live, yours or ours? Who fight against the Worship and all good, who are the thieves and murderers, who tell the lies, you or we?   We wish peace, but you will have war.   We like Missi and the Worship, but you hate them and say, 'Take him to your own land!'   It is our land on which he now lives; it is his own land which he bought from you, but which our fathers sold Missi Turner long ago.   The land was not yours to sell; it was really ours.   Your fathers stole it from us long ago by war; but we would not have asked it back, had you not asked us to take Missi away.   Now we will defend him on it, and he will teach us and our people in our own land!"

So meeting after meeting broke into fiery speech, and separated with many threats.

To the next great meeting I was invited, but did

not go, contenting myself with a message pleading that they should live at peace and on no account go to war with each other. But Ian himself came for me.

I said, "Ian, I have told you my whole heart. Go not to that meeting. I will rather leave the island or die, than see you going to war about me!"

He answered, "Missi, come with me, come now!"

I replied, "Ian, you are surely not taking me away to kill me? If you are, my God will punish it."

His only reply was, "Follow me, follow me quickly."

I felt constrained to go.

He strode on before me till we reached the great village of his ancestors. His followers, armed largely with muskets, as well as native weapons, filled one half the Village Square or dancing ground. Miaki, Nouka, and their whole party sat in manifest terror upon the other half. Marching into the centre, he stood with me by his side, and proudly looking round, exclaimed,—

"Missi, these are my men and your friends! We are met to defend you and the Worship." Then pointing across to the other side, he cried aloud, "These are your enemies and ours! The enemies of the Worship, the disturbers of the peace on Tanna! Missi, say the word, and the muskets of my men will sweep all opposition away, and the Worship will spread and we will all be strong for it on Tanna. We will not shoot without your leave; but if you

P.   20

refuse they will kill you and persecute us and our children, and banish Jehovah's Worship from our land."

I said, "I love all of you alike. I am here to teach you how to turn away from all wickedness, to worship and serve Jehovah, and to live in peace. How can I approve of any person being killed for me or for the Worship? My God would be angry at me and punish me, if I did!"

He replied, "Then, Missi, you will be murdered and the Worship destroyed."

I then stood forth in the middle before them all and cried, "You may shoot or murder me, but I am your best friend. I am not afraid to die. You will only send me the sooner to my Jehovah God, whom I love and serve, and to my dear Saviour Jesus Christ, who died for me and for you, and who sent me here to tell you all His love. If you will only love and serve Him and give up your bad conduct, you will be happy. But if you kill me, His messenger, rest assured that He will in His own time and way punish you. This is my word to you all; my love to you all!"

So saying, I turned to leave; and Ian strode sullenly away and stood at the head of his men, crying,—

"Missi, they will kill you! they will kill us, and you will be to blame!"

Miaki and Nouka, full of deceit, now cried out,—

"Missi's word is good! Let us all obey it. Let us all worship."

An old man, Sirawia, one of Ian's under-chiefs, then said,—

"Miaki and Nouka say that the land on which Missi lives was theirs; though they sold it to him, and he has paid them for it, they all know that it was ours, and is yet ours by right; but if they let Missi live on it in peace, we will all live at peace, and worship Jehovah. And if not, we will surely claim it again."

Miaki and his party hereon went off to their plantations, and brought a large present of food to Ian and his men as a peace-offering. This they accepted; and the next day Ian and his men brought Miaki a return present and said,—

"You know that Missi lives on our land? Take our present, be friends, and let him live quietly and teach us all. Yesterday you said his word was good, obey it now, else we will punish you and defend the Missi."

Miaki accepted the token, and gave good promises for the future. Ian then came to the hill-top near our house, by which passed the public path, and cried aloud in the hearing of all,—

"Abraham, tell Missi that you and he now live on our land. This path is the march betwixt Miaki and us. We have this day bought back the land of our fathers by a great price to prevent war. Take of our bread-fruits and also of our cocoa-nuts what you require, for you are our friends and living on our land, and we will protect you and the Worship!"

For some time things moved on quietly after this. An inland war, however, had continued for months. As many as ten men, they said, were sometimes killed in one day and feasted on by the warriors. Thousands had been thereby forced down from the mountains, and sought protection under Ian and his people. All the people claiming connection with his Tribe were called Naraimini; the people in the Volcano district were called the Kaserumini; and the Harbour Tribes were the Watarenmini; and so on all over the island. In such divisions, there might be from two to twenty Chiefs and Villages under one leader, and these stood by each other for purposes defensive and offensive. Now Nouka and Miaki had been frustrated in all their plans to get the Inland and the Harbour people involved in the war, as their own followers were opposed to it. In violation of his promises, however, Nouka invited all the men who wished to go to the war to meet him one morning, and only one appeared! Nouka, in great wrath, marched off to the war himself, but, as no one followed, he grew faint-hearted, and returned to his own village. On another morning, Miaki summoned all his fighting men; but only his own brother and six lads could be induced to accompany him, and with these he started off. But the enemy, hearing of his coming, had killed two of his principal allies the night before, and Miaki, learning this, turned and fled to his own house, and was secretly laughed at by his tribe.

Next day, Nouka came to me professing great friendship and pleading with me to accompany him and Miaki to talk with the Kaserumini, and persuade them to give up the war. He was annoyed and disappointed when I refused to go. Nowar and others informed me, two days thereafter, that three persons had died in that district, that others were sick, and that the Heathen there had resolved to kill me in revenge as the cause of all. As Nouka's wife was one of the victims, this scheme was concocted to entrap me. I was warned on no account to leave my house at night for a considerable time, but to keep it locked up and to let no one in after dark. The same two men from that district who had tried to kill Mr. Johnston and me, were again appointed and were watching for Abraham and me, lurking about in the evenings for that purpose. Again I saw how the Lord had preserved me from Miaki and Nouka! Truly all are safe who are in God's keeping; and nothing can befall them, except for their real good and the glory of their Lord.

Chafed at the upsetting of all their plans and full of revenge, Nouka and Miaki and their allies declared publicly that they were now going to kill Ian by sorcery, *i.e.*, by Nahak, more feared by the poor Tannese than the field of battle. Nothing but the grace of God and the enlightenment of His Spirit through the Scriptures, has ever raised these Natives

above that paralyzing superstition. But, thank God,
there are now, while I write this (1887), about twelve
thousand in the New Hebrides who have been thus
enlightened and lifted out of their terrors, for the
Gospel is still, as of old, the power of God unto salvation! Strange to say, Ian became sick shortly
after the Sacred Men had made the declaration about
their Nahak-sorcery. I attended him, and for a time
he recovered, and appeared very grateful. But he
soon fell sick again. I sent him and the Chief next
under him a blanket each; I also gave shirts and
calico to a number of his leading men. They wore
them and seemed grateful and pleased. Ian, however,
gradually sank and got worse. He had every symp-
tom of being poisoned, a thing easily accomplished, as
they know and use many deadly poisons. His sufferings were very great, which prevented me from ascrib-
ing his collapse to mere superstitious terror. I did all
that could be done; but all thought him dying, and
of course by sorcery. His people were angry at me
for not consenting before to their shooting of Miaki;
and Miaki's people were now rejoicing that Ian was
being killed by Nahak.

One night, his brother and a party came for me to
go and see Ian, but I declined to go till the morning
for fear of the fever and ague. On reaching his
village, I saw many people about, and feared that I
had been led into a snare; but I at once entered into
his house to talk and pray with him, as he appeared
to be dying. After prayer, I discovered that I was

left alone with him, and that all the people had retired from the village; and I knew that, according to their custom, this meant mischief. Ian said,—

"Come near me, and sit by my bedside to talk with me, Missi."

I did so, and while speaking to him he lay as if lost in a swoon of silent meditation. Suddenly he drew from the sugar-cane leaf thatch close to his bed, a large butcher-like knife, and instantly feeling the edge of it with his other hand, he pointed it to within a few inches of my heart and held it quivering there, all a-tremble with excitement. I durst neither move nor speak, except that my heart kept praying to the Lord to spare me, or if my time was come to take me home to Glory with Himself. There passed a few moments of awful suspense. My sight went and came. Not a word had been spoken, except to Jesus; and then Ian wheeled the knife around, thrust it into the sugar-cane leaf, and cried to me,—

"Go, go quickly!"

Next moment I was on the road. Not a living soul was to be seen about the village. I understood then that it had been agreed that Ian was to kill me, and that they had all withdrawn so as not to witness it, so that when the Man-of-war came to inquire about me Ian would be dead, and no punishment could overtake the murderer. I walked quietly till quite free of the village, lest some hid in their houses might observe me. Thereafter, fearing that they, finding I had escaped, might overtake and murder me, I ran for my life a weary four miles till I reached the Mission House, faint, yet praising God for such a deliverance. Poor Ian died soon after, and his people strangled one of his wives and hanged another, and took out the three bodies together in a canoe and sank them in the sea.

Miaki was jubilant over having killed his enemy by Nahak; but the Inland people now assembled in thousands to help Sirawia and his brother to avenge that death on Miaki, Nouka and Karewick. These, on the other hand, boasted that they would kill all their enemies by Nahak-sorcery, and would call up a hurricane to destroy their houses, fruit trees, and plantations. Miaki and a number of his men also came to the Mission House; but, observing his sullen countenance, I asked kindly after his wife who was about to be confined, and gave a blanket, a piece of calico, and a bit of soap as a present for the baby. He seemed greatly pleased, whispered something to his men, and peaceably withdrew. Immediately after Miaki's threat about bringing a storm, one of their great hurricanes actually smote that side of the island and laid everything waste. His enemies were greatly enraged, and many of the injured people united with them in demanding revenge on Miaki. Hitherto I had done everything in my power to prevent war, but now it seemed inevitable, and both parties sent word that if Abraham and I kept to the Mission House no one would harm us. We had little faith in any of their promises, but there was no alternative for us.

On the following Saturday, 18th January, 1862, the war began. Musket after musket was discharged quite near us, and the bush all round rang with the yell of their war-cry, which if once heard will never be forgotten. It came nearer and nearer, for Miaki fled, and his people took shelter behind and around our house. We were placed in the heart of danger, and the balls flew thick all around us. In the afternoon Ian's brother and his party retired, and Miaki quickly sent messengers and presents to the Inikahimini and Kaserumini districts, to assemble all their people and help him "to fight Missi and the Tannese who were friends of the Worship." He said,—

"Let us cook his body and Abraham's, and distribute them to every village on this side of the island!"

Yet all the while Miaki assured me that he had sent a friendly message. The war went on, and poor Nowar the Chief protected us, till he had a spear broken into his right knee. The enemy would have carried him off to feast on his body; but his young men, shouting wildly his name and battle-cry, rushed in with great impetuosity and carried their wounded Chief home in triumph. The Inland people now discharged muskets at my house and beat against the walls with their clubs. They smashed in the door and window of our store-room, broke open boxes and casks, tore my books to pieces and scattered them

about, and carried off everything for which they cared,
including my boat, mast, oars, and sails. They broke
into Abraham's house and plundered it; after which
they made a rush at the bedroom, into which we
were locked, firing muskets, yelling, and trying to
break it in. A Chief, professing to be sorry for us,
called me to the window, but on seeing me he sent a
tomahawk through it, crying,—

"Come on, let us kill him now!"

I replied, "My Jehovah God will punish you; a
Man-of-war will come and punish you, if you kill
Abraham, his wife, or me."

He retorted, "It's all lies about a Man-of-war!
They did not punish the Erromangans. They are
afraid of us. Come on, let us kill them!"

· He raised his tomahawk and aimed to strike my
forehead, many muskets were uplifted as if to shoot,
so I raised a revolver in my right hand and pointed
it at them. The Rev. Joseph Copeland had left it
with me on a former visit. I did not wish it, but he
insisted upon leaving it, saying that the very knowledge that I had such a weapon might save my life.
Truly, on this occasion it did so. Though it was
harmless, they fell back quickly. My immediate
assailant dropped to the ground, crying,—

"Missi has got a short musket! He will shoot
you all!"

After lying flat on the ground for a little, they all
got up and ran to the nearest bush, where they continued yelling about and showing their muskets.

Towards nightfall they left, loaded with the plunder of the store and of Abraham's house. So God once more graciously protected us from falling into their cruel hands.

In the evening, after they left, I went to Miaki and Nouka. They professed great sorrow at what had taken place, and pretended to have given them a present of food not to do us further injury. But Nowar informed us that, on the contrary, they had hired them to return and kill us next morning and plunder everything on the Mission premises. Miaki, with a sneer, said,—

"Missi, where was Jehovah to-day? There was no Jehovah to-day to protect you. It's all lies about Jehovah. They will come and kill you, and Abraham, and his wife, and cut your bodies into pieces to be cooked and eaten in every village upon Tanna."

I said, "Surely, when you had planned all this, and brought them to kill us and steal all our property, Jehovah did protect us, or we would not have been here!"

He replied, "There was no Jehovah to-day! We have no fear of any Man-of-war. They dare not punish us. They durst not punish the Erromangans for murdering the Gordons. They will talk to us and say we must not do so again, and give us a present. That is all. We fear nothing. The talk of all Tanna is that we will kill you and seize all your property to-morrow."

I warned him that the punishment of a Man-of-war can only reach the body and the land; but that Jehovah's punishment reached both body and soul in Time and in Eternity.

He replied: "Who fears Jehovah? He was not here to protect you to-day!":

"Yes," I said, "my Jehovah God is here now. He hears all we say, sees all we do, and will punish the wicked and protect His own people."

After this, a number of the people sat down around me, and I prayed with them. But I left with a very heavy heart, feeling that Miaki was evidently bent on our destruction.

I sent Abraham to consult Nowar, who had defended us till disabled by a spear in the right knee. He sent a canoe by Abraham, advising me to take some of my goods in it to his house by night, and he would try to protect them and us. The risk was so great, we could only take a very little. Enemies were on every hand to cut off our flight, and Miaki, the worst of all, whose village had to be passed in going to Nowar's. In the darkness of the Mission House, we durst not light a candle for fear of some one seeing and shooting us. Not one of Nowar's men durst come to help us. But in the end it made no difference, for Nowar and his men kept what was taken there as their portion of the plunder. Abraham, his wife, and I waited anxiously for the morning light. Miaki, the false and cruel, came to assure us that the Heathen would not return that day. Yet, as daylight came in, Miaki himself stood and blew a great conch not far from our house. I ran out to see why this trumpet-shell had been blown, and found it was the signal for a great company of howling armed savages to rush down the hill on the other side of the bay and make straight for the Mission House. We had not a moment to lose. To have remained would have been certain death to us all, and also to Matthew, a Teacher just arrived from Mr. Mathieson's Station. Though I am by conviction a strong Calvinist, I am no Fatalist. I held on while one gleam of hope remained. Escape for life was now the only path of duty. I called the Teachers, locked the door, and made quickly for Nowar's village. There was not a moment left to carry anything with us. In the issue, Abraham, his wife, and I lost all our earthly goods, and all our clothing except what we had on. My Bible, the few translations which I had made into Tannese, and a light pair of blankets I carried with me.

To me the loss was bitter, but as God had so ordered it, I tried to bow with resignation. All my deceased wife's costly outfit, her piano, silver, cutlery, books, etc., with which her dear parents had provided her, besides all that I had in the world ; also a box worth £56, lately arrived, full of men's clothing and medicine, the gift of my dear friends, Samuel Wilson, Esq., and Mrs. Wilson, of Geelong. The Sandal-wood Traders bought all the stolen property for tobacco, powder, balls, caps, and shot. One Trader gathered together a number of my books in a sadly torn and

wasted condition and took them to Aneityum, demanding £10 from Dr. Geddie for his trouble. He
had to pay him £7 10s., which I repaid to him on
my second return to the Islands. This, by way of
digression, only to show how white and black
Heathenism meet together.

Let us return to the morning of our flight. We
could not take the usual path along the beach, for
there our enemies would have quickly overtaken us.
We entered the bush in the hope of getting away
unobserved. But a cousin of Miaki, evidently secreted
to watch us, sprang from behind a bread-fruit tree,
and swinging his tomahawk, aimed it at my brow
with a fiendish look. Avoiding it, I turned upon him
and said in a firm bold voice,—

" If you dare to strike me, my Jehovah God will
punish you. He is here to defend me now !"

The man, trembling, looked all round as if to see
the God who was my defender, and the tomahawk
gradually lowered at his side. With my eye fixed
upon him, I gradually moved backwards in the track
of the Teachers, and God mercifully restrained him
from following me.

On reaching Nowar's village unobserved, we found
the people terror-stricken, crying, rushing about in
despair at such a host of armed savages approaching.
I urged them to ply their axes, cut down trees, and
blockade the path. For a little they wrought vigorously at this; but when, so far as eye could reach,
they saw the shore covered with armed men rushing

on towards their village, they were overwhelmed with fear, they threw away their axes and weapons of war, they cast themselves headlong on the ground, and they knocked themselves against the trees as if to court death before it came. They cried,—

'"Missi, it's of no use! We will all be killed and eaten to-day! See what a host are coming against us."

Mothers snatched up little children and ran to hide in the bush. Others waded as far as they could into the sea with them, holding their heads above the water. The whole village collapsed in a condition of indescribable terror. Nowar, lame with his wounded knee, got a canoe turned upside-down and sat upon it where he could see the whole approaching multitude. He said,—

"Missi, sit down beside me, and pray to our Jehovah God, for if He does not send deliverance now, we are all dead men. They will kill us all on your account, and that quickly. Pray, and I will watch!"

They had gone to the Mission House and broken in the door, and finding that we had escaped, they rushed on to Nowar's village. For, as they began to plunder the bed-room, Nouka said,—

"Leave everything. Missi will come back for his valuable things at night, and then we will get them and him also!"

So he nailed up the door, and they all marched for Nowar's. We prayed as one can only pray when in

the jaws of death and on the brink of Eternity. We
felt that God was near, and omnipotent to do what
seemed best in His sight. When the savages were
about three hundred yards off, at the foot of a hill
leading up to the village, Nowar touched my knee,
saying,—

"Missi, Jehovah is hearing! They are all standing
still."

Had they come on they would have met with no
opposition, for the people were scattered in terror.
On gazing shorewards, and round the Harbour, as far
as we could see, was a dense host of warriors, but all
were standing still, and apparently absolute silence
prevailed. We saw a messenger or herald running
along the approaching multitude, delivering some
tidings as he passed, and then disappearing in the
bush. To our amazement, the host began to turn,
and slowly marched back in great silence, and entered
the remote bush at the head of the Harbour. Nowar
and his people were in ecstasies, crying out,—

"Jehovah has heard Missi's prayer! Jehovah has
protected us and turned them away back."

We were on that day His trusting and defenceless
children; would you not, had you been one of our
circle, have joined with us in praising the Lord God
for deliverance from the jaws of death? I know not
why they turned back; but I have no doubt it was
the doing of God to save our lives.

We learned that they all assembled in a cleared
part of the bush and there held a great wrangling

palaver. Nouka and Miaki advised them first to
fight Manuman and his people. They said,—

"His brother, the Sacred Man Kanini, killed Ian
by Nahak. He is a friend of Missi and of the Worship.
He also sent the hurricane to destroy us. They
have plenty of yams and pigs. Let us fight and
plunder them, and when they are out of the way, we
will be strong to destroy Missi and the Worship."

On this the whole mass went and attacked
Manuman's first village, where they murdered two of
his men, two women, and two children. The inhabitants fled, and all the sick, the feeble, and the
children who fell into their hands were reported to
us to be murdered, cooked, and eaten. Led on by
Miaki, they plundered and burned seven villages.

About mid-day, Nouka and Miaki sent their cousin
Jonas, who had always been friendly to me, to say
that I might return to my house in safety, as they
were now carrying the war inland. Jonas had spent
some years on Samoa, and been much with Traders in
Sydney, and spoke English well ; but we felt they
were deceiving us. That night, Abraham ventured
to creep near the Mission House, to test whether we
might return, and save some valuable things, and get
a change of clothing. The house appeared to stand
as when they nailed up the door. But a large party
of Miaki's allies at once enclosed Abraham, and, after
asking many questions about me, they let him go
since I was not there. Had I gone there, they would
certainly that night have killed me. Again, at mid-

P.   21

night, Abraham and his wife and Matthew went to the Mission House, and found Nouka, Miaki, and Karewick near by, concealed in the bush among the reeds. Once more they enclosed them, thinking I was there too, but Nouka, finding that I was not, cried out,—

"Don't kill them just now! Wait till Missi comes."

Hearing this, Matthew slipped into the bush and escaped. Abraham's wife waded into the sea, and they allowed her to get away. Abraham was allowed to go to the Mission House, but he too crept into the bush, and after an anxious waiting they all came back to me in safety. We now gave up all hope of recovering anything from the house.

Towards morning, when Miaki and his men saw that I was not coming back to deliver myself into their hands, they broke up my house and stole all they could carry away. They tore my books, and scattered them about. They took away the type of my printing-press, to be made into bullets for their muskets. For similar uses they melted down the zinc lining of my boxes, and everything else that could be melted. What they could not take away, they destroyed. I lay on the ground all night, concealed in an outhouse of Nowar's, but it was a sleepless and anxious night, not only to me and my Aneityumese, but also to Nowar and his people.

Next day, the attack was renewed by the three Chiefs on the district of my dear friend Manuman. His people fled ; the villages were burned ; all who came in their way were killed, and all food and property carried away. At night they returned to keep watch over Nowar and me. When darkness was setting in, Miaki sent for me to go and speak with him, but Nowar and the Aneityumese were all so opposed to it that I did not go. Messages were sent to Nowar, threatening to kill him and his people for protecting me, and great excitement prevailed.

Another incident added horror to the memories of this day. A savage from Erromanga, living with Nowar, had gone to the war that day. He got near a village unobserved, climbed into a tree, and remained there watching. After midday, Kamkali, a true friend of mine, the Chief of his village, came home wearied from the war, got his blanket, stealthily crept into a quiet place in the bush, rolled himself up, and lay down to sleep; for, according to their custom, the leading warriors in times of conflict seldom sleep in their own houses, and seldom twice in the same place even in the bush, for fear of personal danger. The Erromangan, having watched till he was sound asleep, crept to where he lay, raised his club and smashed in his skull. He told, when he came home, how the blood ran from nose, mouth, and ears, with a gurgling sound in his throat, and after a few convulsive struggles all was over! And the people around Nowar praised him for his deed. Cocoa-nuts were brought for him to drink, and food was presented before him in large quantities, as to one who had done something noble. For safety, he was put into the same house where I had to sit, and even Nowar honoured him. I watched for the workings of a natural man's conscience under the guilt of murder. When left alone, he shook every now and then with agitation, and started round with a terrified gaze. He looked the picture of a man who felt that he had done to his neighbour what he would not have liked another to do to him. I wonder if that consciousness ever dies out, in the lowest and worst, that last voice of God in the soul?

That very night, Nowar declared that I must leave his village before morning, else he and his people would be killed for protecting me. He advised me, as the sea was good, to try for Mr. Mathieson's Station; but he objected to my taking away any of my property—he would soon follow with it himself! But how to sail? Miaki had stolen my boat, mast, sails, and oars, as also an excellent canoe made for me and paid for by me on Aneityum; and he had threatened to shoot any person that assisted me to launch either the one or the other. The danger, however, was so great that Nowar said,—

"You cannot remain longer in my house! My son will guide you to the large chestnut tree in my plantation in the bush. Climb up into it, and remain there till the moon rises."

Being entirely at the mercy of such doubtful and vacillating friends, I, though perplexed, felt it best to obey. I climbed into the tree, and was left there alone in the bush. The hours I spent there live all before me as if it were but of yesterday. I heard the frequent discharging of muskets, and the yells of the savages. Yet I sat there among the branches, as safe in the arms of Jesus! Never, in all my sorrows, did my Lord draw nearer to me, and speak more soothingly in my soul, than when the moonlight flickered among these chestnut leaves, and the night air played on my throbbing brow, as I told all my heart to Jesus. Alone, yet not alone! If it be to glorify my God, I will not grudge to spend many nights alone in such a tree, to feel again my Saviour's spiritual presence, to enjoy His consoling fellowship. If thus thrown back upon your own soul, alone, all, all alone, in the midnight, in the bush, in the very embrace of death itself, have you a Friend that will not fail you then?

Gladly would I have lingered there for one night of comparative peace! But, about midnight, Nowar sent his son to call me down from the tree, and to guide me to the shore where he himself was, as it was now time to take to sea in the canoe. Pleading for my Lord's continuing presence, I had to obey. My life and the lives of my Aneityumese now hung upon a very slender thread, and was almost equally at risk from our friends so-called, and from our enemies. Had I been a stranger to Jesus and to prayer, my reason would verily have given way, but my comfort and joy sprang up out of these: "I will never leave thee, nor forsake thee; lo, I am with you alway!" Pleading these promises, I followed my guide. We reached the beach, just inside the Harbour; at a beautiful white sandy bay on Nowar's ground, from which our canoe was to start. A good number of the Natives had assembled there to see us off. Arkurat, having got a large roll of calico from me for the loan of his canoe, hid it away, and then refused the canoe, saying that if he had to escape with his family he would require it. He demanded, for the loan of his canoe, an axe, a sail for his canoe, and a pair of blankets. As Karis had the axe and another had the quilt, I gave the quilt to him for a sail, and the axe and blankets for the canoe. In fact, these few relics of our earthly all at Nowar's were coveted by the savages and endangered our lives, and it was as well to get rid of them altogether. He cruelly proposed a small canoe for two; but I had hired the canoe for five, and insisted upon getting it, as he had been well paid for it. As he only laughed and mocked us, I prepared to start and travel overland to Mr. Mathieson's Station. He then said,—

'My wrath is over! You may take it and go."

We launched it, but now he refused to let us go till daylight. He had always been one of my best friends, but now appeared bent on a quarrel, so I had to exercise much patience with him and them. Having launched it, he said I had hired the canoe but not the paddles. I protested,—

"Surely you know we hired the paddles too. What could we do without paddles?"

But Arkurat lay down and pretended to have fallen asleep, snoring on the sand, and could not be awaked. I appealed to Nowar, who only said,—

"That is his conduct, Missi, our conduct!"

I replied, "As he has got the blankets which I saved to keep me from ague and fever, and I have nothing left now but the clothes I have on, surely you will give me paddles."

Nowar gave me one. Returning to the village, friends gave me one each till I got other three. Now Arkurat started up, and refused to let us go. A Chief and one of his men, who lived on the other side of the island near to where we were going, and who was hired by me to go with us and help in paddling the canoe, drew back also and refused to go. Again I offered to leave the canoe, and walk overland if possible, when Faimungo, the Chief who had refused to go with us, came forward and said,—

"Missi, they are all deceiving you! The sea is so rough, you cannot go by it; and if you should get round the weather point, Miaki has men appointed to shoot you as you pass the Black Rocks, while by land all the paths are guarded by armed men. I tell you the truth, having heard all their talk. Miaki and Karewick say they hate the Worship, and will kill you. They killed your goats, and stole all your property yesterday. Farewell!"

The Teachers, the boy, and I now resolved to enter the canoe and attempt it, as the only gleam of hope left to us. After Faimungo came, the man to whom the canoe belonged had withdrawn from us, it having transpired that Miaki would not attack us that night, as other game had attracted his savage eyes. My party of five now embarked in our frail canoe; Abraham first, I next, Matthew after me, the boy at the steering paddle, and Abraham's wife sitting in the bottom, where she might hold on while it continued to float. For a mile or more we got away nicely under the lee of the island, but when we turned to go south for Mr. Mathieson's Station, we met the full force of wind and sea, every wave breaking over and almost swamping our canoe. The Native lad at the helm paddle stood up crying,—

"Missi, this is the conduct of the sea! It swallows up all who seek its help."

I answered, "We do not seek help from it but from Jehovah Jesus."

Our danger became very great, as the sea broke over and lashed around us. My faithful Aneityumese, overcome with terror, threw down their paddles, and Abraham said,—

"Missi, we are all drowned now! We are food for the sharks. We might as well be eaten by the Tannese as by fishes; but God will give us life with Jesus in heaven!"

I seized the paddle nearest me; I ordered Abraham to seize another within his reach; I enjoined Matthew to bail the canoe for life, and the lad to keep firm in his seat, and I cried,—

"Stand to your post, and let us return! Abraham,

where is now your faith in Jesus? Remember, He is Ruler on sea as on land. Abraham, pray and ply your paddle! Keep up stroke for stroke with me, as our lives depend on it. Our God can protect us. Matthew, bail with all your might. Don't look round on the sea and fear. Let us pray to God and ply our paddles, and He will save us yet!"

Dear old Abraham said,—

"Thank you for that, Missi. I will be strong. I pray to God and ply my paddle. God will save us!"

With much labour, and amid deadly perils, we got the canoe turned; and after four hours of a terrible struggle, we succeeded, towards daylight as the tide turned, in again reaching smooth water. With God's blessing we at last reached the shore, exactly where we had left it five hours ago!

Now drenched and weary, with the skin of our hands sticking to the paddles, we left the canoe on the reef and waded ashore. Many Natives were there, and looked sullen and disappointed at our return. Katasian, the lad who had been with us, instantly fled for his own land; and the Natives reported that he was murdered soon after. Utterly exhausted, I lay down on the sand and instantly fell into a deep sleep. By-and-by I felt some one pulling from under my head the native bag in which I carried my Bible and the Tannese translations—the all that had been saved by me from the wreck! Grasping the bag, I sprang to my feet, and the man ran away. My Teachers had also a hedging knife,

a useless revolver, and a fowling-piece, the sight of
which, though they had been under the salt water for
hours, God used to restrain the savages. Calling my
Aneityumese near, we now in united prayer and
kneeling on the sands committed each other unto the
Lord God, being prepared for the last and worst.

As I sat meditating on the issues, Faimungo, the
friendly Inland Chief, again appeared to warn us of
our danger, now very greatly increased by our being
driven back from the sea. All Nowar's men had
fled, and were hid in the bush and in rocks along the
shore; while Miaki was holding a meeting not half
a mile away, and preparing to fall upon us. Faimungo said,—

"Farewell, Missi, I am going home. I don't wish
to see the work and the murders of this morning."

He was Nowar's son-in-law. He had always been
truthful and kindly with me. His home was about
half-way across the island, on the road that we
wanted to go, and under sudden impulse I said,—

"Faimungo, will you let us follow you? Will you
show us the path? When the Mission Ship arrives, I
will give you three good axes, blankets, knives, fish
hooks, and many things you prize."

The late hurricanes had so destroyed and altered
the paths, that only Natives who knew them well
could follow them. He trembled much and said,—

"Missi, you will be killed. Miaki and Karewick
will shoot you. I dare not let you follow. I have

only about twenty men, and your following might endanger us all."

I urged him to leave at once, and we would follow of our own accord. I would not ask him to protect us; but if he betrayed us and helped the enemy to kill us, I assured him that our God would punish him. If he spared us, he would be rewarded well; and if killed against his wishes, God would not be angry at him. He said,—

"Seven men are with me now, and thirteen are to follow. I will not now send for them. They are with Miaki and Nouka. I will go; but if you follow, you will be killed on the way. You may follow me as far as you can!"

Off he started to Nowar's, and got a large load of my stolen property, blankets, sheets, etc., which had fallen to his lot. He called his seven men, who had also shared in the plunder, and, to avoid Miaki's men, they ran away under a large cocoa-nut grove skirting the shore, calling,—

"Be quick! Follow and keep as near to us as you can."

Though Nowar had got a box of my rice and appropriated many things from the plunder of the Mission House besides the goods entrusted to his care, and got two of my goats killed and cooked for himself and his people, yet now he would not give a particle of food to my starving Aneityumese or myself, but hurried us off, saying,—

"I will eat all your rice and keep all that has been

left with me in payment for my lame knee and for
my people fighting for you!"

My three Aneityumese and I started after Faimungo and his men. We could place no confidence
in any of them; but, feeling that we were in the
Lord's hands, it appeared to be our only hope of
escaping instant death. We got away unobserved
by the enemies. We met several small parties of
friends in the Harbour, apparently glad to see us trying to get away. But about four miles on our way,
we met a large party of Miaki's men, all armed, and
watching as outposts. Some were for shooting us,
but others hesitated. Every musket was, however,
raised and levelled at me. Faimungo poised his
great spear and said, "No, you shall not kill Missi
to-day. He is with me." Having made this flourish,
he strode off after [his own men, and my Aneityumese followed, leaving me face to face with a ring of
levelled muskets. Sirawia, who was in command of
this party, and who once like Nowar had been my
friend, said to me, Judas like, "My love to you, Missi."
But he also shouted after Faimungo, "Your conduct
is bad in taking the Missi away; leave him to us to
be killed!"

I then turned upon him, saying, "Sirawia, I love
you all. You must know that I sought only your
good. I gave you medicine and food when you and
your people were sick and dying under measles;
I gave you the very clothing you wear. Am I not
your friend? Have we not often drunk tea and eaten

together in my house? Can you stand there and see your friend shot? If you do, my God will punish you severely."

He then whispered something to his company which I did not hear; and, though their muskets were still raised, I saw in their eyes that he had restrained them. I therefore began gradually to move backwards, still keeping my eyes fixed on them, till the bush hid them from my view, whereon I turned and ran after my party, and God kept the enemy from following. I would like to think that Sirawia only uttered the cruel words which I heard as a blind to save his own life; for at this time he was joined to Miaki's party, his own people having risen against him, and had to dissemble his friendly feelings towards me. Poor Sirawia! Well I knew that Miaki would only use him as a tool for selfish interests, and sacrifice him at last. All this showed how dangers grew around our path. Still we trusted in Jehovah Jesus, and pressed on in flight. A second hostile party encountered us, and with great difficulty we also got away from them. Soon thereafter a friendly company crossed our path. We learned from them that the enemies had slaughtered other two of Manuman's men, and burned several villages with fire. Another party of the enemy encountered us, and were eager for our lives. But this time Faimungo withstood them firmly, his men encircled us, and he said, "I am not afraid now, Missi; I am feeling stronger near my own land!"

Hurrying still onwards, we came to that village on their high ground called Aneai, *i.e.,* Heaven. The sun was oppressively hot, the path almost unshaded, and our whole party very exhausted, especially Faimungo, carrying his load of stolen goods. So here he sat down on the village dancing ground for a smoke, saying,—

"Missi, I am near my own land now. We can rest with safety."

In a few minutes, however, he started up, he and his men, in wild excitement. Over a mountain, behind the village and above it, there came the shoutings, and anon the tramp, tramp of a multitude making rapidly towards us. Faimungo got up and planted his back against a tree. I stood beside him, and the Aneityumese woman and the two men stood near me, while his men seemed prepared to flee. At full speed a large body of the tallest and most powerful men that I had seen on Tanna came rushing on and filled the dancing ground. They were all armed, and flushed with their success in war. A messenger had informed them of our escape, probably from Miaki, and they had crossed the country to intercept us. Faimungo was much afraid, and said,—

"Missi, go on in that path, you and your Aneityumese; and I will follow when I have had a smoke and a talk with these men."

I replied, "No, I will stand by your side till you go; and if I am killed, it will be by your side. I will not leave you."

He implored us to go on, but that I knew would be certain death. They began urging one another to kill us, but I looked round them as calmly as possible, saying, "My Jehovah God will punish you here and hereafter, if you kill me or any of His servants."

A killing-stone, thrown by one of the savages, grazed poor old Abraham's cheek, and the dear soul gave such a look at me, and then upwards, as if to say, "Missi, I was nearly away to Jesus." A club was also raised to follow the blow of the killing-stone, but God baffled the aim. They encircled us in a deadly ring, and one kept urging another to strike the first blow or fire the first shot. My heart rose up to the Lord Jesus; I saw Him watching all the scene. My peace came back to me like a wave from God. I realized that I was immortal till my Master's work with me was done. The assurance came to me, as if a voice out of Heaven had spoken, that not a musket would be fired to wound us, not a club prevail to strike us, not a spear leave the hand in which it was held vibrating to be thrown, not an arrow leave the bow, or a killing-stone the fingers, without the permission of Jesus Christ, whose is all power in Heaven and on Earth. He rules all Nature, animate and inanimate, and restrains even the savage of the South Seas. In that awful hour I saw His own words, as if carved in letters of fire upon the clouds of Heaven: "Seek, and ye shall find. Whatsoever ye shall ask in My name, that will I do, that

the Father may be glorified in the Son." I could
understand how Stephen and John saw the glorified
Saviour as they gazed up through suffering and persecution to the Heavenly Throne ! Yet I never could
say that on such occasions I was entirely without fear.
Nay, I have felt my reason reeling, my sight coming
and going, and my knees smiting together when thus
brought close to a violent death, but mostly under
the solemn thought of being ushered into Eternity
and appearing before God. Still, I was never left
without hearing that promise in all its consoling and
supporting power coming up through the darkness.
and the anguish, " Lo, I am with you alway." And
with Paul I could say, even in this dread moment
and crisis of being, " I am persuaded that neither
death nor life . . . nor any other creature, shall
be able to separate us from the love of God which is
in Christ Jesus our Lord."

Faimungo and others now urged us to go on in the
path. I said, " Faimungo, why are we to leave you?
My God heard your promise not to betray me. He
knows now what is in your heart and in mine. I
will not leave you ; and if I am to die, I will die by
your side."

He replied, " Now, I go on before; Missi, keep
close to me."

His men had gone, and I persuaded my Aneityumese to follow them. At last, with a bound, Faimungo started after them. I followed, keeping as
near him as I could, pleading with Jesus to protect

me or to take me home to Glory. The host of armed men also ran along on each side with their weapons ready; but leaving everything to Jesus, I ran on as if they were my escort, or as if I saw them not. If any reader wonders how they were restrained, much more would I, unless I believed that the same Hand that restrained the lions from touching Daniel held back these savages from hurting me! We came to a stream crossing our path. With a bound all my party cleared it, ran up the bank opposite, and disappeared in the bush. "Faint yet pursuing," I also tried the leap, but I struck the bank and slid back on my hands and knees towards the stream. At this moment I heard a crash above my head amongst the branches of an overhanging tree, and I knew that a killing-stone had been thrown, and that that branch had saved me. Praising my God, I scrambled up on the other side, and followed the track of my party into the bush. The savages gazed after me for a little in silence, but no one crossed the stream; and I saw them separate into two, one portion returning to the village and another pressing inland. With what gratitude did I recognise the Invisible One who brought their counsels to confusion!

I found my party resting in the bush, and amazed to see me escaped alive from men who were thirsting for my blood. Faimungo and his men received me with demonstrations of joy; perhaps feeling a little ashamed of their own cowardice. He now ascended

the mountain and kept away from the common path
to avoid other Native bands. At every village enemies
to the Worship were ready to shoot us. But I kept
close to our guide, knowing that the fear of shooting
him would prevent their shooting at me, as he was the
most influential Chief in all that section of the island.

One party said, "Miaki and Karewick said that
Missi made the sickness and the hurricanes, and we
ought to kill him."

Faimungo replied, "They lie about Missi! It is
our own bad conduct that makes us sick."

They answered, "We don't know who makes the
sickness; but our fathers have taught us to kill all
foreign men."

Faimungo, clutching club and spear, exclaimed,
standing betwixt them and us, "You won't kill Missi
to-day!"

In the flight we passed springs and streamlets, but
though parched with sickening thirst, not one of us
durst stoop down to drink, as we should have been
almost certainly killed in the act. Faimungo now
sent his own men home by a near path, and guided
us himself till we were close upon the shore. There,
sitting down he said,—

"Missi, I have now fulfilled my promise. I am so
tired, I am so afraid, I dare not go farther. My love to
you all. Now go on quickly! Three of my men will go
with you to the next rocks. Go quickly! Farewell."

These men went on a little, and then said, "Missi,
we dare not go! Faimungo is at war with the

people of the next land. You must keep straight along this path."

So they turned and ran back to their own village.

To us this district was especially perilous. Many years ago the Aneityumese had joined in a war against the Tannese of this tribe, and the thirst for revenge yet existed in their hearts, handed down from sire to son. Besides, Miaki had incited the people here to murder the Teachers and me if we attempted to escape this way. Most providentially the men were absent on a war expedition, and we saw only three lads and a great number of women and children, who ran off to the bush in terror. In the evening the enraged savages of another district assaulted the people of the shore villages for allowing us to pass, and, though sparing their lives, broke in pieces their weapons of war—a very grievous penalty. In the next district, as we hasted along the shore, two young men came running after us, poising their quivering spears. I took the useless revolver out of my little native basket, and raising it cried,—

"Beware! Lay down your spears at once on the sand, and carry my basket to the next landing at the black rocks."

They threw their spears on the sand, lifted the bag, and ran on before us to the rocks which formed the march betwixt them and their enemies. Laying it down, they said appealingly, "Missi, let us return to our home!" And how they did run, fearing the pursuit of their foes.

In the next land we saw none. After that we saw crowds all along, some friendly, others unfriendly, but they let us pass on, and with the blessing of Almighty God we drew near to Mr. Mathieson's Station in safety. Here a man gave me a cocoanut for each of our party, which we greatly required, having tasted nothing all that day, and very little for several days before. We were so weak that only the struggle for life enabled us to keep our feet; yet my poor Aneityumese never complained and never halted, not even the woman. The danger and excitement kept us up in the race for life, and by the blessing of God we were now approaching the Mission House, praising God for His wonderful deliverances.

Hearing of our coming, Mr. Mathieson came running to meet me. They had heard of my leaving my own Station, and they thought I was dead! They were themselves both very weak; their only child had just been laid in the grave, and they were in great grief and in greater peril. We praised the Lord for permitting us to meet; we prayed for support, guidance, and protection; and resolved now, in all events, to stand by each other till the last.

Before I left the Harbour I wrote and left with Nowar letters to be given to the Captains of any vessels which called, for the first, and the next, and the next, telling them of our great danger, that Mr. Mathieson was almost without food, and that I would reward them handsomely if they would call at the Station and remove any of us who might be spared thence to Aneityum. Two or three vessels called, and, as I afterwards learned, got my letters ; but, while buying my stolen property from the Natives for tobacco, powder, and balls, they took no further notice of my appeals, and sailed past Mr. Mathieson's straight on to Aneityum. "The tender mercies of the wicked are cruel!"

Let me now cull the leading events from my Journal, that intervened betwixt this date and the final break-up of the Mission on Tanna—at least for a season—though, blessed be God! I have lived to see the light rekindled by my dear friends Mr. and Mrs. Watt, and shining more brightly and hopefully than ever. The candle was quenched, but the candle-stick was not removed!

On Wednesday, 22nd January, 1862, we heard that other three of Manuman's people had been killed and a district burned with fire. Though this poor man was one of Nowar's chief friends, yet I heard him say before my flight, "When so many children are being killed, why do they not send one for food to me and my family? They are as tender and good as the young fowls!" A remark like this lets you see deep into the heart of a Cannibal, and he a sort of half-converted one, if I may use such an expression ; certainly not one of the worst type by any means.

On the 23rd January, Mr. Mathieson sent for Taura, Kati, and Kapuku, his three principal Chiefs, to induce them to promise protection till a vessel called to take us away. They appeared friendly, and promised to do their best. Alas! the promises of the Tannese Chiefs had too often proved to be vain.

On Friday, 24th January, report reached our Station that Miaki and his party, hearing that a friendly Chief had concealed two of Manuman's young men, compelled him to produce them and club them to death before their eyes. Also, that they surrounded Manuman's party on a mountain, and hemmed them in there, dying of starvation and trying to survive on the carcases of the dead and on bark and roots. Also, that Miaki had united all the Chiefs, friends and foes alike, in a bond of blood, to kill every one pertaining to the whole Mission on Tanna. Jesus rules!

On Sunday, the 26th January, thirty persons came to worship at the Mission House. Thereafter, at great risk, we had Worship at three of the nearest and most friendly villages. Amidst all our perils and trials, we preached the Gospel to about one hundred and sixteen persons. It was verily a sowing time of tears; but, despite all that followed, who shall say that it was vain! Twenty years have passed, and now when I am writing this, there is a Church of God singing the praises of Jesus in that very district of Tanna. On leaving the second village, a young lad affectionately took my hand to lead me to the next village; but a sulky, down-browed savage, carrying a ponderous club, also insisted upon accompanying us. I led the way, guided by the lad. Mr. Mathieson got the man to go before him, while he himself followed, constantly watching. Coming to a place where another path branched off from ours, I asked which path we took, and, on turning to the left as instructed by the lad, the savage getting close behind me, swung his huge club over his shoulder to strike me on the head. Mr. Mathieson, springing forward, caught the club from behind with a great cry to me; and I, wheeling instantly, had hold of the club also, and betwixt us we wrested it out of his hands. The poor creature, craven at heart however blood-thirsty, implored us not to kill him. I raised the club threateningly, and cau_ed him to march in front of us till we reached the next village fence. In terror lest these Villagers should kill him, he gladly received back his club, as well as the boy his bow and arrows, and they were lost in the bush in a moment. At the village from which this man and boy had come, one savage brought his musket while we were conducting worship, and sat sullen and scowling at us all the time. Mocking questions were also shouted at us, such as—"Who made the rains, winds, and hurricanes? Who caused all the disease? Who killed Mr. Mathieson's child?" They sneered and scoffed at our answers, and in this Taura the Chief joined the rest. They retorted that trading vessels had called at the Harbour, and that all my clothes and property had been sold for muskets, powder, caps, and balls, so that Miaki and his men had plenty of ammunition for fighting purposes now! After this, feeling that no one could be trusted, we ceased visiting these villages, and refrained from exposing ourselves at any distance from the Mission House.

On the 27th, at daylight, a vessel was seen in the offing, as if to tantalize us. The Captain had been at the Harbour, and had received my letter from Nowar. I hoisted a flag to induce him to send or come on shore, but he sailed off for Aneityum, bearing the plunder of my poor Mission House, purchased for ammunition and tobacco from the Natives. He left the news at Aneityum that I had been driven from my Station some time ago, and was believed to have been murdered.

On the 29th January, the young Chief Kapuku came and handed to Mr. Mathieson his own and his father's war-gods and household idols. They consisted chiefly of a basket of small and peculiar stones, much worn and shining with use. He said,—

"While many are trying to kill you and drive the worship of Jehovah from this island, I give up my gods, and will send away all Heathen idols from my land."

On the 31st, we learned that a party of Miaki's men were going about Mr. Mathieson's district inciting the people to kill us. Faimungo also came to inform us that Miaki was exerting all his artifice to get us and the Worship destroyed. Manuman even sent, from inland, Raki, his adopted son, to tell me of the fearful sufferings that he and his people were now passing through, and that some were killed almost every day. Raki's wife was a Chief's daughter, who, when the war began, returned to her father's care. The savages of Miaki went to her own father's house and compelled him to give her up as an enemy. She was clubbed and feasted on.

. On Sabbath, 2nd February, thirty-two people attended the morning service. I addressed them on the Deluge, its causes and lessons. I showed them a doll, explaining that such carved and painted images could not hear our prayers or help us in our need, that the living Jehovah God only could hear and help. They were much interested, and after Worship carefully examined the doll. Mr. Mathieson and I, committing ourselves to Jesus, went inland and conducted worship at seven villages, listened to by in all about one hundred people. Nearly all appeared friendly. The people of one village had been incited to kill us on our return ; but God guided us to return by another way, and so we escaped.

During the day, on 3rd February, a company of Miaki's men came to the Mission House, and forced Mrs. Mathieson to show them through the premises. Providentially, I had bolted myself that morning into a closet room, and was engrossed with writing. They went through every room in the house and did not see me, concluding I had gone inland. They discharged a musket into our Teacher's house, but afterwards left quietly, greatly disappointed at not finding me. My heart still rose in praise to God for another such deliverance, neither by man nor of man's planning !

Worn out with long watching and many fatigues, I

lay down that night early, and fell into a deep sleep. About ten o'clock the savages again surrounded the Mission House. My faithful dog Clutha, clinging still to me amid the wreck of all else on Earth, sprang quietly upon me, pulled at my clothes, and awoke me, showing danger in her eye glancing on me through the shadows. I silently awoke Mr. and Mrs. Mathieson, who had also fallen asleep. We committed ourselves in hushed prayer to God and watched them, knowing that they could not see us. Immediately a glare of light fell into the room! Men passed with flaming torches; and first they set fire to the Church all round, and then to a reed fence connecting the Church and the dwelling-house. In a few minutes the house, too, would be in flames, and armed savages waiting to kill us on attempting an escape! Taking my harmless revolver in the left hand and a little American tomahawk in the right, I pled with Mr. Mathieson to let me out and instantly again to lock the door on himself and wife. He very reluctantly did so, holding me back and saying,—

"Stop here and let us die together! You will never return!"

I said, "Be quick! Leave that to God. In a few minutes our house will be in flames, and then nothing can save us."

He did let me out, and locked the door again quickly from the inside; and, while his wife and he prayed and watched for me from within, I ran to the burning reed fence, cut it from top to bottom, and

tore it up and threw it back into the flames, so that
the fire could not by it be carried to our dwelling-
house. I saw on the ground shadows, as if something
were falling around me, and started back. Seven or
eight savages had surrounded me, and raised their
great clubs in air. I heard a shout—"Kill him!
kill him!" One savage tried to seize hold of me,
but, leaping from his clutch, I drew the revolver
from my pocket and levelled it as for use, my heart
going up in prayer to my God. I said,—

"Dare to strike me, and my Jehovah God will
punish you! He protects us, and will punish you
for burning His Church, for hatred to His Worship
and people, and for all your bad conduct. We love
you all; and for doing you good only you want to
kill us. But our God is here now to protect us and
to punish you."

They yelled in rage, and urged each other to strike
the first blow, but the Invisible One restrained them.
I stood invulnerable beneath His invisible shield, and
succeeded in rolling back the tide of flame from our
dwelling-house.

At this dread moment occurred an incident, which
my readers may explain as they like, but which
I trace directly to the interposition of my God.
A rushing and roaring sound came from the South,
like the noise of a mighty engine or of muttering thunder. Every head was instinctively turned
in that direction, and they knew, from previous hard
experience, that it was one of their awful tornadoes

of wind and rain. Now, mark, the wind bore the flames away from our dwelling-house, and had it come in the opposite direction, no power on Earth could have saved us from being all consumed! It made the work of destroying the Church only that of a few minutes; but it brought with it a heavy and murky cloud, which poured out a perfect torrent of tropical rain. Now, mark again, the flames of the burning Church were thereby cut off from extending to and seizing upon the reeds and the bush; and, besides, it had become almost impossible now to set fire to our dwelling-house. The stars in their courses were fighting against Sisera! The mighty roaring, of the wind, the black cloud pouring down unceasing torrents, and the whole surroundings, awed those savages into silence. Some began to withdraw from the scene, all lowered their weapons of war, and several, terror-struck, exclaimed,—

"That is Jehovah's rain! Truly their Jehovah God is fighting for them and helping them. Let us away!"

A panic seized upon them; they threw away their remaining torches; in a few moments they had all disappeared in the bush; and I was left alone, praising God for His marvellous works. "O taste and see that God is good! Blessed is the man that trusteth in Him!"

Returning to the door of the Mission House, I cried,—

"Open and let me in. I am now all alone."

Mr. Mathieson let me in, and exclaimed,—

"If ever, in time of need, God sent help and protection to His servants in answer to prayer, He has done so to-night! Blessed be His holy name!"

In fear and in joy we united our praises. Truly our Jesus has all power, not less in the elements of Nature than in the savage hearts of the Tannese. Precious Jesus! Does He not chide us, saying,— "Hitherto ye have asked nothing in My Name. Ask and ye shall receive, that your joy may be full!"? How much help, blessing, and joy we lose every day, because we do not take all to Jesus as we ought! Often since have I wept over His love and mercy in that deliverance, and prayed that every moment of my remaining life may be consecrated to the service of my precious Friend and Saviour!

All through the remainder of that night I lay wide awake keeping watch, my noble little dog lying near me with ears alert. Early in the morning friends came weeping around us. Our enemies were loudly rejoicing. It had been finally resolved to kill us at once, to plunder our house and then to burn it. The noise of the shouting was distinctly heard as they neared the Mission premises, and our weeping, friendly Natives looked terror-struck, and seemed anxious to flee for the bush. But just when the excitement rose to the highest pitch, we heard, or dreamed that we heard, a cry higher still, "Sail O!" We were by this time beginning to distrust almost our very senses; but again and again that cry came rolling up from the shore, and was repeated from crowd to crowd all along the beach, "Sail O ! Sail O !" The shouts of those approaching us gradually ceased, and the whole multitude seemed to have melted away from our view. I feared some cruel deception, and at first peered out very cautiously to spy the land. But yonder in very truth a vessel had sailed into the bay. It was the *Blue Bell*, Captain Hastings. I set fire to the reeds on the side of the hill to attract his attention. I put a black shawl as a flag on one end of the Mission House and a white sheet on the other.

This was one of the vessels that had been to Port Resolution, and had sailed past to Aneityum some time ago. I afterwards saw the mate and some of the men wearing my shirts, which they had bought from the Tannese on their former visit. At the earnest request of Doctors Geddie and Inglis, Mr. Underwood, the owner, had sent Captain Hastings to Tanna to rescue us if yet alive. For this purpose he had brought twenty armed men from Aneityum, who came on shore in two boats in charge of the mate, the notorious Ross Lewin. He returned to the ship with a boat-load of Mr. Mathieson's things, leaving ten of the Natives to help us to pack more and carry them down to the beach, especially what the Missionary thought most valuable.

The two boats were now loaded and ready to start. It was about two o'clock in the afternoon, when a strange and painful trial befell us. Poor dear Mr.

Mathieson, apparently unhinged, locked himself all
alone into what had been his study, telling Mrs.
Mathieson and me to go, for he had resolved to
remain and die on Tanna. We tried to show him
the inconsistency of praying to God to protect us or
grant us means of escape, and then refuse to accept
a rescue sent to us in our last extremity. We argued
that it was surely better to live and work for Jesus
than to die as a self-made martyr, who, in God's
sight, was guilty of self-murder. His wife wept aloud
and pled with him, but all in vain! He refused to
leave or to unlock his door. I then said,—

"It is now getting dark. Your wife must go with
the vessel, but I will not leave you alone. I shall
send a note explaining why I am forced to remain ;
and as it is certain that we shall be murdered whenever the vessel leaves, I tell you God will charge you
with the guilt of our murder."

At this he relented, unlocked the door, and accompanied us to the boats, in which we all immediately left.

Meantime, having lost several hours, the vessel had
drifted leeward ; darkness suddenly settled upon us,
and when we were out at sea we lost sight of her
and she of us. After drifting about for some hours
in a heavy sea and unable to find her, those in charge
of the boats came near for consultation, and, if possible, to save the lives of all. We advised that they
should steer for Port Resolution by the flame of the
Volcano—a never-failing light-house, seen fifty miles

away—and there await the vessel. The boats were
to keep within hearing of each other by constant
calling; but this was soon lost to the ear, though on
arriving in the bay we found they had got to anchor
before us. There we sat in the boats and waited for
the coming day. As the light appeared, we anchored
as far out as possible, beyond the reach of musket
shots; and there without water or food we sat under
a tropical sun till mid-day came, and still there was
no sign of the vessel. The mate at last put all the
passengers and the poorest seamen into one boat
and left her to swing at anchor; while, with a strong
crew in the other, he started off in search of the
vessel.

In the afternoon, Nowar and Miaki came off in a
canoe to visit us. Nowar had on a shirt, but Miaki
was naked and frowning. He urged me to go and
see the Mission House, but as we had seen a body
of men near it I refused to go. Miaki declared that
everything remained as I had left it, but we knew
that he lied. Old Abraham and a party had slipped
on shore in a canoe, and had found the windows
smashed and everything gone except my books,
which were scattered about and torn in pieces. The
armed men there wanted to kill the Aneityumese,
but others said, "Not till we get Missi killed too!"
They learned that Miaki had sold everything that he
could sell to the Traders. The mate and men of the
Blue Bell had on my very clothes. They boasted
that they had bought them for a few figs of tobacco

and for powder, caps, and balls. But they would
not return a single shirt to me, though I was without
a change! We had all been without food in the
boat since the morning before, so Nowar brought
us off a cocoa-nut each, and two very small roasted
yams for the ladies. Those, however, only seemed
to make our thirst the more severe, and we spent a
trying day in that boat under a burning sun. Miaki
said,—

"As our fathers did not destroy Missi Turner's
house, we will not destroy yours."

But after a time, failing to persuade me to accompany him and fall into a trap, he muttered,—

"We have taken everything your house contained,
and would take you too if we could; for we hate
the Worship, it causes all our diseases and deaths;
it goes against our customs, and it condemns the
things we delight in."

Nowar informed me that only a few nights before
this, Miaki and his followers went inland to a village
where last year they had killed ten men. Having
secretly placed a savage at the door of every house,
at a given signal they yelled, and when the terrified
inmates tried to escape they killed almost every man,
woman, and child. Some fled into the bush, others
rushed to the shore. A number of men got into a
canoe to escape, but hearing women and children
crying after them they returned, and taking those
they could with them they killed the rest lest they
should fall alive into Miaki's hands. These are

P.   23

surely " they who through fear of death are all their
lifetime subject to bondage." The Chief and nearly
his whole village were cut off in one night! Not an
uncommon thing in those Islands, where war becomes
chronic, and the thirst for blood becomes insatiable.
The dark places of the Earth are "full of the habita-
tions of horrid cruelty." To have actually lived
amongst the Heathen and seen their life gives a man
a new appreciation of the power and blessings of
the Gospel, even where its influence is only very
imperfectly allowed to guide and restrain the passions
of men. Oh, what will it be when all men in all
nations love and serve the glorious Redeemer!

This Miaki and his followers were a scourge and
terror to the whole island of Tanna. They intensely
hated Nowar, because he would not join in their
cruelties. Yet he and Manuman and Sirawia and
Faimungo continued to survive long after war and
death had swept all the others away. The first three
lived to be very old men, and to the last they made
a profession of being Christians, though their knowledge was very limited and their inconsistencies very
grave and very numerous. Happy is it for us that
we are not the judges, for souls either of the white
or the dark skin, as to how many and grievous
things may be forgiven, and whether there be or be
not that spark of love, that grain of faith which the
Lord the Pitiful will graciously accept and increase![1]

[1] See Appendix A. "The Prayer of the Tannese," etc.

About five o'clock in the evening the vessel hove in sight. Before dark we were all safely on board, and were sailing for Aneityum. Though both Mr. and Mrs. Mathieson had become very weak, they stood the voyage wonderfully. Next day we were all safely landed. We had offered Captain Hastings £20 to take us to Aneityum, but he declined any fare. However, we divided it amongst the mate and crew, for they had every one shown great kindness to us on the voyage. After arriving on Aneityum, Mrs. Mathieson gradually sank under consumption, and fell asleep in Jesus on 11th March, 1862, in the full assurance of a glorious resurrection, and was interred there. Mr. Mathieson, becoming more and more depressed after her death, went over to Mr. Creagh's Station, on Maré, and there died on 14th June, 1862, still trusting in Jesus, and assured that he would soon be with Him in Glory. Never more earnest or more faithful souls entered the Mission field, but they both suffered from weakness and ill-health during all their time on Tanna, and had frequently to seek change by removal for a short period from the island. Their memory is very fragrant to me as fellow-labourers in the Gospel of Jesus.

After their death, I was the only one left alive in all the New Hebrides Mission north of Aneityum to tell the story of those pioneer years, during which were sown the seeds of what is now fast becoming a glorious harvest. Twenty-five years ago, all these dear brethren and sisters who were associated with

me in the work of the Mission were called home to
Glory, to cast their crowns at the feet of Jesus and
enjoy the bliss of the redeemed, while I am privileged
still to toil and pray for the salvation of the poor
Islanders, and plead the cause of the Mission both
in the Colonies and at home, in which work the
Lord has graciously given me undreamt-of success.
My constant desire and prayer are that I may be
spared to see at least one Missionary on every island
of the group, to unfold the riches of redeeming love
and to lead the poor Islanders to Jesus for salvation.

What could be taken in three boats was saved out
of the wreck of Mr. Mathieson's property; but my
earthly all perished, except the Bible and the translations into Tannese. Along with the goods pertaining to the Mission, the property which I had to leave
behind would be undervalued at £600, besides the
value of the Mission House, etc. Often since have I
thought that the Lord stripped me thus bare of all
these interests, that I might with undistracted mind
devote my entire energy to the special work soon to
be carved out for me, and of which at this moment
neither I nor any one had ever dreamed. At any
rate, the loss of my little earthly all, though doubtless
costing me several pangs, was not an abiding sorrow
like that which sprang from the thought that the
Lord's work was broken up at both Stations, and that
the Gospel was for the time driven from Tanna.

In the darkest moment, I never doubted that
ultimately the victory there, as elsewhere, would be

on the side of Jesus, believing that the whole Earth would yet be filled with the glory of the Lord. But I sometimes sorely feared that I might never live to see or hear of that happy day! By the goodness of the Ever-merciful One I have lived to see and hear of a Gospel Church on Tanna, and to read about my dear fellow-Missionaries, Mr. and Mrs. Watt, celebrating the Holy Supper to a Native Congregation of Tannese, amid the very scenes and people where the seeds of faith and hope were planted not only in tears, but tears of blood,—" in deaths oft."

My own intention was to remain on Aneityum, go on with my work of translating the Gospels, and watch the earliest opportunity, as God opened up my way, to return to Tanna. I had, however, got very weak and thin; my health was undoubtedly much shaken by the continued trials and dangers through which we had passed; and therefore, as Dr. and Mrs. Inglis were at home carrying the New Testament through the press in the language of Aneityum, and as Tanna was closed for a season, Dr. Geddie, the Rev. Joseph Copeland, and Mr. Mathieson all urged me to go to Australia by a vessel then in the Harbour and leaving in a few days. My commission was to awaken an interest among the Presbyterian Churches of our Colonies in this New Hebrides Mission which lay at their doors, up till this time sustained by Scotland and Nova Scotia alone. And further, and very specially, to raise money there, if possible, to purchase a new Mission Ship for the work of God in the New Hebrides,—a clamant necessity, which would save all future Missionaries some of the more terrible of the privations and risks of which a few examples have in these pages already been recorded.

After much prayerful deliberation with my brethren and with my own heart before God, I somewhat reluctantly felt constrained to undertake the task. If my story was to be the means of providing more Missionaries for the Islands, and of providing a commodious Ship for the service of the Mission alone, to keep open their communications with the outer world and with Christian influences, not to speak of carrying their provisions at fixed periods, or rescuing them when in troubles and perils from the jaws of death, I was not unwilling to tell it again and again, if the Lord would open up my path. God knows my heart, and any one who really knows me will easily admit, that no selfish or egotistical motive has influenced me in reciting through all the Australasian Colonies, New Zealand, Scotland, and latterly in many parts of England and Ireland, the incidents of my career and experience, first of all on Tanna, and thereafter for nearly twenty years—as the Second Part of my biography will relate—on the neighbouring island of Aniwa; an island entirely given to me by the Lord, the whole population of which became Christian; and they and their race will be my crown of joy and rejoicing in the day of the Lord Jesus.

With regrets, and yet with unquenchable hope for these Islands, I embarked for Australia, having received the solemn promise of my brethren, that in entering upon this great effort I was to be left absolutely free of all control, and empowered to carry out the work as God might seem to guide me, and open up my way. I had only spoken to one man in Sydney; all the doors to influence had therefore to be unlocked, and I had no helper, no leader, but the Spirit of my Lord. The Second Part of this Autobiography, should God spare me to write it, will record His marvellous goodness in using my humble voice and pen and the story of my life for interesting thousands and tens of thousands in the work of Missions, and especially for binding together the children of the Sabbath Schools of Australasia in a Holy League of help to the New Hebrides, which has already borne precious fruit to His glory, and will continue to do so for ages to come.

Oftentimes, while passing through the perils and defeats of my first years in the Mission field on Tanna, I wondered, and perhaps the reader hereof has wondered, why God permitted such things. But on looking back now, I already clearly perceive, and the reader of my future pages will, I think, perceive, that the Lord was thereby preparing me for doing, and providing me materials wherewith to accomplish the best work of all my life—the kindling of the heart of Australian Presbyterianism with a living affection for these Islanders of their own Southern Seas—the binding of all their children into a happy league of shareholders, first in one Mission Ship, and

finally in a larger and more commodious Steam-Auxiliary, and, last of all, in being the instrument under
God of sending out Missionary after Missionary to
the New Hebrides, to claim another island and still
another for Jesus. That work, and all that may
spring from it in time and Eternity, never could have
been accomplished by me, but for first the sufferings
and then the story of my Tanna enterprise !

Some unsophisticated souls who read these pages
will be astonished to learn, but others who know
more of the heartless selfishness of human creatures,
will be quite prepared to hear, that my leaving
Tanna was not a little criticized, and a great deal of
nonsense was written, even in Church Magazines,
about the breaking up of the Mission. All such
criticism came, of course, from men who were themselves destitute of sympathy, and who, probably,
never endured one pang for Jesus in all their comfortable lives. Conscious that I had, to the last inch
of life, tried to do my duty, I left all results in the
hands of my only Lord, and all criticisms to His
unerring judgment. Hard things also were occasionally spoken to my face. One dear friend, for instance, said,—

"You should not have left. You should have
stood at the post of duty till you fell. It would have
been to your honour, and better for the cause of the
Mission, had you been killed at the post of duty like
the Gordons and others."

I replied,—" I regard it as a greater honour to live

and to work for Jesus, than to be a self-made martyr.
God knows that I did not refuse to die; for I stood
at the post of duty, amid difficulty and danger, till
all hope had fled, till everything I had was lost, and
till God, in answer to prayer, sent a means of escape.
I left with a clear conscience, knowing that in doing
so I was following God's leading, and serving the
Mission too. To have remained longer would have
been to incur the guilt of self-murder in the sight of
God."

Never for one moment have I had occasion to
regret the step then taken. The Lord has so used
me, during the five-and-twenty years that have
passed over me since my farewell to Tanna, as to
stamp the event with His own most gracious ap-
proval. Oh, to see a Missionary, and Christian
Teachers, planted on every island of the New
Hebrides! For this I labour, and wait, and pray.
To help on the fulfilment thereof is the sacred work
of my life, under God. When I see it accomplished,
or in a fair way of being so, through the organization
that will provide the money and call forth the men,
I can lay down my head as peacefully and gratefully
as ever warrior did, with the shout of victory in his
ears,—" Lord, now lettest Thou Thy servant depart
in peace!   *   *

                    *

For the present, my pen is here laid aside. I shall
wait to see what use the Lord makes of Part First of
my autobiography, before I prosecute the theme. If

the Christian public seems not to find in it the help
and quickening that some friends think it likely to
bestow on those who read, the remainder need not be
written. Part Second, if called for, will contain a
record, in many respects, an utter contrast to all that
has gone before, and yet directly springing there-
from, as will be seen by all who look beneath the
surface. I am penning these words in 1887, and
five-and-twenty years lie betwixt this date and my
farewell to Tanna. These years, if ever published,
will tell the story of my visiting all the Colonial
Churches, and collecting the purchase money of our
white-winged Mission Ship, the *Dayspring;* my return
to Scotland, visiting all the home congregations in
1864, and securing several new Missionaries to follow
me to the New Hebrides; my second marriage, and
settlement on Aniwa, with her whom the good Lord
still spares to me, the mother of our happy family,
and my God-given helpmeet in all the work of the
Gospel ; the conversion of that whole island of Aniwa
from idolatry, and the planting there of a Church
and Congregation of Christ, from which have since
gone forth many Native Evangelists and Teachers.
Then there will fall to be recorded my call from the
Islands in recent years to revisit all the Colonial
Presbyterian Congregations once again, telling them
the story of the Conversion of Aniwa—the sinking of
the well, and other incidents, which turned an entire
people from idols and from cannibalism to the
service of the living and true God—whereby the

Churches, and especially the children, were led more and more to make the New Hebrides their own very harvest field in the Heathen world. And finally, I will have to tell how I was again sent home to Scotland in 1884 to raise money for the purchase or building of a steam-auxiliary Mission Ship, now urgently required in the interests of the Mission, both because of the great increase in the number of the Missionaries and the necessities of so many families; and also and chiefly to avert the dreadful disappoint-ments and loss of time, and thereby sometimes of life itself, caused by the frequent becalming of our little *Dayspring* in these thickly-islanded seas. That part of the story will show the fruits of the education and perils and experiences of a lifetime, in the marvellous impression produced by the simple and unadorned recital of the story of Tanna and Aniwa, amongst the Christian people of Scotland, Ireland, and England. Multitudes were blessed in almost every town where a meeting was granted me. Three Missionaries devoted themselves to the New Hebrides, and are already labouring there; while others consecrated themselves to several of the great seats of Foreign Mission enterprise in Africa and Asia. I returned to my own Church of Victoria with a sum of nearly £9,000, of which £6,000 was for the new Missionary Steam-Auxiliary, and the remainder for the outfit and support of more Missionaries for the Islands; and that money I handed over to the Australian Church, where it awaits, at interest in the bank, the arrangements being made by all the Colonies to take each their due share in the future up-keep of the Ship. For this—for everything—for all, praise be to the Lord! I never asked one subscription, except in prayer and in my public appeals. The Lord sent in all freely to me through the hands of His people; to Him be all the glory. I went back to Aniwa, and found the work of the Lord going forward there as if in a regularly settled Congregation at home, fostered and guided by an occasional visit of my ever dear and genuine friends, Mr. and Mrs. Watt, from old stern-hearted but at last relenting Tanna. The Church of Victoria has again summoned me to visit the Colonial Congregations, to tell the story of my Mission life, and to promote the interests of its now grand and growing Foreign Scheme. It is in the midst of such labours, while addressing at least one meeting every day, and three or four every Sabbath day, that I have penned the preceding pages; and I leave them to speak for themselves, without any attempt at ornament or style. The Lord whom I serve in the Gospel knows my motive and my hope, and I very calmly leave this book to His disposal, and the succeeding volume to His guidance, if such there shall ever be—as the reader well knows I have had to leave heavier and darker issues in the same blessed Hands. I offer every one, who has done me the favour to read or to listen, my kindly greeting. May you and I meet in the glory of Jesus, and continue our fellowship there! Good-bye.

APPENDIX.

APPENDIX A.

(*See p.* 354.)

THE PRAYER OF THE TANNESE,
WHO LOVE THE WORD OF JEHOVAH,
TO THE GREAT CHIEF OF SYDNEY.

[*Written at the urgent request and dictation of the Missionary's friends on Tanna to be presented to the Governor of New South Wales. Literally translated by me, John G. Paton.*]

TO the Chief of Sydney, the servant of Queen Victoria of Britannia, saying—We great men of Tanna dwell in a dark land. Our people are very dark hearted. They know nothing good.

Missi Paton the man, Missi Mathieson the man, and Missi Mathieson the woman, have dwelt here four yams (=years) to teach us the worship of Jehovah. Their conduct has been straight and very good; therefore we love these three Missionaries, and the worship of Jehovah which they three have taught us, the Tannese.

Alas! a part, as it were, only three of our Chiefs,

whose names are Nauka, Miaki, and Karewick, besides Ringian, Enukarupi, Attica, and Namaka, they
and their people hate the worship and all good
conduct like that which the Word of Jehovah teaches
us and the people of all lands. These men all
belong to four Villages only. They have stolen all
Missi's property; they have broken into his house.
They have cut down his bananas. They have
scolded and persecuted him; and they desire to kill
Missi and to eat him, so that they may destroy the
Worship of God from the land of Tanna.

We hate exceedingly their bad conduct, and pray
you, the Great Chief of Sydney, to punish these dark
Tannese, who have persecuted Missi, who have
deceived Missi, who have altogether deceived the
Great Chief (= Commodore Seymour) and the Chief
(= Captain Hume) of the men-of-war, and who deceived the Chief and the Missionaries in the *John
Williams,* who murdered one of Missi Paton's Aneityum Teachers, who fought Missi Turner and Missi
Nisbet, who killed Vasa and his Samoan people, who
killed the foreigners, who have now fought and
driven away our three Missionaries. Their conduct
has been exceedingly bad. They destroy the Kingdom of Tanna, kill the people and eat them, and are
guilty of bad conduct every day. Our hearts hate
their bad conduct; we are pained by it.

Therefore we earnestly pray you, the Chief of
Sydney, to send quickly a man-of-war to punish
them, and to revenge all their bad conduct towards

Missi. Then truly we will rejoice; then it will be good and safe for the three Missionaries to dwell here, and to teach us, men of the devil. Our hearts are very dark; we know nothing; we are just like pigs. Therefore it is good for Missi to teach us the Word and the Worship of Jehovah the Great King. Long ago He was unknown here. Missi brought His knowledge to us.

Our love to you, the Great Chief of Sydney, the servant of Queen Victoria, and we earnestly pray you to protect us, and to protect our Missionaries and the Worship of God in our land, the land of Tanna. We weep for our Missionaries. They three gave us medicine in our sickness, and clothing for our bodies; taught us what is good conduct, and taught us the way to Heaven. Of all these things long ago we had no knowledge whatever; therefore we weep, and our hearts cling to these three, our Missionaries. If they three are not here, who will teach us the way to Heaven? Who will prevent our bad conduct? Who will protect us from the bad conduct of foreigners? And who will love us, and teach us all good things?

Oh, compassionate us, Chief of Sydney! Hold fast these three, our Missionaries, and give them back to us, and we will love you and your people. You and your people know the Word of Jehovah; you are going on the path to Heaven; you all love the Word of Jehovah. Oh, look in mercy on us, dark-hearted men, going to the bad land, to the great eternal fire, just like our fathers who are dead!

May Jehovah make your heart and the hearts of your people sweet towards us, to compassionate us, and to look in mercy on our dark land; and we will pray Jehovah to make you good, and give you a rich reward.

The names of us, the Chiefs of Tanna, who worship towards Jehovah :—

Yarisi,	× his mark.	Manuman,	× his mark.
Ruawa,	× his mark.	Nuara,	× his mark.
Kapuka,	× his mark.	Nebusak,	× his mark.
Taura,	× his mark.	Kaua,	× his mark.
Faimungo,	× his mark.	Nowar,	× his mark.

APPENDIX

NOTES ON THE NEW HEBRIDES.

By the Editor.

THE SOUTH SEAS—so named by Vasco Nugnez de Balboa, who in 1513 first saw the Ocean on the other side of Darien, and marched into it as far as he durst, waving his sword, and taking possession of it in name of his master, the King of Spain.

The PACIFIC OCEAN—so named by Ferdinand Magellan, who in 1521 sailed westwards in his *Victory* seven thousand miles, and found the sea exceptionally *peaceful*—for that trip at least.

The NEW HEBRIDES—so named by Captain Cook, who in 1773 first fully explored and described the whole of the group. As far back, however, as 1606, Captain Pedro Fernandez de Quiros had landed on the largest and most northerly island of the group. He at once fancied it to be the great *Southern* Continent, deemed to be essential to balance the great Continents of the North, and eagerly looked for both by sailors and men of science. He named the bay, *Vera Cruz,*—the river that flowed into it, *Jordan,*—and the city which he founded there, *New Jerusalem.* The land itself he called by the preposterous designation of *Tierra Australis del Espiritu Santo.* In 1768 a French explorer, Bougainville, sailed round *Santo,* discovering that it was but an island, and through the *Straits* that still bear his name ; whereon, finding many islands all around, he re-baptized them *L'Archipel des Grandes Cyclades.* But Cook, being the first who sailed in and out amongst all the group, and put on record the most faithful descriptions and details, which to this hour remain generally authori-. tative, considered himself entitled to name them the *New Hebrides ;* and history since has been well pleased to adopt his views, seeing, doubtless, the geographical analogy betwixt the multitudinous scat- tered isles and islets of the *old* Hebrides and those of the *new.*

From Santo in the north to Aneityum in the south, a distance of about 400 miles, there are scat- tered over the Ocean thirty islands, twenty being well inhabited, and eleven of them being of considerable size, from Aneityum, which is forty miles in circum- ference, to Santo, which measures seventy miles by forty. The Islands lie 1,000 miles to the North of New Zealand, 1,400 miles North-East from Sydney, 400 miles West of Fiji, and 200 East of New Cale- donia. The population is now estimated at 70,000 ; but, in the early days of Missions, before Traders and Kanaka-collectors, and the new Epidemics of Civili- zation (!) had decimated them, their numbers were certainly three times greater.

The general appearance of the Islands is that of

a range of mountains bursting up out of the sea,
clothed with forests, and severed from each other
by deep valleys, through which the tides now flow.
They are all volcanic in origin, but the lava has
poured itself out over a bed of coral, and the mountains have reared themselves up on a coral base.
The fires are still active on Tanna, Ambrym, and
Polevi—the volcano on Tanna being now, as in the
days of Cook, a pillar of cloud by day and of fire by
night, a far-shining light-house for the sailor, kindled
by the finger of God Himself. The climate is moist
and humid, with a thermometer seldom below 60°
and seldom above 90° in the shade; their winter is
called the Rainy Season, and their vegetation is
tropical in its luxuriance.

On one Island may be found a hundred varieties
of ferns alone. The damara or kauri-pine, so prized
in New Zealand, grows there, as also the bread-fruit
tree, the banana, the papua-apple, the chestnut, and
above all the cocoa-nut, which for refreshing drink
competes with the vine of other lands, and for varied
uses and services to man almost rivals the very palm-
tree of Palestine. The sandal-wood, for its sacred
odours and idol incense, has been almost swept
entirely away,—as much as £70,000 worth being
carried off from Erromanga alone !

Among native foods, the yam and the taro hold
the foremost place, not inferior to our finest potatoes ;
besides the banana, the sugar-cane, the bread-fruit,
and the cocoa-nut, which flourish to perfection. Their

arrowroot is in some respects the finest in the world, and is kept only for special uses as yet, but may develop into a great and valuable industry, as Commerce opens up her markets and stretches out her hands. The English cabbage has been introduced and grows well; also the planting of cotton and of coffee.

The scarcity of animals is marvellous. The pig, the dog, and the rat are their only four-footed creatures; and some affirm that the rat is the alone indigenous quadruped in all the New Hebrides! Lizards and snakes abound, but are declared not to be poisonous. There are many small and beautiful pigeons, also wild ducks and turkeys, besides multitudes of ordinary fowls. Goats have now been largely introduced, as well as sheep, and various European animals. Fish, of course, swarm in millions around the shores, and a whaling station on Aneityum sent into the market £2,000 worth of oil in a year.

The Natives are practically quite naked, till induced by the Missionary to "wear a shirt".—the first sign of renouncing Heathenism and inclining towards Christianity. They are Cannibals of a very pronounced type, and Savages without any traces of civilization, except those connected with war (!),—without a literature, and almost without a religion, except only the dread of evil spirits, the worship of ancestors, and the lowest forms of fetishism, trees, stones, etc. They are partly Malay and partly Papuan,—a mixture of Ham and of Shem,—some with hair crisp and woolly, stuck full of feathers and shells, others with hair long and wavy, twisted into as many as 700 separate whipcords on a single head, and taking five years to finish the job! Their bows and arrows, tomahawks, clubs and spears, are sometimes elaborately carved and adorned; and they can twist and weave grasses and fibres into wondrously beautiful mats, bags, and girdles. They make bracelets out of shells, sliced and carved in marvellous ways, as also ear-rings and nose-rings; and in many similar methods they show some savage sense of beauty.

Polygamy, with all its accompanying cruelties and degradations, universally prevails. Infanticide is systematically practised; and even the despatch of parents, when they grow old and helpless. Widows' are put to death on almost every island to bear their husbands company into the spirit world. There is not an unmentionable vice hinted at in Romans i. which is not unblushingly practised on those Islands, wheresoever the Gospel has not dawned.

For the best published information on all these subjects, consult the work by Dr. John Inglis: "IN THE NEW HEBRIDES" (Nelson & Sons, 1887),— Reminiscences of noble Missionary Service for three-and-thirty years.

Butler & Tanner, The Selwood Printing Works, Frome, and London.

CPSIA information can be obtained
at www.ICGtesting.com
Printed in the USA
LVOW13s0045301116
515049LV00010B/179/P